Education for Tomorrow

A Biocentric, Student-Focused Model for Reconstructing Education

Michael Risku and Letitia Harding
University of the Incarnate Word, San Antonio, Texas, USA

SENSE PUBLISHERS
ROTTERDAM/BOSTON/TAIPEI

A C.I.P. record for this book is available from the Library of Congress.

LB
41
.R57
2013

ISBN: 978-94-6209-156-6 (paperback)
ISBN: 978-94-6209-157-3 (hardback)
ISBN: 978-94-6209-158-0 (e-book)

Published by: Sense Publishers,
P.O. Box 21858,
3001 AW Rotterdam,
The Netherlands
https://www.sensepublishers.com/

Printed on acid-free paper

CONTENTS

CONTENTS

PREFACE

About This Book

So if today I had a young mind to direct, to start on the journey of life, . . .
I would, for its welfare, unhesitatingly set that child's feet in the path of my
forefathers. I would raise him to be an Indian!

Luther Standing Bear, *The Land of the Spotted Eagle*

Over the past few years, there have been many books on the market that have
discussed indigenous ways of knowing, and bemoaned Western society's seeming
lack of interest in anything other than scientific, fact-based knowledge. Equally
plentiful are the writings of critical theorists who decry today's public education
system as divisive and manipulated by those in power to ensure that *their* children
have the educational advantages needed to maintain the hierarchical status quo, thus
leaving not only the children of indigenous people, but also those of most minorities
and the poor in a never-ending cycle of inequality.

   In this book, we bring both of these topics together by first examining the ways
that indigenous people and women of all cultures acquire and pass on knowledge,
and the effects that enforced Eurocentric systems have had on that process. Next,
we turn to public schools to explore the effects, both good and bad, that today's
programs have on the distribution of opportunities afforded *all* children in the United
States. For what are they being prepared? Finally, we apply the findings of liberatory
pedagogies by offering suggestions for a revolutionary education system that
highlights the need for all students to have the freedom and encouragement to look
critically and rationally at their lives. With such freedom, students know that they
can question their social status, and work toward equality, freedom, and change. This
can be achieved by looking both back to the pedagogical methods of our indigenous
ancestors, and forward to a time when all children, regardless of gender, or of ethnic
or socio-economic heritage, are taught in such a way that every aspect of their lives
is addressed, nurtured, and valued, not just their ability to either make money or to
serve those who do.

   Since its inception in 2002, the No Child Left Behind (NCLB) Act has been the
focal point of public primary and secondary education in the United States. The
opening paragraph of the document states boldly that its purpose is *to ensure that
all children have a fair, equal, and significant opportunity to obtain a high-quality
education.*[1] These are, undoubtedly, noble sentiments that must be applauded. The
reality, however, is that the education system in this country is still far removed

from offering all students an equal learning experience, and that the overemphasis on assessment has proven to be extremely profitable for testing corporations but a logistical nightmare for teachers. Teaching to the test has become the norm in many schools, especially those whose students are most in need of the help and attention that NCLB promises.

Today, the education system in the United States forces students and teachers to focus on the few aspects of life that are deemed necessary to succeed in Western society—and that, in and of itself, is not a bad thing. It is, however, tragic that ways of knowing that do not fall in line with the system are considered worthless and are actively discouraged. We are then left with young people who are prepared for assessment in reading, math, and science, but whose intuition, relationship with nature, and traditions of their forebears have been abandoned.

One of the main intentions of this work is to highlight the ancient ways of knowing that have been either discarded or forgotten or never known by most people living in the Western world, and to offer ways in which they could be reintroduced into our education system to form a new type of pedagogy which emphasizes the need to educate the whole child, intellectually, psychologically, physically, and spiritually, so that our young people can become citizens who would be considerate of every aspect of the world.

The study of indigenous epistemology is difficult in the United States; research and dialogue on the subject is in its infancy, mainly because many scholars deem it unworthy of study and too far removed from accepted Western thinking. Some Canadian scholars, on the other hand, have been more willing to recognize and value the importance that native people place on knowledge acquisition; thus, much of the fieldwork and research for this work was undertaken among that country's First Nations and Métis population.

Although a number of universities in this country emphasize that they have Native American writers as members of faculty (for example, Diné poet, writer, and librettist, Laura Tohe, is a professor at Arizona State University, and Diné poet and writer, Luci Tapahonso, holds the position of professor of American Indian Studies and English at The University of Arizona), many less acclaimed native scholars who are not creative writers but are studying or carrying out research on native issues within the United States university system find that, unless they adhere to quantifiable Western topics and methods of study, they often fail to see their work recognized or published. We hope that our work will, in some way, lead to more research in this important field.

With regard to terminology, the use of identifying terms such as indigenous, natives, Indians, Western culture, and civilization, comes from Western education, and we are painfully aware that the English language is *terminological quicksand*. Moreover, references to Western society, the Western world, or Western culture are not geographically based, but indicate the cultural system founded upon Greco-Roman classical influences. Specific terms may be more correct, but not as easily interpreted. Thus, for the purpose of being more readily understood by all readers, we have adopted the commonly accepted usages, and we apologize for any breached sensitivities.

It is important for readers to understand that the intentions behind this work are two-fold; first we wish to offer an overview of the importance of indigenous ways of knowing in today's world, despite society's persistent attempt to discredit them, and second, we are suggesting ways in which today's public education system could be enhanced by embracing the worldviews and needs of all its students.

Finally, the personal narratives that precede each chapter are the work of the first author.

ACKNOWLEDGEMENTS

I want to thank my parents, Emil and Ernestine (Pat) Risku for raising me among the woods and waters of Northern Minnesota, my Grandfather Ernest Rioux, and my neighbor and mentor, Wayne Miller. They all helped me forge an enduring worldview. I want to thank Jenna Hegerstom, Moraya Cortez and Serena Bahe for all their many efforts toward developing this manuscript. I especially want to thank my ever-patient wife, Julaine, for her loving support. I also thank my pack-mates, "Lady," "Lily," and "Lacy," who have taught me much more than I have them. Kafka was right.

MTR

First, I would like to thank Michael for suggesting this collaboration; the process has been long, but well worth all of the efforts. I would also like to thank my family on both sides of the Atlantic for all of their support and interest in this project. I am particularly grateful to my husband, Richard, whose selfless patience has been the greatest gift.

LH

NOAA AND THE DEERFLY

A few summers ago, I was in Northwest Ontario, Canada, on a Native Reserve carrying out the initial stages of my search for indigenous wisdom and knowledge. I wasn't having much luck, so one day I decided to visit local Native mounds, hoping for some insight. The day was warm and sultry with severe thunderstorm warnings posted for that afternoon and evening; my weather radio accessed information services from both the United States National Oceanic and Atmospheric Administration (NOAA) and its Canadian counterpart. The forecast was important, because I had to travel a significant distance to and from the mounds by boat over a large stretch of water.

My mound tour was uneventful, except for the bugs, particularly the deerflies, so after a respectable time wandering through the woods, I turned toward the small interpretive center. Being hot and thirsty, I went into the café announcing to no one in particular how warm and humid it was and that surely it was going to storm soon. Besides a waitress, the small café's only other occupant was an elderly Native gentleman who was wearing a Detroit Tigers baseball cap. He was eating a piece of pre-bingo blueberry pie. A minute or two after my professorial pontification, he muttered, "deerflies bite?" After a moment of reflection, I told him "no." He said, "Hmm." There it was. Of course, at the time I didn't realize the significance of his gift to me.

The boat trip back to my island cabin was uneventful and the apocalyptic thunderstorms never materialized. The next morning, I walked down to the dock and was promptly bitten by a deerfly. I got it – the bite and the lesson. If there are deerflies around and they are biting, it will storm. The storms hit the area within the hour. Perhaps the old man only wanted to know if he could get home after bingo without getting wet, but I would like to believe that he was educating me, even though he said only three words. No Doppler radar necessary; deerflies don't show up on radar anyway.

CHAPTER 1

INTRODUCTION

> Objectivity requires an ability to stand apart – but there is no "apart." We are
> inescapably of the universe.
>
> John Broomfield, *Other Ways of Knowing*

That deerflies only bite before a storm is not lost knowledge, but rather knowledge that is being or has been ignored or disregarded as irrelevant. How many other examples are there of untapped knowledge that could benefit today's society and, on a larger scale, alter the way that Westernized human beings view the world and their place in it?

Since the days of Plato and Aristotle, scholars in the Western world have come to consider knowledge as being derived either from an authoritative source or through scientific objectivity; the latter being a way of learning that strips away all that is not derived deductively. Herein, however, lies a paradox; to be objective, researchers must shed their cultural lens and the cultural implications of their subjects: and by doing so, they are forced to ignore intuitively and experientially-derived knowledge, and the myriad educational or cultural outliers that they have been taught to deem irrelevant to scholarly investigation. Failure to siphon such data leaves them vulnerable to criticism that their research is "soft" and therefore not to be taken seriously within academic institutions. It is unlikely that any meteorology program teaches deerfly behavior.

Over the past twenty or so years the works of "new-age philosophers" such as James Redfield,[1] Carlos Castaneda,[2] and Colin Wilson[3] have gained a steady and significant place in bookstores and, indeed, on personal bookshelves throughout the Western world. It is perhaps hard to imagine how, or why, such volumes have touched modern, technology-dependent consumers, but Redfield's *The Celestine Prophecy*,[4] that he had to self-publish as a paperback in 1993 before a hardcover version was produced commercially in 1994, has enjoyed enormous success both in the United States and abroad, including more than two years on the New York Times best seller list. By 2004, according to Redfield's website *Celestinevision.com*,[5] he had over 20 million books in print in over 50 languages.

The writings of Carlos Castaneda, notably *The Teachings of Don Juan*,[6] also need to be taken seriously. This is not because they were all best sellers and wildly popular among the general public, but because their meaning is anything but simplistic, and most academics seem unwilling, or unable, to critique them. Colin Wilson's novel, *The Philosopher's Stone*,[7] albeit somewhat less popular than the aforementioned works, provides a fascinating vision of human potential that few can imagine, and suggests that an extraordinary untapped power resides within humans.

The popularity of this group of authors may lie in their ability to make important philosophical ideas accessible and interesting to the general public by including cultural-based thinking in their sphere of knowledge, and thus positing new theories that include pre-literate knowledge as a way of knowing. While authors such as these have endured their share of ridicule and derision from "learned" critics, many readers conclude that their message ought to be heeded. After all, they of all writers seem to have provided the general public with alternative worldviews for the future, and a grounded sense of purpose that many people of Western society have lost as they engage in the constant struggle to keep up with technological progress and the pressure to achieve.

At the other extreme are the "academic philosophers" who reach only a select few. An interesting article, entitled "The Care and Feeding of the Reader,"[8] in the September 14, 2007 issue of *The Chronicle of Higher Education* shows that of the almost 1.5 million books sold in the United States during 2006, only 483 sold more than 100,000 copies. The article's author, Rachel Toor, comments that very few of the 483 had been written by academics, and of those even fewer were actually read, because "…many books by academics are, frankly, nothing more than data dumps. Their authors assume that information is enough."[9] Yet these are the people who define and control what is considered knowledge. So why is it that non-academics are able to connect with their readers more successfully than those who dedicate their lives to garnering and disseminating knowledge? According to Toor, writers who succeed in reaching a wide audience do so because they care about their readers enough to ensure, not just that they are informed, but also that they find pleasure in reading the text.[10] The writers of best sellers are not writing to ensure tenure or promotion, or to be able to add a line to their curriculum vitae. They are writing because they have a story to tell, or perhaps because they feel that they have an answer to a societal problem.

University professors, whose audiences are often limited, make sparse mention in their scholarly texts of knowledge derived through non-Western ways. Some would also say that by using language that is exclusive only to fellow scholars, the educational elite is ensuring that they determine how knowledge is derived, what is worthy of learning, and how it will be taught. Non-academics could be forgiven for thinking that the system is designed intentionally to exclude the general public. That would explain why the new-age philosophers are considered by those in the academic world to be *outliers*, despite their significant popular success, and why they are, for the most part, not only ignored as Western research demands, but also, and even worse, scorned and discredited throughout the temples of empiricism. But the phenomenal success of *The Celestine Prophecy* and *The Teachings of Don Juan* series surely suggests that scientifically-derived knowledge is failing to serve *all* the needs of Western society. One main difference between the traditional academic writing and the work of the so-called *outliers* is that the latter embraces divergent means of acquiring knowledge; traditional and non-traditional, ancient and modern, deductive and inductive.

Of equal concern, however, is the knowledge that the educational curriculum in United States schools is, to a large extent, determined by these same academics, and thus promotes only information or subjects that they value. Of course, the political system of the country also plays a large part in determining what will be taught in schools, because the politics of public school funding and the ideology promoted in the curriculum are closely linked. The result is that young people in the United States are herded into an education system that is designed to favor one type of student; the English-speaking, relatively wealthy American with no special needs, and whose parents have been able to choose to live in an affluent school district. At school, these students have access to the latest technology and textbooks, experienced teachers who are *highly qualified*[11] to teach in their particular field, athletic facilities to ensure fitness, and ample counselors to provide scholarship opportunities. At the same time, they tend to have parents who have the educational background, determination, and time to encourage and support active learning, and a peer group that shares their educational goals. These young people expect, and are expected, to become tomorrow's leaders, thus continuing their parents' legacy and sense of entitlement.

On the other side of this educational divide are young people whose experiences with the educational process leave them with few skills and even fewer career options. For these students, school offers little hope for the future; the schools are often under-funded (there is no wealthy Parent Teacher Association (PTA) here), the overall standard of teaching is poor (experienced and effective teachers have the freedom to chose their workplace, and tend to prefer the security and comfort of affluent school districts), parents usually have neither the education nor the means to support their children's aspirations, and, importantly, their peer group does not want them to succeed ("crabs in the bucket" syndrome).[12] Unfortunately, this is the daily reality for many minority students. While people in this country talk incessantly about multiculturalism and the benefits of a diverse society, the education system continues to favor those of Northern European descent—the very people whose societal norms have been dictated by Greek and Roman doctrine and methods of teaching. Native people, minority citizens, and immigrants from other parts of the world, especially those who are not native English speakers, are often marginalized because their ways of learning and prior knowledge are not consistent with traditional scientifically objective methodology.

Many observers of indigenous people and their ways of knowing and accumulating knowledge have learned and, thus, continually insist that before people can take part fully in all aspects of humanity, they must integrate additional ways of learning into every facet of their lives. And, if education is the means by which young people become knowledgeable and useful members of society, their course of study must integrate both Western and native ways of knowing. This can be achieved by adopting a unified approach to education that equips students with the tools to embrace not only empirical science, but also the many less easily defined criteria that indigenous people have known for millennia and are necessary for a better future.

The subsequent chapters in this book will look at: how people, both indigenous and Western, gain and use knowledge (chapters 2–5); how harmful a forced education system can be (chapter 6); the different ways that people use language to communicate and learn (chapter 7); and the alienating effects of separating people from their knowledge base and culture (chapter 8). In the final three chapters (9–11), we will suggest ways in which the present Western education model, which is, by all accounts, failing our children, should be replaced by a new system that educates every aspect of every child. A plan that calls for a total rethink of our education system seems to be a tall order and will be discounted by some as a preposterous notion, but most of us know that our present system is broken and that our children deserve much better.

THE BUTTERFLY TREE

I recall that in my youth I often wondered why at certain times of the year all the Monarch butterflies suddenly started flying south. This wonder was recently revisited when I realized I live near a "butterfly tree." Most evenings I walk my dog near a pond in south Texas, and I have found that for just a few evenings each fall, a particular tree next to the pond becomes alive with hundreds, if not thousands, of butterflies. Astonishingly, the surrounding trees have no butterflies. This tree, or its location, is special, but the mystery is, how do all the butterflies in the area not only find it, but also know that it is theirs? Surely there are many such trees that serve as hostels for the Monarchs during their long journey, and as evening comes, butterflies go to them, but it is the accuracy of their navigation that is fascinating. As I watch, these beautiful insects are not wandering around looking for a place to rest; they simply fly from all different directions directly to this particular tree. My observations help me to recall the sacred connection between animal and place. There was a time when I had seemingly forgotten, but no matter where my wanderings lead, something always reminds me.

I was taught to hunt and fish as a child and learned that both were important rituals within my community. As an adult, I am always struck by how much more attuned I am to my surroundings after only a relatively short time in the woods. I certainly see and hear things during the first few days, but as time passes, my sense of hearing, seeing, and intuiting increase profoundly as my city-born dullness dissipates. It is as if a fog has lifted. The very presence of the natural world seems to wash out the sensory pollution of the modern materialistic society.

For those who live in a city with a large population, the grime is thicker and takes longer to cleanse. I live in a large city and, although near an extensive green area, I am always aware of constant ambient noise—even during the so-called quiet times of the day. During rush hour, there is a background din that must surely take its toll on the senses. When I retreat to the woods of the Minnesota-Canadian border region, I am always surprised by the silence and by the slow pace of life. The first few days are busy, but once I have completed my post-arrival tasks, it is difficult to overcome feelings of boredom and inertia. That is surely a product of my modern way of life. Unfortunately, not only has Western culture taught us to be continuously occupied, but also today's society suggests that if we are not multitasking, we are underachieving. This constant activity has, however, made us unaware and unresponsive to our natural surroundings. The prime danger here is that our educational process is teaching us how to be in the world but not a fully integrated part of it. Fortunately for me, my early upbringing taught me to value my connection with nature, and so the longer I stay in the woods, the more comfortable I become with my place in the natural world.

INDIGENOUS WAYS OF KNOWING

> There is a way in which the collective knowledge of mankind expresses itself, for the finite individual, through mere daily living . . . a way in which life itself is sheer knowing.
>
> Laurens van der Post, *Venture to the Interior*

Indigenous people traditionally acquire knowledge from two spheres; via an axis from above, that is, from the spirit world, and from the earth below. Within this system of learning, science, art, and religion are integrated, and education brings knowledge of how to live and how to be moral. This is a simple model of being human. Culture and education are enhanced through critical consciousness, but they are not liberatory; on the contrary, they are acquired through community life and thus strengthen social bonds.

Indigenous or aboriginal people have traditionally been hunters and gatherers, but the majority of such people today neither hunts nor gathers. Throughout the world there are still some indigenous people who follow their ancestors' way of life, but few have managed to remain nomadic. For those who do maintain an itinerant lifestyle, it is common that they have contact with, and utilize, resources from outside their culture. It is extremely rare for indigenous cultures today to avoid contact with people outside their group, but a small number do prefer to inhabit areas that are isolated from modern society. For these people, the greatest threat to their way of life is modern man's invasion of their territory as he seeks to satisfy his insatiable need to acquire more and more land. Yet, it is from the small populations of those who do preserve the ways of their ancestors that we get a true glimpse of people whose lifestyles are totally different from our own Western *civilized* model. The following pages offer examples of indigenous people from whom we can gain insight: they are the Mashco-Piro of Peru[1], the Sng'oi of Malaysia[2], the Bushmen of the Kalahari[3], and the Australian Aborigines. While most of these people are finding it increasingly difficult to maintain their autonomy, we were heartened to hear that in the spring of 2008 the Brazilian government released aerial pictures of a previously unknown tribe, along with claims that there may be as many as 50 uncontacted tribes remaining in Brazil and Peru.

Indigenous people who have succeeded in maintaining a distance from the modern world retain ancient practices and ways of knowing that most of us have long forgotten, and now can only imagine. But if we are prepared to set aside skepticism and open our minds, we can learn much from these people and from the few who have been privileged to meet them. The rub, however, is that documentation of these meetings is inevitably recorded through a cultural lens and so must be regarded as interpretative. Nevertheless, any insight into the lives and knowledge base of people who have remained true to the way of life of their distant forebears has to be better than total ignorance of these branches of humanity.

People of Western cultures have a tendency to see indigenous people as "others," and to assess their practices and beliefs with a conscious or unconscious bias that stems from their own culture and education. Moreover, not only do we consider them as distinctly "other," but we also often see their practices and beliefs as bizarre or alien. Yet it is through their uniqueness that most can be learned. Of great concern, however, is the seemingly unstoppable encroachment of modern humans upon these cultures—and its devastating consequences.

In 2005, the government of Peru began working to develop a series of "transitory territorial reserves"[4] to protect nomadic indigenous communities who roam the Amazon jungle. Unfortunately, because of the many economic interests in the proposed areas, the engines of bureaucracy have almost ground to a halt and little progress has been made. The Amazon rainforest area houses the greatest number of isolated indigenous people in the world. Among these are the Mashco-Piro, one of the area's indigenous groups who, since the oppressive days of the rubber barons, have resolutely defended their traditional way of life by voluntarily distancing themselves from other cultures. The proposed area lies within the 2.7 million hectare Alto Purús National Park[5] and offers the Mashco-Piro, of whom there is thought to be no more than 800 (and even that number is considered by some to be extremely optimistic), the freedom to maintain their traditional ways and, most importantly, to avoid the outside world. The Mashco-Piro, according to anthropologist Linda Lema Tucker, "are nomads who move freely through the forest, subsisting on what they are able to gather, hunt or fish. They have survived like fugitives in order to protect themselves from the outside world, which they continue to see as a threat,"[6] and that threat is real. Logging, both legal and illegal, tourism, and missionary work are just some of the many activities that bring Western people close to the Mashco-Piro, and the encounters have proven to be fatal at times for both sides. The indigenous people have been known to attack and kill loggers who have encroached upon their settlements, and, of course, non-indigenous people bring deadly diseases into the area with devastating results for the indigenous groups. According to sociologist Tarcila Rivera, who works with the Peruvian government's Center for Indigenous Cultures, there are laws to protect the "uncontacted" as they are sometimes called. Unfortunately, however, because of their lifestyle, they are seldom considered to be like regular Peruvian citizens and are thus "...outside the protection offered to the rest of the citizens."[7] Sebastiao Manchineri of the Association of Indigenous Organizations of the Amazon Basin bemoans the fact that, "[t]he economic system does not respect cultural diversity, and indigenous groups who have voluntarily isolated themselves are considered obstacles. ...Without the help of their governments, those communities wishing to live apart from 'civilization' will become extinct, and there is nothing we can do about it."[8] The most recent threat to their existence is a plan to build a highway through the Communal Purus Reserve and the Alto Purus National Park. The project, which is being opposed by many local groups and the national park authorities, would, according to indigenous leader Julio Cusurichi "lead to 'ethnocide' of the uncontacted Indians."[9]

The thought of these people disappearing from the face of the earth and the subsequent loss of ancient knowledge is devastating, and some researchers are keen to learn as much as possible before it is too late. In the first part of the PBS documentary series, *Millennium: Tribal Wisdom and the Modern World*,[10] anthropologist David Maybury-Lewis describes his quest to locate the Mashco-Piro. He explains that, unlike other explorers, he and his colleagues recognize the need to film from a distance so that they do not risk bringing disease and death to the already fragile indigenous group. Others have told him about Mashco-Piro women who have been seen close to the river's edge, and one observer recounted that he saw the native women walking on all fours and later heard them talking with "great sadness."[11] One of the older women was said to have been "carrying herself with great delicacy . . . walking like a priest,"[12] and having an eerie and seemingly inappropriate laugh. The film tracks Maybury-Lewis and his team as they approach the boundary of Mashco-Piro territory by boat. Suddenly, one (non-Mashco-Piro) indigenous guide points to the riverbank and shouts "Mashco-Piro." One woman rises and leaves while another sits talking with her hands lifted upward; is she perhaps calling to someone? Maybury-Lewis, noting the distance between his boat and the women, mourns his inability to communicate—he has promised to stay away, and this only deepens the sense of mystery that surrounds these women.[13] It is reasonable to believe that viewers of the series see almost as much of the Mashco-Piro as does Maybury-Lewis, and watching these women as they sit along the bank of a tributary of the Manu River offers a glimpse into another world. Sadly, it is only a glimpse, and little can be learned from such a fleeting encounter. Fortunately, however, Robert Wolff's description of his encounters with the Sng'oi of Malaysia offers a fuller picture of an indigenous lifestyle.

In his book *Original Wisdom: Stories of an Ancient Way of Knowing*, Wolff recounts his experiences with Malaysia's aboriginal people, the Sng'oi, most of whom, according to Wolff, live in remote jungle areas far removed from all signs of Malaysian modern civilization. As Wolff grew to know and love these people, he came to recognize their innate contentment and joy. Instead of competing for, and craving, material possessions, they seem to desire nothing that nature cannot provide. They live a pre-agricultural, semi-nomadic lifestyle, hunting a little but mainly existing on jungle fare. When food around their settlement becomes scarce, they move.

Wolff's book is important because he corroborates what others have said by experiencing what it is like to live with truly aboriginal people. He is quick to point out, however, that he is not an anthropologist; nor does he claim membership of the tribe just because he spent time with them. He is a Western-educated psychologist who was raised in Indonesia. But by being open-minded and non-judgmental, by learning the natives' language and living with the Sng'oi, he was able to experience an indigenous way of life and way of knowing, and then to share his newfound knowledge. He describes his experience as being bathed in an overwhelming sense of oneness and of having a deep feeling of belonging. He also suggests that his relationship with the Sng'oi has lit a light deep inside himself. Wolff found that the Sng'oi follow their feelings, and when they do so they find reason for their actions. In Wolff's words, "you followed your intuition and whatever happened was the reason for having the intuition."[14]

Wolff found that, in much the same way as the people described by Plato in his "Allegory of the Cave," the Sng'oi believe that human beings live in a shadow world and that the real world is beyond the shadow. The similarities in the process toward enlightenment are striking, but with Plato the purpose was to convince his pupils to strive toward an absolute source for the betterment of society: "The Good." Those in authority, of course, provide the definition of what "The Good" and betterment mean. For the Sng'oi, the reason for gaining enlightenment is to achieve oneness with nature. It is important to note, however, that while Plato's cave dwellers lived in a shadow-world of ignorance, and were persuaded that only education and literal enlightenment could lead them to the goodness and light of the real world—the world of ideas, according to Wolff, the only way for the Sng'oi to learn about the real world is through their dreams, because life is lived in the shadow-world, and the real world is only visited at night. Wolff recounts part of a common early morning ritual in which the Sng'oi gather together to share and interpret their dreams. From an amalgamation of those dreams a narrative emerges: "The story that was created around the memories that four or five people brought back from the real world set the tone for the day."[15] Interestingly, James Redfield in his *The Celestine Vision* concludes that "dreams are an obscured form of intuition."[16] Wolff seems to agree with Redfield's belief that dreams are a form of intuition, but he takes the notion a step further by suggesting that, like the Sng'oi, not only our dreams but also our intuition should be central to our decision making process. It is safe to assume that Wolff's life was greatly influenced by his experiences with the Sng'oi, as he confides that it was through his Western education that he "began to feel alienated from the earth and from [his] fellow humans."[17] It could be said that his life of dreams, dream narratives, and intuitive-based activities with the Sng'oi became more 'real' than his Western way of life.

Dreams and the dream world are consistent themes among indigenous people, and their importance in creating links between ancient and contemporary dimensions cannot be underestimated; hence the prominence of shamans who are often called upon to interpret meaning from dreams, and to explain their relevance to present circumstances. It is probable that the shaman is selected for this task because of his or her apparent ability to communicate with otherworldly beings.

The idea of dream interpretation is not new to Western readers. In the old Babylonian heroic poem, *The Epic of Gilgamesh*, Gilgamesh, the king of Uruk, prays for dreams that will bring him favorable messages from the sun god, Shamash.

Unfortunately, his dreams fill him only with dread and uncertainty until his devoted friend, the primitive, uncivilized Enkidu, interprets them in a positive light. The presence of Gilgamesh in the Western Canon cannot, however, be taken as evidence that spiritual connections are readily accepted by Western civilizations. Gilgamesh is often described as being set in so-called mythic time when gods moved freely between the earth and the heavens using humans as their playthings, while the part god/part human epic heroes such as Gilgamesh, Odysseus, and Achilles acted as links between the two worlds. Today's Western readers who recognize nothing but historical, linear time see little or no parallel between these stories and their concept of reality.

The Western and indigenous worlds can, however, be seen to come together in the number of dream catchers that are seen hanging from the rear view mirrors of modern cars. These native works of art are thought to be tools to ward off evil spirits, but in reality were used by most indigenous people as a means of communicating with the nether world. In his 2001 novel, *Dreamcatcher*, Steven King portrays a Down syndrome man as a dream catcher; a concept that seems much more understandable than the more popular idea of endowing an object with such qualities. Furthermore, this interpretation helps to explain how people, far removed from cultures that recognize the dream world, claim to hear from, or see glimpses of, other dimensions. Farfetched as this idea may seem, Albert Einstein spent a lifetime theorizing about, and demonstrating mathematically, dimensions that ran parallel to our own. Recent developments in *string theory* and the study of the effects of membranes, *m theory,*[18] posit not just a fourth dimension—time/light, but a world with multiple dimensions or universes that continually collide with each other, to which we might move if only we knew how. Unless they are physicists, most people have no idea about how string theory works, or how its impact through vibration affects our lives, but that does not mean that the forces and matter explained through string theory do not exist. Sadly, one of the best explanations of string theory has been cartoon-like, and was on the SyFy channel. But phenomena that exist outside our senses are difficult to understand. Light, specifically as described in the theory of *astral light,* is a good example. The one true constant is neither time nor space; it is light. We don't know much about light, except that it has a significant impact on all living things, yet virtually all indigenous and ancient cultures use the metaphor of light in describing the spirit and natural world. It is not surprising, therefore, that among indigenous populations, special places that are considered sacred are described as having an energy, feel, and luminosity that foster intuition. Perhaps the sacred places revered by the indigenous and the theoretical constructs created by Einstein and other scientists have more in common than most people believe.

Einstein's ideas resulted in the Einstein-Rosen bridge theory that raises the possibility that parallel universes can attract one another to the point that they become connected by means of a wormhole. And now, Steven Hawking has suggested that during the short time that these wormholes are open, they could even offer a means of time travel.[19] Reading Wolff's narrative, it is easy to feel that he has transcended *his* reality and crossed over into another time and reality. He has not lost touch with the real world as we know it, nor is he psychotic; he has moved into a parallel universe and rather than a scary place, has found it to be wonderful. Wolff's experience with the Sng'oi suggests a journey resulting in a state of oneness with nature, a complete sense of belonging, and an understanding that meaning in life is not exclusive to any one group of people. Again, Wolff is not indigenous; he was educated in the Western tradition and possesses no inordinate skills or ability, learned or otherwise, which has brought him the gift of another sense. Wolff claims that we all, to a degree, have the ability to achieve this inner quality, some perhaps more than others. He also claims that he now frequently uses this extra sense in the same way he would a muscle and feels that it must be exercised to keep it strong. Wolff moved from Asia to a city in the United States and realized that he had to make significant adjustments to his lifestyle, because the environment in the city was so full and busy that it created a feeling of sensory overload. His time with the Sng'oi had heightened his sense of awareness of other people, but he found that he did not want to know what the city people thought because they were so filled with "resentment and bitterness." Wolff believes that Western modern ways of living have made us "deaf and blind" to all that is important in life.[20]

The Sng'oi did not learn how to inhabit the jungle of Malaysia successfully by reading survival guides. On the contrary they, like other indigenous people, are experientialists, believing only what they experience personally or learn through the experiences of others. Epistemologically, they watch, listen, and wait for meaning to come to them through reflection. This contemplative process is mysterious, particularly for people who have been steeped in Western culture that overvalues the scientific method of learning. The good news is that reflection is not exclusive to indigenous people: as Wolff discovered, it is there for all who are open to trying unfamiliar means of acquiring knowledge.

Many years before Wolff recorded his encounters with the Sng'oi, Laurens van der Post[21] wrote about the Bushmen of the Kalahari in his 1958 *The Lost World of the Kalahari*. Van der Post was perhaps the most obvious Westerner to seek and then to study the Bushmen, because he was raised in an area that had historically been "Bushman country." Yet throughout much of the book, his account of the elusive nomadic people seems to be little more than a recording of hearsay and legend as he continues a painful search, beset by false hopes and disappointments, until it would appear that he is too late and that the Bushmen have been rendered extinct. It is natural, therefore, that when he actually meets Nxou, a young member of a colony of about thirty Bushmen, his readers share his relief that he "had made contact at last!"[22] This event occurs within the last fifty pages of the book but provides the evidence that confirms and justifies all of van der Post's hopes and dreams.

Growing up in Africa, surrounded by the spirit of the Bushmen, van der Post found himself relating to all of the myths and fairy tales that he heard about these native people. Indeed, the tales of the Bushmen are not unlike the Western stories of our own epic heroes with their extraordinary attributes and adventures. And, no doubt, the stories that he grew up hearing greatly influenced his drive to prove that at least some Bushmen still existed, and to find them. The quest, however, at times seemed futile, because modern man's voracious appetite for more and more land has left little or no opportunity for nomadic indigenous people to survive.

The picture that Van der Post paints in the early stages of his book is of a people who are small in stature, have vision like no other human, and move "with a flame-like flicker of gold like a fresh young Mongol."[23] These pre-contact descriptions have a colonial ring to them with paternalistic statements about the "child-man," and, at the same time, offer a non-human, anatomical description of his physical features, such as the shape of his buttocks, the color of his skin, the shape of his face, and his power of vision, all of which are noted in much the same way as one would depict the characteristics of a wild animal. It is not until after Van der Post actually spends time with them that he begins to describe them as peaceful, content, and spiritual—that is, as having human characteristics.

Between the tales that he learned as he grew up and from his own experience, Van der Post has portrayed a people who were such natural botanists and organic chemists that they "used different poisons on different animals, the strongest for the eland and the lion, and less powerful variants for the smaller game."[24] The Bushmen also made a repellant that allowed them to traverse lion territory without fear and actually use lions to herd other game. Van der Post asked them if they ever climbed trees to find game, and they asked why they would want to do that, for seeing the animals' tracks told them all they needed to know of their whereabouts. Van der Post states the Bushmen "knew the animal and vegetable life, the rocks and the stones of Africa as they have never been known since."[25] It is important to note, however, that Van der Post is not describing people who were in control of their surroundings. Unlike modern man, the Bushman "was utterly committed to Africa . . . he was back in the moment . . . when birds, beasts, plants, trees and men shared a common tongue, and the whole world, night and day, resounded like the surf of a coral sea with universal conversation."[26] As in a fairy tale where animals and humans talk, Van der Post, having being raised among the descendants of nomadic Bushmen, always believed that they understood the language of each animal. Renowned hunters, they never killed except for food, and were both apprehensive and sorry afterwards for having to kill an animal. They owned nothing that they could not carry and made no permanent structures. They neither domesticated any animal nor planted any crop. They lived where they made a large animal kill or near a water supply. Many of these water holes were either unknown or undetectable by others. The Bushmen truly lived in harmony with the land. They considered other animals as "persons of the early race."[27] Thus, Darwin may not have been the first to discover evolution. It could be said that he simply *rediscovered* what the Bushmen *knew* at least 8,000 years earlier. Van der Post claims that the Bushmen were the oldest inhabitants in southern Africa and that the black Africans were northern immigrants. He also states that many black Africans feel that the Bushmen were the first people of Africa, and thus the oldest form of human life left in the world.[28] Unfortunately, but characteristically, colonials used the Bushman's integration with nature as evidence of his inferiority—"He built no home of any durable kind, did not cultivate the land and did not even keep cattle or other domestic chattel, and this seemed to prove to his enemies that he was a human 'untouchable' and not far removed from the beasts of the veld."[29]

Since the time of van der Post's narrative, mystery has continued to surround the story of the Bushmen. Have they vanished under the pressures of modern development, or is there a chance that some have survived? Rupert Isaacson, a London-based writer, grew up surrounded by African artifacts and listening to stories of the Bushmen. His mother was South African and his father was Rhodesian. In *The Healing Land*, Isaacson takes up van der Post's story recounting his own compulsion to discover the Bushmen's fate. And yes, he did succeed. But while some were following some semblance of a traditional lifestyle, Isaacson describes scenes of drunkenness, poverty, in-fighting, and prostitution. Some saw the presence of white people as a means of making money: "Maybe people like you – tourists – might come here and see our life. There is money in this…"[30] Isaacson's tale is one of broken people and broken promises; land claims have been filed and won, but corporate greed seems to always prevail. A Botswana government official explained, "We all aspire to Cadillacs. [The Bushmen] can no longer be allowed to commune with flora and fauna."[31] The discovery of diamonds in the Central Kalahari Game Reserve did nothing to advance the Bushmen's cause. To force the Bushmen off their land, the government destroyed their only water well. And without a secure source of water, the Bushmen's land could not sustain them. In January 2011, the BBC reported that an appeals court had ruled that Bushmen could drill new water wells on their traditional lands. Despite the good news, however, the future of the traditional Bushman is still tenuous. Young tribal members are unskilled in the traditional way of life and many do not wish to follow the old ways. They have become accustomed to the trappings of modern living and cannot imagine living any other way. To compound the problems, the wells are failing to produce enough water to supply the needs of those trying to return to the lands of their forefathers. One of the greatest difficulties that endangers the future of the Bushmen, and indeed, almost every other indigenous people trying to live a traditional lifestyle, is the chasm between their way of seeing and interpreting life and that of Westerners. The Bushmen's worldview is like that of all other indigenous people, that of a circle. The Bushmen also believe that we are but "a dream dreaming us."[32] The similarities between the Bushmen, the Sng'oi, and the Australian Aborigine with regard to the importance of dreams are so striking and diverse from Western interpretation that it demands that we revisit our meaning of the dream world.

The indigenous Australian culture may be one of the oldest of any that still exists, and is arguably the most difficult for Eurocentric[33] minds to understand. Furthermore, although they share similar beliefs about the importance of dreams with other indigenous people, it is the Aborigine's sense of time and *Dreamtime* that sets them apart. It is from this culturally isolated population that we can learn much since their strangeness (to our minds), and our lack of understanding, correlates with their isolation. What is *Dreamtime*? It is the time that exists below the surface of wakeful awareness, and it is also the time before the world as we know it was fully created and whole: a time within a time. Dreaming and then believing that what has been dreamed still exists in a physically distinct geographic place is unique to the Aborigine. Physical places are important among all indigenous populations because they serve as portals that people can use to connect with their ancestors and the spirit world. For most indigenous people, buttes, mountaintops, waterfalls, and valleys are their churches. It is from these places that they learn and integrate visual and oral traditions into their cosmology.[34] Physical places are therefore not separate from spirituality, and different gods, spirits, and ancestors dwell in different places. But for the Australian Aborigine there is no portal; it is all present in the here and now.

Like the Australian Aborigines, Native Americans recognize the spiritual aspect of the wind and sky, and of dreaming, in their cosmology, and there are similarities between the aboriginal *Dreamtime* and Native American spirituality. Both particularly emphasize the importance of *places* versus *events* and the difference in the knowledge of men and women, and each relies on the connections between language and geography as a means of acquiring knowledge and determining meaning: linear time as we know it does not exist, and there is no history. Clearly, Aborigines and the indigenous Bushmen provide a glimpse into a different world that is beyond ancient history. Van der Post experienced this when he found two hunters and offered them a ride in his truck. While the vehicle was going "full speed" across the desert, one, on sight of an animal he wished to track, "hurled himself from the vehicle." With no further ado, he got up and continued the hunt as if nothing had happened.[35] Why did he step off a moving truck? Probably, it was his unfamiliarity with the dangers of unnatural speed, and his belief in the natural laws of motion. This incident may highlight the difference in the way indigenous people perceive the world around them. While the time for learning from the Bushmen themselves may be gone, there is perhaps a chance that we may learn from their libraries—yes— libraries. As Van der Post states, "how mistaken is the common assumption that literature exists only where there is a system of writing."[36]

The Bushmen's intricate color paintings and symbols on the walls of caves and overhangs that exist throughout much of southern Africa are their libraries. Historically, Western people have gone to great pains to decipher written language, but little effort has been expended on symbolic languages that use pictures rather than words. This is understandable. According to Tim Jones, director of the Saskatchewan Archaeological Society,

> Trying to determine the meaning of the paintings from a modern perspective and a different cultural context, especially when some of them may represent the very personal religious experiences of individuals, is an exercise fraught with potential pitfalls. . . . Appreciating the general cultural context is, maybe, as deep as we can get.[37]

Written languages correlate with the means by which the authoritative sources of the three major Western religions transmit knowledge while the use of symbolic writing and animal-like images has generally been linked to aboriginal people. The latter have always been considered primitive and less sophisticated than the former, primarily because to treat both forms of language equally would have been seen as humanizing the Bushmen and others, making it more difficult to displace them and to justify treating them as less than human; a practice that was widespread during colonial times and has yet to be fully eradicated. For those who care to look, the Bushmen's influence may be seen from the Iberian Peninsula to Egypt to the far reaches of southern Africa: these were Paleolithic people who roamed all of Africa, and it would be comforting to think that some who share their ways of knowing and living still do.

There is much we can learn from ancient and indigenous people, but there may be as much if not more that we can learn from our fellow animals. The deerfly of Chapter 1 spoke through the old Indian, "I will not bite you unless a storm is imminent."[38] The old Indian learned from his elders about deerflies as a means of forecasting the weather, and also from his experience of being bitten and the subsequent storm. It is the behavior of the deerfly that creates this knowledge, but it is the wisdom of the person that allows him or her to translate the behavior into meaning.

On November 4, 2007, the people of the small village of San Juan Grijalva in the southern state of Chiapas, Mexico, woke to find all their cattle running up the mountainside. Fearing the loss of their cattle, most of the 600 villagers chased them, only to witness, from the safety of the high ground, their village being swallowed by a mudslide from the neighboring mountain. Like the survivors who also followed animals to higher ground before the 2004 tsunami struck Asia, the villagers may not have made the connection between their animals' behavior and the pending disaster. They chased their cattle for economic reasons, but the behavior of the animals foretold the event: deerflies and storms are more numerous than cattle and mudslides, and thus the correlation is more observable. Maybe Kafka was right when he said, "All knowledge, the totality of all questions and all answers, is contained in the dog."[39]

The stories of indigenous people tell us that there was a time when humans and animals could speak to one another. Now people try to control animals and, indeed, all aspects of nature. Animals are afraid of humans, and with good cause: humans have butchered them, often killing for the sake of killing. The recent popularity of horse and dog "whisperers" harbors back to the time when animals could trust mankind. Although we don't understand how humans and other animals communicate with one another, we have come to recognize that there are people who do seem to have a way to connect with animals, and a means by which to communicate with them. We talk a lot about animals, have pets, watch documentaries on animals and visit zoos, yet we are androcentric in the extreme. We talk at animals, but if we listen they will try to communicate with us, and when they once again learn to trust us as they did in the past, perhaps they will enlighten us about things that they know and we do not. But today if people were to say that they talk with animals, not only would we not believe them, but we would be concerned about their mental health when just the opposite should be true. *Ancestral connectiveness* includes our fellow animal species.

Human intelligence does not set us apart from other animals; forgotten knowledge has caused our separation from the natural world. We understand Darwinism, yet we continue to think of humans as separate from its evolutionary mandate. The grounds for this separation are legitimized by the Hebrew influence in Genesis: "Be fertile and increase, fill the earth and master it; and rule the fish of the sea, the birds of the sky, and all the living things that creep on earth."[40] And while it is not right to lay this all at the feet of the Jews and Greeks, David Abram reminds us that it was they who carved it in stone:

> So the ancient Hebrews, on the one hand, and the ancient Greeks on the other, are variously taken to task for providing the mental context that would foster civilization's mistreatment of nonhuman nature. Each of these two ancient cultures seems to have sown the seeds of our contemporary estrangement— one seeming to establish the spiritual or religious ascendancy of humankind over nature, the other effecting a more philosophical or rational dissociation of the human intellect from the organic world.[41]

These two rich cultures, as much as they have brought to the modern world, on a darker side provide the ingredients and, via the written word, a recipe for the definition of the priest-king hegemony.[42] This unholy marriage of religion and philosophy spawned an ecological and epistemological holocaust beyond our imagination. The result is a mindset that allows humans who have been raised and educated in the Western tradition to set themselves both above and apart from all other living beings, and to dismiss their actions, beliefs, and lifestyles as obsolete, alien, and naïve.

One such common belief among indigenous people is the concept of shape-shifting: a term used to describe the ability of animals to change their form dimensions. It includes the ability not just to see or hear entities within another dimension, but to move one's physical self, part or whole, between dimensions. A deer may disappear before a hunter's eyes, but this usually has more to do with the latter's hunting ability. Among northern American Indians, Windego stories were often told to scare small children into behaving, and every culture, ancient or modern, has some type of "boogieman." Interestingly, the Bugis (upon whom the boogieman myth is based) are a seafaring people who live in Indonesia. The Bugis resisted European colonization and were labeled by the Dutch as fierce pirates, and hence the term "boogiemen." Windego is a popular name that is commonly used for parks and streets, but you may not want to live on Windego Lane. The Windego was a shape-shifter between moose and man who flew through the forest looking for people, usually lost children and bad men, to eat. The rational adult mind suspects that the Windego is no more than a mythical character in a campfire story that was told to keep children close to home, or in a tribal story that explained the scorn of banishment, or to tell the fate of someone who simply got lost and died in the woods. It was also used in the past as an odious but plausible means of explaining away starvation and cannibalism. But regardless, the principle of shape-shifting was a commonly held belief that had to come from somewhere. Shape-shifting is but another difficult concept for Westerners to understand because it does not fit into our worldview. Has shape-shifting been relegated to fairy tale status by monotheism? For animists, people who are in tune with the natural world, or students of Einstein or Newton, it can be real. Einstein believed that dimensions can intertwine, and Newton believed that natural elements could be combined to create something entirely different; so how much of a stretch is shape-shifting? And it has been real to too many different people across too many different lands to be ignored—here is its premise:

In the very earliest time,

when both people and animals lived on earth,

a person could become an animal if he wanted to

and an animal could become a human being.

Sometimes they were people

and sometimes animals

and there was no difference.

All spoke the same language.

That was the time when words were like magic.

The human mind had mysterious powers.

A word spoken by chance

might have strange consequences.

It would suddenly come alive

and what people wanted to happen could happen.

All you had to do was say it.

Nobody could explain this,

that's the way it was.[43]

There is a widespread interest today, particularly among young female readers, in one aspect of shape-shifting thanks to the widely popular *Twilight* series written by Stephanie Meyer. In this vampire narrative, a resident coven is challenged by a group of young Quileutes who are able to transform into wolves. As with many works of fiction, this story has some grounding in truth, or in this case, in tribal legend. According to Quileute mythology the tribal name is derived from *Kwoli* (Quileute for wolf) because its people are descended from wolves who changed into people.

But people tend not to accept as knowledge, information that cannot be quantified because quantification means control. Knowledge through sensation is difficult to control; hence we are both skeptical and fearful of it because it seems dangerous. The rational mind has difficulty with the infinite or sensual. Thus, the creation of "truth" is something we are told is concrete and onto which we can mentally hold. And we are often taught not to question truth lest we stare into the abyss of the infinite. Yet while we cling to the idea of truth to keep our feet firmly on the ground, religious faith offers freedom to transcend our physical world. It is this constructed faith that is important, and the spiritual process of sustaining that faith allows us to believe in eternal life, our human understanding of the infinite. The concept of shape-shifting should be no more difficult to accept than eternal life, or heaven and hell (other dimensions) but, because it is sensory and includes other animals, it has been rejected as mythical. Shape-shifting may be a heightened form of "synaesthesia," the synergistic blending of the auditory and visual aspects of all natural things.

Our senses are the base of our experiences and our experiences are our life, but to believe this is considered "nonsense," which goes a long way toward understanding why modern humans feel so disconnected and adrift from meaning and purpose in their lives. The idea that a cure for "losing your mind" is to "come to your senses" suggests that we know better. We have, however, been so programmed by idealism and realism that we rarely do come to our senses and, although escaping from our constructed realities will free us from artificial and mechanical thinking, we often feel guilty for doing so. Ironically, like Plato's chained prisoners in the cave, we would rather see the shadow than learn the truth. We are programmed to accept that progress is always for the best, and so we strive to learn new things and move forward. Yet many answers to societal problems lie in the distant past, waiting for us to rediscover them. One strategy should be to look to the behavior of the ancients and of the animals around us for help. Animal behavior is not dictated by a clock, an appointment book, or the need to be seen to be progressing; they have in-built mechanisms that control all that they need to survive.

Like the monarch butterflies, all animals, including humans, have a circadian clock, and researchers have found that the monarchs as well as other animals have cryptochrome proteins, which allow for navigation using the sun's position. So butterflies have a built-in global positioning system (GPS) that allows them to know exactly where they are at all times relative to fixed points, all in their pinpoint size brains. Steven Reppert, a neurobiologist from the University of Massachusetts, has been studying monarchs and their circadian rhythms as it relates to sleep disorders and depression. It is no wonder then that ancient seafarers traversed the Pacific using stars; the wonder is how and why we humans now need a GPS to go to the grocery store. And how is losing this ancient ability good? Hopefully, we can relearn what we have lost and use this reclaimed knowledge to reconnect humans with the natural world. The result will be that we view the natural world through new, or renewed, lenses. The revised mindset will allow people to see the world not as an entity to be controlled and stripped of its resources, but as a life support system for all living beings to be nurtured, cherished, and revered.

BIOCENTRIC CONNECTIONS TO THE LAND AND THE SEA

Being raised next to Lake Superior I found it difficult to ignore its spirit. My father and his commercial fishing buddies frequently talked about the lake as a living entity rather than as a mere body of water. Living next to such a strong spirit will eventually convert anyone, so although the North Shore of Lake Superior was mostly inhabited by Scandinavian Christians, the belief system of the men who lived near and worked on the lake developed into an amalgamation of Christianity and the lake spirits. They still attended the Lutheran churches that were sprinkled among the small communities, but I could tell that their hearts and minds were elsewhere. Their wives lured them to church with casseroles, cake, and coffee, so they returned to their Lutheran roots for the day, but back on the surface of Lake Superior they took a short side-step to the spirit world of their ancient past. So although I was raised neither in a native culture, nor much of a Christian one for that matter, my life was nevertheless strongly influenced, and surrounded, by aspects of a worldview that suggested an ancient natural spiritual presence and something more.

Two personal experiences have led me to this conclusion. One was unusual because of the setting. I was in graduate school and living in Milwaukee, Wisconsin. It was morning, and I had just boarded a city bus heading for class. I lived near Lake Michigan and the bus route went along the shore before turning inland. There were only ten people or so on the bus, and I settled into an empty bench seat. Upon sitting down, I immediately felt that I was in the presence of someone; that there was someone actually sitting next to me, but there was no one within several rows. I then felt a hand-like touch on my shoulder. Startled, I quickly turned around, but there was no one near me. I did not experience the touch again, but I still felt the presence. I thought that perhaps a draft had come through one of the doors, but they were all closed, or that some form of static electricity from my jacket had caused the sensation (I actually tried to generate static electricity to no avail), but the nature and magnitude of the touch lead me to believe that it was something else. I suspect that from my reactions, my fellow passengers may have thought I was seeing things or hearing voices. That was not the case; I was feeling things. I have no idea what caused the sensation, but I know that I was touched by something, that something had a presence, and that although I continued to feel the presence for several minutes, I never felt afraid. I might have chalked the incident up to a freak draft and not given it much thought had it not been for an event that occurred several years earlier.

During the spring of 1981, I was on a fishing trip with an acquaintance into the Pukasawa National Park in Northwest Ontario. It was my first visit to this large wilderness area that borders the far northern shore of Lake Superior, so I knew very little about the area other than that few traveled here because it was very remote and deemed dangerous. The area is large and only accessible from Lake Superior – hence the danger, as there are long stretches of the shoreline with rock cliffs several hundred feet high that provide no refuge from the sudden weather changes that plague this inland ocean. The wilderness shoreline is 140 miles long and in some places over 70 miles from the nearest road or residence. The area has a reputation of being beautiful but deadly to the unprepared.

For over a week we had been near the middle of the park within neither sight nor sound of another human being, and had, to that point, enjoyed excellent trip conditions. We started our return journey, traveling close to the shoreline looking for streams to fish. With the shoreline providing such scant relief from storms, streams are an important source of both sport and refuge. In times of bad weather, our small, but seaworthy boat could be pulled or motored upstream into estuaries where we could camp until kinder weather allowed us to move on. One afternoon as we continued the exploration of streams along the shoreline, the sea started to build, so I started looking for a place to put in. I eventually found a small cove with a nice beach. It seemed an idyllic spot, and as we entered the channel we felt relieved to be leaving the lake. Immediately upon entering the small bay, however, I began to feel discomforted. I could not explain what I was feeling, and I suppressed my unease as we busied ourselves setting up camp.

During the next 18 hours my worldview and reliance on science to explain everything was shattered. Once the chores of setting up camp had been completed, my unease intensified into anxiety. Looking around the immediate area, I noticed that there was no sign of birds, small animals, or fish. Although physically beautiful, the bay was strangely silent and sterile. The wind and waves of Lake Superior were but a few yards away, yet the air was heavy and still. I tried my best to explain away my disquiet and the environmental abnormalities, but I could not. By evening I concluded that something bad had happened here and that evil was present. All the while, however, my fishing partner was feeling just fine. I mentioned my unease and physical observations, but he did not see or feel anything unusual. In retrospect, I think we were in different places.

I don't think I slept much that night, and although the wind was down the next morning the lake swells made travel marginal, but I insisted that we leave as soon as possible. My rationale was that the wind and waves would get higher, stopping us from traveling any time soon. Of course that was not the reason I wanted to leave. I wanted to put as much distance between me and that bay as possible, and we traveled a good 20 miles up the lake before next putting ashore. I carefully assessed our next campsite and was relieved to find that the surrounding woods were alive and peaceful and that my dread had passed.

I have never returned to that little bay despite having made several trips to and within the area. Truth be told, I have not looked for it, because I will never forget the feelings that were evoked there, and I am not keen to relive them. What I do know is that both the place and the experience were real. I embarked on that trip as a pragmatic, high school social science teacher, but upon entering that bay, I crossed over into another place, a place I had heard stories about but never really knew existed, and although curious, I do not want to experience it again. This is why when I felt the hand on my shoulder and presence years later on that Milwaukee bus I was so startled.

I may have been happier before my experiences, when knowledge was finite and obtainable and verifiable through science and study. Now I'm not so confident about what I know, or even about the importance of what I have spent years learning. As a student of history and philosophy, I have come to learn that history often is not true, and philosophy and reason alone leave one with little to grasp other than the belief that there is much that we have either lost or just don't know.

CHAPTER 3

INTUITION AND ATTITUDES TOWARD WOMEN

The unconscious mind may include all man's past; but it also includes all his future.

Colin Wilson, *New Pathways in Psychology*

Intuition is an ancient mode of deriving knowledge that many Westerners feel has all but disappeared within most present-day humans, but there are still many instances of intuitive practices by indigenous people throughout the world. One such occurrence was demonstrated during the December 2004 Asian tsunami that devastated much of the shoreline bordering the Indian Ocean resulting in the loss of more than 200,000 lives. India's Andaman and Nicobar archipelago islanders were directly in the path of the tsunami, yet they survived with a relatively small number of casualties. Many of these Paleolithic islanders either left their islands well before the tsunami struck, riding the big waves far out to sea in canoes, or they retreated ahead of the tsunami to the highest elevations of the islands. After the tsunami devastated the area, Indian journalist, Neelesh Misra, interviewed local environmentalist and lawyer, Ashish Roy, who explained, "They can smell the wind. They can gauge the depth of the sea with the sound of their oars. They have a sixth sense which we don't possess."[1] According to Misra, "Government officials and anthropologists believe that ancient knowledge of the movement of wind, sea and birds may have saved the five indigenous tribes on the Indian archipelago of Andaman and Nicobar Islands from the tsunami that hit the Asian coastline Dec. 26."[2]

The intuitive power of the Andaman and Nicobar archipelago islanders is certainly not without precedence. It is well documented that the ancient people of Oceania traveled over millions of square miles of the Pacific Ocean. These people's "wayfinding" relied on using their senses to interpret the ocean environment in much the same way as animals do to detect and avoid dangers, as in the 2004 Asian earthquake and subsequent tsunami. According to astronomer and science writer, Leila Belkora, when Captain James Cook travelled from Tahiti to New Zealand accompanied by Tahitian chief and navigator, Tupaia, he was astounded to discover that the Māori and Tupaia shared the same language. He later learned that Hawaiian natives also shared this language.[3] How could this be? Research undertaken throughout the 1960s to 1980s suggests that the people of Oceania possessed a wisdom that allowed them to navigate using their knowledge about "every available feature of the seascape and phenomenon of nature: winds, ocean swells, the habits of land-roosting birds, and how wind and current affects the shape of ocean waves."[4] Their familiarity with the night sky also allowed them to use the stars as guides.

27

They created "star paths," a mental global positioning system, and taught these and other sensory-derived environmental knowledge to their children.[5] A fascinating relatively recent example of this skill was recounted in Ward Goodenough's 1953 booklet *Native Astronomy in the Central Carolines* about a 1908–1910 German South Seas Expedition. It seems that the researchers came across an indigenous navigator who knew the star paths "from every known place to every other known place."[6] Such a person is rare in the extreme in today's world. It would appear that the tradition of passing on knowledge orally has come very close to being lost in Western society because, as a way of learning and educating young people, it is difficult to evaluate, test and, therefore, validate. Thus, this way of acquiring knowledge has been devalued to the point that it is all but lost. Fortunately, the Polynesian Voyaging Society is working to revive and preserve this ancient art and to teach these ancient skills to today's young native islanders.[7] The society was, however, dealt a blow in July 2010 when it was announced that master navigator, Mau Piailug, had died. In 1976, the Micronesian, who worked with the Society to reintroduce ancient navigational skills to Pacific Islanders, "navigated the double-hulled voyaging canoe Hokule'a from Hawaii to Tahiti on its maiden voyage."[8] Fortunately, the society is still very active and keeps its volunteers and supporters up to date with its activities using a variety of social networking sites.[9]

During, and after, the 2004 tsunami, stories also abounded about animals sensing the danger and fleeing affected areas. In the words of NBC correspondent, Charles Sabine, "[a]s a huge black curl of wave started rolling out at sea, humans stood transfixed. But in the animal world there appears to have been an earlier sense of danger, almost a sixth sense that something was terribly wrong."[10] A headline in National Geographic News questions, "Did Animals Sense Tsunami Was Coming?"[11] Reported eyewitness accounts, documented in a bullet list of strange animal behaviors, suggest that they must have:

- Elephants screamed and ran for higher ground.
- Dogs refused to go outdoors.
- Flamingos abandoned their low-lying breeding areas.
- Zoo animals rushed into their shelters and could not be enticed to come back out.[12]

These are just two of many accounts of animals intuiting that something bad was about to happen and reacting to that knowledge. Of course, journalists like a good story, and a tale of animal mythical powers is hard to resist, but while it is certain that some animals were lost in the tsunami, it seems clear that many did have some type of inner ability to read nature's signs and move to safety.

Unlike most other animals, the human species has no preformed pattern of behavior, and apparently no innate releasing mechanism that is so often referred to as instinct. Human brains are, however, clearly hardwired for survival, sex, hunting, and gathering. But in carrying out these impulses, we do not all behave in the same way. Humans generally have the same sense organs as other animals, but other animals use their much more limited intellectual capabilities to learn from their sense experiences and then adjust to their environment. These sensory-derived experiences are inherently important, but they are not considered knowledge within the Western education system, and have been given little academic attention because they do not lend themselves to traditional teaching, testing, or research methods. They are thus often either ignored, or considered to be pseudo-science. Knowledge gained through sensations is difficult to control and hence it seems dangerous and is mistrusted. The logical mind has difficulty with information that is infinite or sensual. Episodes of déjà vu and synchronicity, for example, are impossible to correlate with Western rational thinking, yet people generally accept the terms and the veracity of such experiences without much anxiety. The first is commonly used to describe happenings that seem to have been experienced in an identical manner before, while the second denotes occasions when perfect strangers meet, only to feel that they already know one another. There have also been ongoing questions surrounding *how* we know things commonly attributed to intuition. People in Western societies have a tendency to discredit or discount knowledge that is not learned through cognitive activities, but equally, they seem willing to accept, at least to some extent, the existence of intuition. Nevertheless, as we stated earlier in this chapter, that does not mean that intuition carries any official value in schools or in the workplace.

It seems to be commonly accepted that women possess more intuition than men. That belief in women's intuition has not, however, always proven beneficial to their wellbeing. Indeed, a lack of understanding of the source of this mysterious knowledge has often fueled the idea that women are more susceptible to the forces of evil, specifically sorcery and witchcraft, than their male counterparts and has thus been used against them. Throughout history, the authoritative sources of the dominant monotheistic religions of the Western world have been devastatingly effective in providing a rationale for condemning and subjugating women. The Bible's Ecclesiastics, for example, says, "More bitter than death is woman";[13] and "Blessed Art Thou O Lord our God, King of the Universe, who has not made me a heathen, who has not made me a slave, who has not made me a woman,"[14] is a prayer for Jewish men. Finally, in his first letter to Timothy, Paul wrote, "Let the woman learn in silence with all subjection. But I suffer not a woman to teach, nor to usurp authority over the man, but to be in silence. For Adam was first formed, then Eve. And Adam was not deceived, but the woman being deceived, was the transgression."[15]

Contrary to these biblical professions, the Book of Proverbs ascribes "Wisdom" a feminine persona. Wisdom speaks of being present at God's side and helping Him during the process of creation. She permeates all things, and is the reflection of the eternal light. She was made by God, yet sits at His side, and points the way to God and to eternal life:

Yahweh created me, [Wisdom] first-fruits of his fashioning, before the oldest of His works. From everlasting, I was firmly set, from the beginning, before the earth came into being. The deep was not, when I was born, nor were the springs with their abounding waters. Before the mountains were settled, before the hills, I came to birth; before He had made the earth, the countryside, and the first elements of the world.

When He fixed the heavens firm, I was there, when He drew a circle on the surface of the deep, when He thickened the clouds above, when the sources of the deep began to swell, when He assigned the sea its boundaries and the waters will not encroach on the shore when He traced the foundations of the earth, I was beside the master craftsman, delighting Him day after day, ever at play in His presence, at play everywhere on His earth, delighting to be with the children of men.[16]

While it may seem uncharacteristic to give such an important "figure" female attributes, it makes ultimate sense when we recollect that the original text was written in Hebrew and the word for wisdom in that language takes the feminine form. Regardless of the explanation behind Wisdom's gender, the most important aspect of a believer's understanding is that she is the guide that will lead to God and to eternal life, and it is important to remember that religious affiliation has always come with rules to obey, sacrifices to make, and an ecclesiastical hierarchy to ensure continued spread of the faith on earth and a path to Heaven for its followers. It is interesting to note that more and more people today question the male designation that tends to be automatically assigned to God.

If, after the crucifixion of Jesus Christ, Christianity had any chance of establishing a place for itself among traditional religions, its followers had to have a relatively safe way to worship without attracting too much attention to themselves and their activities. One successful strategy was to align Christian celebrations with already established religious traditions. This became common practice and even today, many of the most prominent Christian holidays fall in line with other religious celebrations. By the Middle Ages, folklore and miracles were well integrated in Christian worship. The Church allowed for the incorporation of some pagan symbolism and practices to maintain an aura of familiarity and thus keep the peasants from returning to ancient ways. But also during the Middle Ages, and for about 200 years after that time, the Christian Church encouraged and exploited people's fears of Satan to use as a form of control and to explain away plagues, Church wealth, and overall bad times. Fear of Satan lead to the Inquisition and the sanctioning of witch-hunts and the subsequent killing of women who demonstrated knowledge derived from outside the Bible, most notably, intuitive sources. Two Dominicans, Heinrich Kramer and Jacob Sprenger claimed papal sanction for their 15th century witch-hunting manual, *The Malleus Maleficarum*,[17] and even inserted a statement of support from the Catholic Church, despite the fact that (or perhaps because) the Church placed the book on the index of forbidden works; yet between 1487 and 1669 it was reprinted 29 times. The manual provided the rationale and legal means for killing women in countless numbers. In Germany, one judge, Benedikt Carpzov, sentenced 20,000 women to death as witches.[18] The Christian churches are not, however, by any means the only religious bodies to have abused women.

Followers of Islam, the newest of the Western monotheistic religions, may have the best history when it comes to educating women, but the worst perception regarding the abuse and discrimination of them. Although it is no excuse, the reason for their mistreatment comes from the example of their monotheistic predecessors, Jews and Christians, which in turn clearly caught the virus from the Greeks. Well before the days of Islam, patriarchy was solidly entrenched in the pre-Islamic Middle East. The practice of girls and women staying at home and being covered and veiled when outside the home was present in Byzantine society and, indeed, many of the repressive practices attributed to Muslims were inherited from their Byzantine past. Byzantine society was most influenced by pre-Christian Greek culture. Leila Ahmed, in her *Women and Gender in Islam: Historical Roots of a Modern Debate*, writes that,

> Aristotle's influence was widespread and enduring. His theories in effect codified and systematized the social values and practices of that society. They were presented, however, as objective scientific observations and were received by both Arab and European civilizations (or by major figures within these civilizations) as the articulation of eternal philosophical and scientific verities.[19]

Interestingly, the status of women and girls would have been significantly higher in the Middle East had there been more Egyptian influence. It has been well documented that Egypt was much more liberal, and by some accounts men and women were fairly equal. But, according to Ahmed, Egypt was conquered and colonized by Greeks and eventually also became a male-dominated society.[20] By the Arab conquest, Muslims simply continued the Christian, Jewish, Greek, and Roman attitudes and mores with regard to women and girls. Thus, Islam started its history at a time when women and girls were less educated than men and boys, although they did learn to read, write, and count. Moreover, because they were restricted in movement and contact and confined mostly to their homes, their sequestering created opportunities for women to serve each other in their highly segregated society and as men were not allowed contact with them, gave rise to a need for women who were educated as teachers, midwives, and doctors. This separation of women and the contrast in education and opportunity highlights the difference in the way male and female education was valued. Women's education was considered less valuable than that of men, yet it was more developed and advanced than previously experienced in Middle Eastern cultures. The objective of women's education was, however, restricted to better service of their more highly educated husbands and sons, and ministry to each other.

The treatment of women in the Jewish tradition differs markedly according to which arm of the faith is pursued. But overall, the Talmud states that women are a *divine presence*. A divine presence may be a good thing, but it makes a woman an "other." The ancient Jewish role of a woman has often been relegated to that of a spectator, and while that is not perhaps as repressive as in other religions, it most certainly does not allow her much say in how to run her life. Her primary role has traditionally been to ensure the well-being and the education of her husband and sons. Historically the lot of a Jewish woman was to nurture the learning of others, thus her own education was not necessary. The fostering of such high expectations for husbands and sons and low expectations for daughters and wives had to play heavily toward the death of women's self-esteem and a sense of identity confusion, especially when their religious authoritative source had suggested that woman sat next to God, was named Wisdom, and was *divine*. Erica Brown in "An Intimate Spectator: Jewish Women Reflect on Adult Study" states that this "highly articulate group of adult women have gone largely unarticulated in educational research."[21] So apparently things have not changed all that much.

However, not only is the Torah more complimentary towards women than the Bible or Koran, but it also provides some interesting metaphoric insight into why women are different from men, and how these differences are not negative (as the Koran and Bible claim) but positive. Judaism suggests that men and women's minds are not the same (and modern science has proven that), but instead of one being superior to the other, each is different but equal, and the whole is greater than the sum of the parts. Because Eve was made of material (rib) from inside Adam's body, the Torah and Judaism suggest that women are thus more internal, insightful, and have more of an "inner reasoning" than men.[22] But these differences go far beyond women's intuition and offer some explanation into the how and the why of human survival. Coupling women's *inner reasoning* and *local environmental awareness* (intuition), and men's external strength and wider environmental awareness can hardly fail to contribute to increased outcomes and evolutionary longevity.[23] Modern research supports the Torah and finds that women are more intuitive (unconsciously environmentally aware), in local surroundings, whereas men only equal women in local surroundings when stimuli is more male-oriented or self relevant.[24]

Evolutionary and gender mandates, such as maternal demands, cause a division of labor, which in turn causes cultural norms that reinforce biological differences. This is a reality for most women, but it is indeed interesting that the ancient Hebrews picked up on the differences and simply attributed them to Godly intervention. Unfortunately, however, they failed to take God's initiative with regard to Wisdom and rather continued patriarchy, albeit using more psychologically than the physically repressive methods favored by Christians and Muslims. Regardless, none of the Western monotheistic religions have ever taken full advantage of the differences and intuitive gifts of women.

It is easy to blame these three religions for the suppression of intuition, but unequal valuing of the attributes of women goes much further into the past, to a time before their great influence on Western culture, indeed to as long ago as 700 B.C.E. when, according to Sarah Pomeroy, the Greek writer Hesiod described "the divine progression from female-dominated generations, characterized by natural, earthy emotional qualities [intuition], to the superior and rational [reason] monarchy of Olympian Zeus."[25] It is important to note Hesiod's use of the word "divine." Pomeroy asserts that it was Zeus' practice to subordinate females; an organizational pattern that eventually became public policy throughout ancient Greece. This is perhaps best articulated by Aristotle who explains that "[t]he relation of male to female is naturally that of superior to inferior—of the ruling to the ruled."[26] Aristotle's decree is not surprising bearing in mind that in *Generations of Animals* he suggests that because "females are weaker and colder in nature" than males, "we must look upon the female character as being a sort of natural deficiency."[27] The three major Western religions thus found their philosophical tenets in the writings and teachings of the ancient Greeks, who not only helped establish patriarchy, but also denigrated women's attributes other than their ability to reproduce.

Women have long been thought to construct knowledge intuitively for the purpose of helping others and for the benefit of society, and indeed, developmental psychologists consider it common knowledge that the moral development of girls and women differs from that of boys and men. In addition, Carol Gilligan and Jane Attanucci argue that traditional means of measuring moral development characterizes male moral reasoning as reflecting a justice orientation, whereas females are socialized toward a care orientation and responsibility for interpersonal relationships.[28] Differences have also been found in the area of ethics and morals in that males demonstrate less guilt and shame than females, and take less personal responsibility for their behavior, a phenomenon commonly referred to as *locus of control*. Males have a higher level of an *external locus of control*, that is, they will tend to blame others or outside influences for their behavior, while females have a higher level of an *internal locus of control*. If you ask a teenage boy why he did poorly on a test, he will probably say it was a stupid test, or he had to do chores so he didn't have time to study. A teenage girl might say she isn't that smart or she has poor time management skills. Moreover, because moral and cognitive development run along parallel lines, women's cognitive development is also different – it is more complex and focuses on connections and collaboration that use intuition, and personally constructed meaning and self-understanding as ways of knowing, yet Western education has traditionally relied strongly upon rational thinking and analytical ways of acquiring knowledge. Thus, in today's Western culture, the under appreciation of women's contributions to society can at least in part be linked to the discounting of intuition and to biases and misinformation. While it is true that working opportunities and conditions for women have improved significantly over the past few decades, many people still see women's primary role as being home-based and domestically centered. The foundation for this bias lies in the Western secondary and post secondary education systems which were created and taught by men for men, and although that has changed, most of the methods and manner of teaching by both men and women educators still predominantly favor boys and men over girls and women. It is not difficult to realize the enormity of the continuing uphill struggle when we hear a recent past-president of Harvard University, Lawrence Summers, suggesting that women are not as successful in math and science because they may have different innate abilities![29] Many in the science community quickly refuted Summers' statement and he resigned his position just one year later under pressure from an increasingly hostile faculty.

In 1970, more than three decades before Summers' statement, William Perry[30], also of Harvard, conducted epistemological research on undergraduates and found no significant differences between male and female students. While Perry's original work included few women subjects, he later replicated his study using only women. This later study confirmed his original findings, but that may be at least partly because his method and instrument were still more androcentric than not. Nevertheless, Perry's work is still considered important because his qualitative phenomenological method indicated not only how women and men are similar, but also provided a means to identify the ways in which women are epistemologically unique. From a pedagogical viewpoint, the most important factor stemming from this type of research is the realization that men and women do not learn the same way and that women have had to *accommodate* to be considered educated. In Western schools, women have traditionally learned that information fed to them is valuable but that their own interpretation of the meaning of that information is not. Thus, in the classroom, women have traditionally had a tendency to be silent and to conform to the ideas of others. Although women generally are more talkative than men, in the classroom the opposite is true. Women are less likely to reflect verbally or to question what they hear; it is rare for a student, especially a female non-Western student to question a professor about knowledge or its source. Women have learned that knowledge originates outside the self, therefore they look to others for their education, often question their own achievements, and believe themselves to be undeserving. In their book, *Women's Ways of Knowing: The Development of Self, Voice, and Mind*, authors Mary Belenky, Blythe Clinchy, Nancy Goldberger, and Jill Tarule suggest that,

> connected knowing comes more easily to many women than does separate knowing [and that] educators can help women develop their own authentic voices if they emphasize connection over separation, understanding and acceptance over assessment, and collaboration over debate; if they accord respect to and allow time for the knowledge that emerges from firsthand experience; if instead of imposing their own expectations and arbitrary requirements, they encourage students to evolve their own patterns of work based on the problems they are pursuing.[31]

Modern all-girls' schools are no longer seen as a means of segregating girls from boys but rather as a sanctuary for young women to learn and grow in a safe and positive environment. But after the passing of Title IX in 1972, these single-sex schools were deemed unfair because they denied equal treatment and equal access to male students. The idea of an all-girls' education began to fade through the 1980s; however, in the early 1990s, educators were revisiting this educational option.

The National Coalition of Girls' Schools saw significant growth in enrollment, as indeed did other single-sex schools. To answer critics of all-girls' schools and to demonstrate their strength in teaching young women, the Coalition organized several conferences in the early 1990s in subjects in which girls are traditionally thought to do poorly – math, science, and technology. The strategies produced at the conference were as follows:

- Using relevant real-world applications from girls' lives
- Drawing on vocabulary metaphors that girls could identify with
- Teaching in collaborative and cooperative ways
- Calling students by name, and waiting for them to reply before moving on to the next student
- Encouraging risk-taking
- Exploring mistakes and acknowledging their value
- Teaching alternative solutions, rather than just a single right answer to a given problem
- Using writing as a means of learning any subject
- Explaining through stories
- Helping students see themselves as sources of knowledge[32]

Perhaps without realizing it, the Coalition developed strategies that would be in line with scientific research - the manner in which girls should be educated is by aligning their education to their nature as is the case with boys. Although environmental factors are certainly important, differences in the brain structure and chemistry seem to be more important. "The tendencies of girls to be more contemplative, collaborative, intuitive, and verbal, and boys to be more physically active, aggressive, and independent in their learning style seemed to stem from brain function and development."[33] The Coalition helped shed light on the educational needs of girls, and the benefits they reap from a single-sex education. The women who attended these schools testified at the conferences to their success, noting that their education had fostered in them a sense of self-awareness and actualization, confidence, and achievement. In their study of ninth grade students in Nigeria, Valerie Lee and Marlaine Lockheed found that girls attending single-sex schools scored better in mathematics and had fewer stereotypical views of the subject than girls attending co-ed schools. The all-girls' schools tended to have a smaller enrollment with a better teacher /student ratio, and the benefits to girls were best seen in these small schools.[34] The researchers also found that the girls' schools provided an advantage by matching female students with female teachers, affording them positive female role models and allowing them to form relationships that were beneficial and supportive.[35] It must be pointed out, however, that the National Coalition of Girls' Schools stresses that equal access and opportunity should not be the focus in the education of girls, but instead the equality of their experiences and outcomes must be examined.[36] Being equal does not have to mean being the same. So it wasn't so much what the president of Harvard actually said, but how and why he said it that was the problem.

Regardless of the comparable size of brains, academic ability, and preferred ways of learning, women may indeed be more receptive than men, and some even more than other women, to intuitive knowledge. At the 2004 Annual Conference of the Society of Neuroscientists, researcher Jeffery Lorberbaum suggested that motherhood permanently alters brain function. Lorberbaum and his colleagues from the Medical University of South Carolina reported that they had found that mothers are much more attuned than men and non-mothers in responding to the emotional responses of their infants, with mothers showing a very different pattern of brain activity when listening to their own babies' cries.[37] Because of a believed chemical change to their bodies after motherhood, women who are mothers have a means of deriving knowledge that is different from men and other women. Lorberbaum's research findings may help to explain why it was not uncommon for ancient cultures and tribes to recognize *knowledge specialists* and shamans of both sexes. In fact, the oldest known and well-preserved upper Paleolithic burial tomb found in Czechoslovakia, which held many shamanic artifacts, was the final earthly resting place of a woman.[38]

But to conclude that women have more intuition than men is questionable – male intuition is, perhaps, simply not as obvious as that of women. One instance of male intuition is perhaps best known as *hunter's intuition,* where a multitude of senses and experiences come together toward creating the knowledge necessary for a successful kill. A hunter's intuition is personified by the lone hunter processing information from his senses and experiences toward bringing home food for his family. This is best achieved in a concentrative state away from others. When hunters collaborate, it is to share knowledge and to draw conclusions from each other's individual experience. They may hunt or fight as a group, but still the group focus is toward an individual result, the acquisition of something, or the defeat of an enemy. Hence, it is usually individually developed skills, not group effort, that create the opportunities to achieve the desired outcomes. Whether 50,000 years ago or today, that is how men hunt and fight, and as old and primitive as it may be, it still tends to be considered a distinctly male attribute. Of course, just as there are exceptions to all rules, some of the best hunters were and are women, but the gender dominance in this area is certainly male. It is important to note that we are talking here about traditional hunting where the skills of hunter and hunted are balanced, not the modern-day idea of luring prey into a bait station where they are "sitting ducks." Luring animals to a place where they can be picked off by people sitting in comfortable blinds or fenced into "hunting ranches" with no opportunity to hide or escape is not hunting; it is just killing for killing's sake.

Ernest Hemingway, in a number of his outdoor writings, claimed a hunter's intuition as extrasensory perception. In the notes for his unfinished memoir, *True At First Light,* he makes frequent reference to African hunters and their profoundly heightened senses. Similarly, the indigenous Bedouin that live removed from villages and towns speak of the "second sight," an additional sense that allows a person to sense danger well before any indication from other senses. These examples are no different from intuition in that they denote instances of indigenous males possessing an ability to sense game or foresee danger from a distance, not because they have any psychic ability, but rather because they are able to read sensory stimuli from afar.

Hunter's intuition is a unique glimpse into chaos theory working in a natural environment away from the bustle of modern life. Successful hunters must open all aspects of their awareness of nature many of which, aside from their observable hunting skills, are hidden from the unskilled observer. These hunters allow themselves to be immersed into a world outside of thought; into a world of pure instinct. Hunter's intuition is the by-product of tension and a state of hyper-awareness that is rarely reproduced in our modern lives, and has often been attributed to embellished campfire stories of successful hunts. It is, however, really much more than that. Even though people know it has happened, it is difficult to explain convincingly, because these instances of knowledge acquisition always take place alone and are thus unobservable. Female intuition is more visible and common because it takes place within local environments. Sex differences in spatial acuity are well established, particularly that men have a significant advantage in large, three dimensional arenas. It is, however, less known that women have an advantage in seeing and understanding smaller local environments. The implication of this is that males are predisposed to explore larger areas while women are more comfortable and keener in smaller spaces (We discuss this idea fully in Chapter 9). Modern Western man has, however, all but lost his extra ability in larger three-dimensional environments since Western society's move from a dependence upon nature to the technologically-driven mass production lifestyle spawned by the Industrial Revolution. This might go some way toward explaining why more males than females are attracted to video gaming.

While the Industrial Revolution undoubtedly brought many advantages to Western nations, it began a trend of separating people, especially males, from nature and from their ability to intuit. Before the Industrial Revolution, people had generally worked outside or as artisans where their product was directly related to nature. Now, instead of working in concert with nature to produce quality items, Western man focuses his energies on producing larger and larger quantities of consumer goods; unfortunately though, as demand for manufactured goods has risen, the ability to provide quality products has diminished. Work now revolves around the idea of production and a person's worth is associated with increased productivity, which is, in turn, driven by materialism and consumption. This worldview not only drives humans further from nature, but it also requires their dominion over it and its finite resources. Giorgio Agamben states in *The Man Without Content* that this separation "begins at the moment when Locke discovers in work the origin of property, continues when Adam Smith elevates it to the source of all wealth, and reaches its peak with Marx, who makes of it the expression of man's very humanity."[39] During and since the Industrial Revolution, people have become used to working in large buildings where their senses are assaulted by multiple forms of sensory pollution, including unnatural lighting, loud monotonous machine noise, and the smells associated with large-scale manufacturing. How long does it take for a person to lose natural sensate power? We can't stop and smell the roses if we don't see the roses, and if we don't see or smell roses, there is no value associated with that experience or even the rose for that matter. Perhaps this is the reason why people living in the West seem to feel that they are no longer an integral part of nature and that they no longer need nature other than as material to control, use, own, and destroy.

Idealists who value knowledge derived from authoritative sources often conclude that intellect that stems from ideas cannot be considered sense-experiences, but in his book, *Ten Philosophical Mistakes*, Mortimer Adler suggests that,

> Sense includes a variety of powers, such as the power of perceiving, of remembering, and of imagining. Intellect also includes a variety of powers, such as the power of understanding, of judging, and of reasoning. We sometimes lump together all the results of exercising our sensitive powers under the head of *sense-experience*. So, too, we lump together all the operations of our intellectual powers under the head of thought.[40]

Thus, while perhaps ideas are intelligible, our sensory experiences are rarely purely sensible. The world of ideas is created only in the human mind, but knowledge from the senses can include the known and unknown natural world, together with the knowledge created by humans. Adler supports this position when he states,

> There is a sense in which knowing is like eating. The edible, before it is eaten, exists quite independently of the eater and is whatever it is regardless of how it is transformed by being eaten. So, too, the knowable exists quite independently of the knower and is whatever it is whether it is known or not, and however it is known.[41]

The human mind includes both intellectual and sensory powers. Reality exists whether we think it or not, and all knowledge comes from our experiences via our senses. But to be considered knowledgeable and educated, we must exhibit a breadth of knowledge that is primarily derived from the intellect and has been constructed by authoritative sources. In other words, if knowledge does not come from an authoritative source and is not supported by evidence and reason, it is either deemed to be mere opinion or dismissed as non-existent. We need look no further than the curricula of our secondary schools and universities to see core requirements that perpetuate this limited scope of knowledge. They are, however, considered valuable. Yet neither knowledge without understanding, nor knowledge that does not promote wisdom is of practical value to anyone, and scholars who are thus trained are of very limited use to any society.

Beyond the obvious abilities to hear what other people are saying to us, to see our surroundings, and to smell the aromas wafting from the kitchen, people living in

Western society tend to decry abilities that are divorced from the immediate use of the senses. Intuition stems from the senses, but how long will it be before all sensory ability apart from the most basic are lost forever? Could this possibility be termed de-evolution? A loss of intuition or sensate ability may be an evolutionary by-product of increased worldwide urbanization. The question is, how many generations does it take until intuitive potential is permanently diminished? This is evolution and people generally tend to assume that evolution always has worked towards making Homo sapiens better, ensuring the survival of our species. Much has changed, however, over the last few years with regard to what we believe about evolution. It was not long ago that we were taught that evolution was a long slow process more linear than not. The Theory of Evolution gained rapid acceptance in Western societies because it fit nicely with linear thinking and it served ideally as the cornerstone of the ideological and social construct of progress. The Theory of Evolution as we knew it was used to legitimize both progress and the domination of non-Western people. The priest and king hegemony was fully united in the ideology of man over nature for progress—more nature to conquer, and it also legitimized man's inhumanity to man as a necessary part of the process. If we believe in the evolution of species, it is easy to deduce that the evolution of man, and hence Western societies, were at the apex of the evolutionary spearhead—the Theory of Evolution fostered the *theory of racism*, and both provided the natural and human fuel necessary to drive the Industrial Revolution. But we now know as Stephen Jay Gould states, "humans are just a little twig on a gigantic bush of evolution . . . not a terminal direction."[42] But the Theory of Evolution itself has suffered for its reliance upon linearity. Eva Jablonka and Marion Lamb in *Evolution in Four Dimensions* write,

> Molecular biology has shown that many of the old assumptions about the genetic system, which is the basis of present-day neo-Darwinian theory, are incorrect.[43]

Jablonka and Lamb's research suggests that our present understanding of the Theory of Evolution is both outdated and incomplete. They conclude their book with a warning:

> We are convinced that for all major changes in evolution one has to think about at least two dimensions of heredity: the genetic and epigenetic. With many animals, a third dimension, that involving behaviorally transmitted information, is also relevant, and for humans the symbolic systems add a fourth dimension. All four ways of transmitting information introduce, to different degrees and in different ways, instructive mechanisms into evolution. All shape evolutionary change. Yet, so far, the existence of the instructive aspect has had little impact on evolutionary thinking. This must soon change. As molecular biology uncovers more and more about epigenetic and genetic inheritance, and as behavioral studies show how much information is passed

on to others by non-genetic means, evolutionary biologists will have to abandon their present concept of heredity, which was fashioned in the early days of genetics, nearly a century ago. If Darwinian Theory is to remain in touch with what is already known about heredity and evolution, efforts must be made to incorporate multiple inheritance systems and the educated guesses they produce.[44]

If the evolutionary tree is not so much a tree but rather more a bush, and the slow steady march is more a wander, full of bursts and stumbles, we can identify times in human history when a branch of the bush, for whatever reason, withered and died, and other times when a different branch grew fast and straight. Yet surely there are other more subtle reasons why one is favored over another. And in the journey of human history, as in most other things, it is a combination of small things that really matters. Further, evolution is thought of as positive, but evolution is as cruel as it is kind. As one species evolves by acquiring traits that ensures its survival, another species also changes in ways that can lead to extinction. Environmental advantages and degradation and blind luck are major factors in survival. But subtle factors and conscious decisions also contribute to a species' fate. Ample and nutritious food is a factor, but so are diseases and toxins. A decision to move from one continent to another can be beneficial to some yet devastating for others, and the decision to maintain a lifestyle divorced from nature may be leading toward ultimate ruin.

It is well documented that humans are the primary cause of the following six changes to the global environment:

the increasing concentration of CO_2 in the atmosphere, alterations to the global biogeochemical cycle of nitrogen and other elements, the production and release of persistent organic compounds such as the chlorofluorocarbons, widespread changes in land use and land cover, hunting and harvesting of natural populations of large predators and consumers, and biological invasions of non-native species.[45]

These changes are caused mainly by human agricultural and industrial activities, which are affected, and whose effects are compounded, by the volatile growth of the human population. These changes can escalate, causing other disturbances to the global environment such as the "loss of biological diversity by causing the extinction of species and genetically distinct populations."[46] The accelerated destruction of species and uniquely diverse populations is troubling because of their unlikely reversal, and "biological invasions contribute substantially to extinction."[47] Researchers note that biological invasions have constantly taken place throughout the history of the world, but it is the increased rate at which they are currently occurring that has caused alarm.[48] Marine ecosystems are the most vulnerable to biological invasions due to their proximity to high concentrations of humans. About sixty percent of the global human population is located near coastlines, and these areas have been modified and decimated by humans.[49] Peter Vitousek and his colleagues note that:

> As of 1995, 22% of recognized marine fisheries were overexploited or already depleted, and 44% more were at their limit of exploitation…. The consequences of fisheries are not restricted to their target organisms; commercial marine fisheries around the world discard 27 million tons of non-target animals annually, a quantity nearly one-third as large as total landings. Moreover, the dredges and trawls used in some fisheries damage habitats substantially as they are dragged along the sea floor.[50]

Both human and industrial growth has had a devastating effect on the rates of animal extinction and we have no one to blame but ourselves;

> . . . as many as one-quarter of Earth's bird species have been driven to extinction by human activities over the past two millennia, particularly on oceanic islands. At present, 11% of the remaining birds, 18% of the mammals, 5% of fish, and 8% of plant species on Earth are threatened with extinction.[51]

What we now consider biodiversity is not nearly as diverse as it once was, and again we are to blame. That is not, however, the whole story; the growth of the human population can also affect human groups. The movement from one area to another by humans, together with all that they take with them, can create disastrous results for not only non-human life forms, but also for other humans. We are aware that infectious diseases, such as smallpox, are carried by human hosts as they move from one area to another.[52] The introduction of disease by foreign entities can immediately reduce a population through a process that is termed *ecological release*. Ecological release occurs when a population for whatever reason leaves its traditional home and moves into another environment; the moving population is significantly reduced because of the shock of moving as well as the exposure to new environs.[53] It is also important to note that immigrant populations have often been known to introduce diseases and illnesses, such as influenza, smallpox, and measles to indigenous populations with disastrous results. The Taino people of the Caribbean, the Inca of South America, and the Australian Aborigines are just a few examples of people who saw their numbers severely reduced shortly after contact with Western explorers. But Charles Mann states that the domestic animals which the explorers brought with them had a much more devastating effect on native populations than human contact between Native Americans and the first Europeans.[54] The Spaniard De Soto found and well documented a vibrant and heavily populated Mississippi Valley. After he left, Europeans did not visit it again for approximately 100 years, and when they did return, they found the same area virtually deserted and the large native towns and villages looking as if they had never existed.

De Soto's accounts were considered wildly inaccurate, but De Soto's expedition travelled with 300 domesticated pigs (the dog was the only domesticated North

American animal at that time). Several researchers have put the death rate caused by zoonotic disease within the Mississippi Valley region as high as 96%. The population level of the Caldo, who lived on the Texas and Arkansas border, was estimated to have dropped shortly after De Soto's visit from 200,000 to 8,500.[55] Those who survived were, however, still not safe. Further exploration and European encroachment bringing other diseases, together with the shock of forced movement from one area to another to avoid disease, led to a probable human environmental disaster greater than any other. The estimated death toll of Europe's Black Death at its height was estimated at 30% of its total population. Yet because of the catastrophic effects of ecological release on early Native American tribes, it is safe to assume that some populations were rendered extinct before their existence was even known. It would be easy to think that this phenomenon is little more than a history lesson for modern Western society, but today's economic globalization, caused by an insatiable appetite for more and cheaper consumer goods, is causing the movement of large numbers of people with its increased risk of ecological release. History has proven how deadly that can be, and it is safe to say that if a rapid extinction of humans happened once, it can happen again. So why don't we learn from the past so that we can avoid avenues of danger now and in the future. Unfortunately, modern living has placed so many pressures on people that it is difficult for most to think past personal day-to-day survival, let alone take steps to protect those who live far away geographically or have yet to be born. And modern human living has people so absorbed in connectivity via business and social networks that it is almost impossible for them to take the time to contemplate their place in the bionetwork.

Far too many people spend their days rushing around trying to finish tasks so that they can get on to the next one. The more things they can cross off their "to do" list the better, for it demonstrates personal productivity. This is a learned behavior that most people feel is necessary in order to be a member of modern society. But instead of feeling more self-actualized, there is rather a feeling that we are more and more *under* actualized. Modern societal membership comes with the degradation of consciousness, which ensures that people go through life in a state of chronic sensory drowsiness, and this degradation may ultimately cost people dearly as sensory retardation will diminish their time for reflection and other metaphysical activities. Spiritualism requires reflection. But it is difficult if not impossible to reflect upon anything while multitasking, which is often necessary in today's hectic lifestyle and has come to be viewed as a positive and necessary attribute. Modern society makes it difficult and, at times, unrealistic to engage in only one thing at a time.

Recently, multitasking has been linked to a new phenomenon called attention deficit trait.[56] Current studies are suggesting that those who are multi-tasking are short changing themselves. People can learn while being distracted, but the learning process is less efficient. Learning while being distracted engages two different parts of the brain, particularly the medial temporal lobe and the striatum, but these two different areas of the brain compete for attention. Involuntarily, the striatum automatically tries to grab attention away from the area of concentration by encouraging the medial temporal lobe to refocus on new stimuli.[57] Interestingly, this is an ancient evolutionary defense mechanism that helped early humans avoid being eaten. The overload of demands on attention, as Edward Hallowell states, causes the brain to begin to panic "reacting just as if that [distraction] were a bloodthirsty, man-eating tiger."[58] Hallowell continues by stating that the most dangerous disability to learning is fear.

> Fear shifts us into survival mode and thus prevents fluid learning and nuanced understanding… if you're trying to deal intelligently with a subtle task, survival mode is highly unpleasant and counterproductive… The deep regions interpret the messages of overload they receive from the frontal lobes in the same way they interpret everything: primitively. They furiously fire signals of fear, anxiety, impatience, irritability, anger, or panic.[59]

It is important to realize that when two competing areas of the brain are engaged, the process not only affects the learning outcome but also dulls a person's perception of external stimuli and causes emotional and physical distress. Subsequently, the quality of the learning outcome is often diminished because the initial learning process is impinged upon by the divergent task. External stimuli purposefully distract the brain and conflict with the quality of the initial task. The metaphor of seemingly having too many things on one's plate might imply that people can lose things off that plate by forgetting them. In reality, they do not actually lose anything by multi-tasking, but the behavior distracts, and thus diminishes their ability to complete any task to its optimum potential.

It should be assumed that as humans continue to develop, any means of acquiring knowledge should be valued nurtured, and included in the educational curriculum. Intuition is the by-product of our experiences, and so it should be accepted into the decision-making process. This is especially the case with experiences in and of our natural environment. To be fully functional members of this planet's animal kingdom, people, both male and female must be allowed to become fully involved in *every* part of life, and that requires the use of all the senses to acquire knowledge. Hence both learned knowledge and experiential intuitively-derived knowledge, which further increases our *value experiences,* must be valued to ensure quality of experience over quantity. It is worrying to realize that we are moving rapidly away from the attributes that have allowed humans to evolve to our present level of development. We have a tendency to neither deny nor recognize the links that intuitively-derived knowledge have contributed to our differences and how these differences complement each other. Sensory-derived knowledge and the intuitive process for both females and males need to be valued and taught in our educational curriculum, the result of which will be an increase in our knowledge and a greater ability to enjoy all the benefits that derive from the diverse sources of knowledge, not just those found and nurtured in human males.

MY TEACHERS: FIRST, BEST, AND UNCERTIFIED

Four men played a pivotal role in my education: my grandfather, my father, Wayne, and Wayne's uncle, Penti. They were my most important teachers.

Fortunately, my grandfather, Grandpa Rioux, lived next door to me. He was a spry French-Canadian who had walked across the border into Minnesota in 1925 to work on the railroad. Once retired, Grandpa Rioux spent countless hours telling me stories while we whittled or walked in and around the local woods.

Around the time my grandfather moved to a boarding home, my father began taking me to hunt and to fish. A few years later we were joined by Wayne, a new neighbor who was roughly ten years younger than my father. When they got together they often spoke Finnish - their native language that was seldom used in public but never forgotten.

Wayne, my father, and I increasingly spent more time with Wayne's uncle, Penti. Penti lived in an even more isolated area than we did. The three generations of men patiently taught me Finnish and more. They made sure I understood what they were saying by translating everything into English when necessary.

Besides telling me, they showed me things and demonstrated tasks which I then replicated. They corrected me when needed, and I would try the tasks again until I reached their level of satisfaction. My youthful behavior was also corrected when appropriate. I acquired dispositions, knowledge, and skills. I learned procedurally and conceptually, as they felt it was really equally important that I understand why I should do something rather than just how to do it. For example, when hunting in a wilderness area it was more important to understand why I needed to use a compass than just read one. I listened a lot and learned much from these four men far beyond woods and water.

Equally important, I learned a lot more than just hunting. For example, the putting up of several deer was very important to the people of the area. Most families needed to kill two to three deer during the two-week hunting season because beef was an expensive luxury.

One particular deer season the hunting had been poor because the deer population was down. On the last day of the season, another hunter, a co-worker of Wayne's, joined us for a deer drive. We selected a remote area that we knew had not been hunted recently. Wayne and I made a drive through a large swamp, and Penti and my father, both older and excellent shots, were posted with the new hunter overlooking trails along the edge of the swamp. After a couple of hours or so of hunting through the dense swamp, Wayne and I both caught a glimpse of a large buck with two does moving on a trail that would lead them to our waiting hunters. Wayne had carefully positioned both of us so that we could corral the deer toward our posted hunters. After a while, there was a shot. I was sure that we had at least one deer and anxiously waited for more shots, but they did not come. We finally met Penti and my father and learned that neither of them had shot. We walked toward the other hunter and were met with him proudly holding up a fox. I had seen fox tracks on the same trail that the deer were following, as wily bucks frequently follow foxes. I had already been taught that upon seeing a fox or fresh fox tracks that I should look closely for following deer.

As we walked back to the trucks after a hard, cold, fruitless day of hunting, I heard Wayne say something to my father and Penti in Finnish. I didn't catch the words, but I could not mistake the meaning as I saw Penti purse his lips and silently shake his head. I didn't hear, but I didn't have to, and I knew I never wanted them to say or think that about me. It was a lesson in ethics and morality. The man shot the fox with no intentions of eating it, and probably cost us a deer or two. His ethical breach went back many thousands of years. Ethics and morals are intricately entwined in education, but sometimes these lessons are the hardest to learn.

TRADITIONAL INDIGENOUS EDUCATION

Even today, when an Aboriginal mother notices the first stirrings of speech in her child, she lets it handle the 'things' of that particular country: leaves, fruit, insects and so forth. The child, at its mother's breast, will toy with the 'thing', talk to it, test its teeth on it, learn its name, repeat its name – and finally chuck it aside. We give our children guns and computer games … They gave their children the land.

Bruce Chatwin, The Songlines

Most descriptions of indigenous teaching methods highlight resistance against Western educational models and their effects on indigenous communities. That is, of course, both natural and necessary. It would be foolhardy to educate a child for a world that has all but disappeared while leaving him or her ignorant of the tools needed to survive in the "real" world. But that is the dilemma facing many indigenous people today. They mourn the loss of their culture and way of life but, at the same time, they have a duty to ensure a future for their children. So what do they do? Is there a way to make a living today and still maintain a traditional lifestyle?

In chapter 2 we discussed the plight of the Bushmen and the struggles they are having as they try to survive. The romantic in us desperately wants them, and all indigenous people trying to maintain some semblance of traditional lifestyle, to turn their back on all things modern and to follow the path of their ancestors. But is that practical? We know that non-contact tribes in South America are in a constant battle against industrial encroachment and loss of land, and, in Africa, since the discovery of diamonds in parts of the Kalahari Desert, the Bushmen are finding it all but impossible to move back onto their ancestral lands. The cold reality is that many indigenous people are given only two choices; to abandon their culture and embrace a modern lifestyle, or to try to eek out some sort of meager living on land that has been deemed of no value to modern man. Thus they face a future of dire poverty and hopelessness for themselves and their offspring. One further option, albeit one that is troublesome to many on both sides of the issue, involves eco-tourism. There has been an upsurge in recent years in the idea of adventure or expedition vacationing with several reputable travel companies offering the wealthy traveller an opportunity to see parts of the world that are exotic and wondrous and have, until relatively recently, been out of reach. Destinations such as Galápagos, the Amazon Rainforest, and Tanzania, to name but a few, entice the traveller with thoughts of recreating the voyages of discovery days of past centuries, only this time with all 'mod cons' and comforts. Along with the chance to see endangered wildlife in its natural environment, many of these expeditions offer the traveller the prospect of taking a step into the world of indigenous people. The National Geographic Expeditions website advertises one of its Tanzania trips as a "cultural safari" in which the traveller is invited to

> set out on foot to experience the wild wonders of Tanzania from the unique perspective of the people who call it home. On the shore of Lake Eyasi, a stunning salt lake in the Rift Valley, live among the timeless Hadza, one of the last hunter-gatherer groups in the world. Then settle into Maasai country, getting to know the culture and hiking the Ngorongoro Highlands, Olduvai Gorge, and the Serengeti Plain with our Maasai hosts.[1]

To many, this type of enterprise sounds as if it offers the best of all worlds to everyone involved – the tourists receive a unique and authentic experience, the travel company makes money, and the indigenous people are paid to maintain their traditional way of life. It sounds like an 'everybody wins' situation: but is it? There are, most certainly, benefits for the indigenous people. National Geographic, for example, awards grants to help them maintain or re-establish traditional skills. One such grantee, Nilda Callañaupa, is a master Andean weaver who leads the Center for Traditional Textiles of Cusco; a project dedicated to reviving and preserving Peruvian Inca textile traditions. Callañaupa, who has travelled extensively demonstrating her skills and her people's work, is grateful for the way her life has turned out:

> When I was young, shepherding in the mountains, I never would have imagined that some day I would receive a degree from the University of Cusco, make trips to the United States and other countries, have friends from different parts of the world and communicate long distances by fax, the internet or e-mail, I never would have imagined that I could create a Center to help my community and other communities of weavers to continue our art.[2]

Callañaupa's story is impressive, as are the women who work in the center. They learned to forego the services of middlemen and to control the sale of their work, much of which is sold to visiting tourists who are brought en masse to demonstrations of traditional arts and crafts. Again, this practice seems to work well for everyone as the indigenous people can make a living while maintaining a traditional lifestyle, and the tourists experience a way of life that is alien to their own. Moreover, through eco-tourism, the funding organizations and the indigenous people have found ways to preserve traditional education practices within the modern world. But the presence of tourists does not always create the best of atmospheres for indigenous people. Grant money is limited, so those who are poor and unskilled are often left to appeal to the visitors in whatever way they can. Thus, tourists are often hounded by people in tired traditional attire selling low quality art and craftwork and souvenirs or even, in some countries, begging. In his book, *The Healing Land*, Rupert Isaacson wrote about the Bushmen's hopes for profitable business partnerships with European tourist companies. The idea of a profit-sharing enterprise sounded perfect for all concerned.

The reality, however, was far different. For most indigenous people there was, and is, no business model or profit-sharing success. Eco-tourist organizations are, on the other hand, doing well, but to promote the exotic nature of their expeditions, they usually sell the idea that indigenous people are locked in a time that the modern world has by-passed. Thus, to attract tourists successfully, indigenous people can become imprisoned by their attempts to enter today's global economy. They must stay living in the past and make money, or evolve and lose the interest of the tourists. According to Isaacson, many of the Bushmen he saw, earned a living,

> by making crafts for tourists whose cars they waved down as they drove along the road to the park. Half the clan had gone to live in a private game reserve far to the south, where they existed as inmates in a human zoo, posing in their skins for tourists' cameras.[3]

In reality, the tourists learn little from these encounters about the traditional life of indigenous people; they learn about the realities of survival in a post-contact world.

While post-contact survival is indeed the reality for the vast majority of indigenous people worldwide, if we are to propose reintroducing some of the traditional ways of knowing and educational practices into today's Western education model, it is imperative that we understand the workings of those practices. Hence, this chapter examines how pre-contact people educated, or indeed still educate, their children to take on the traditional adult roles within their communities. Questions that rapidly come to mind when considering this type of indigenous education often revolve around our own educational experiences and knowledge. Thus, we tend to ask about the educational system; the separation, if any, between home life and school; the role of parents, community members, and other elders in the education process; the age of children deemed in need of education; the composition of a curriculum; and the definition of "critical skills." The answers to most of these questions are, of course, subject to wide variation depending on the location and way of life of the indigenous society, but of vital importance is the change in those education methods necessitated by contact with Western cultures.

Since a major purpose of education should be to transmit a society's cultural values to its young, it naturally follows that this education should be in harmony with the norms and desires of its community, its leaders, and elders. Education and learning is always best and most effective from within this cultural context. Students will value and embrace an education that is controlled by, relevant to, and reflective of, the values and cultural mores of their community. Ethnic differences in educational outcomes have more to do with the relevance of the knowledge being transmitted and a positive cultural climate than with the methods of instruction. Individual students accommodate to most methods to learn successfully, yet when they become educators, the didactic lecture style method often becomes their normal teaching style, because not only have they have been taught in this way, but also rarely are they encouraged to question a method that is so ingrained in traditional educational practice. It is interesting to note, however, that research into indigenous learning styles, including Paul Hughes and Arthur J. More's[4] work on Aboriginal ways of learning concludes that there is scant evidence to suggest that recurrent learning styles dominate among indigenous communities. On the contrary, while recurrent learning styles have been identified in many indigenous communities, it is important to understand that every student, regardless of cultural background, is different, and individual learning preferences among students should not be minimized. That said, cultural traditions are undoubtedly handed down and preserved through education, and an understanding of these facets of indigenous life are necessary to comprehend the rationale behind educational methods and subjects. When Hughes and More investigated Aboriginal ways of learning, they noted several areas of cultural conflict between indigenous recurrent learning styles and those accommodated in today's assimilated schools. According to Hughes and More, aboriginal learning comprised:

- Learning through observation and imitation rather than verbal instruction
- Learning through trial and feedback
- Emphasizing that the group is more important than the individual
- Holistic learning
- Visual-spatial skills
- Imagery
- Contextual learning
- Spontaneous learning[5]

A 1995 Australian government inquiry (resulting in the Blanchard Report) into aboriginal traditional education not only learned how children were educated, but also who in the community was involved in the process. Witnesses testified that, during their early years, children learned a great deal from their close relatives by informally watching and imitating the elders' actions. Only later, during training for initiation or religious ceremonies, did verbal instruction and structured learning at the hands of more distant members of the community enter the process. Regardless of the learning stage, however, the emphasis was always on educating the whole person for his or her role in society.[6]

In her starkly titled essay *Our People's Education; Cut the Shackles; Cut the Crap; Cut the Mustard*, educator and scholar Verna Kirkness, who was born on the Fisher River Reserve in Manitoba, offers insight into the problems encountered by Canadian indigenous students in assimilated programs. But before discussing the difficulties imposed by Western educational practices, Kirkness offers insight into the type of education indigenous children received in their own communities:

It was an education in which the community and the natural environment were the classroom, and the land was regarded as the mother of the people. Members of the community were the teachers, and each adult was responsible for ensuring that each child learned how to live a good life. Central to the teaching was the belief in the sacred, the Great Spirit.[7]

Kirkness continues with a description of a learning process much akin to the Australian aboriginal experience recounted in testimony collected for the Blanchard Report. Educating the whole person was seen as a priority, and children learned "traditional values such as humility, honesty, courage, kindness and respect"[8] through stories about heroes and tricksters. Practical skills that would benefit the family and the community at large were honed by watching and imitating experienced elders. And as the children learned to hunt, fish, gather food, build shelters, and raise other young, they did so with the understanding that they must never forget to respect their environment.[9] One of the most important aspects of indigenous education was its continuous connection to the spiritual life and the cultural continuity of the community. It is not difficult to understand the alienation felt in schools in which the teachers and many of the other children did not share that worldview.

While descriptions of learning styles and educational practices offer an idea of indigenous traditional education, it is only from first-hand accounts that we can really develop an appreciation for the emotional trauma engendered by its loss. In *Land of the Spotted Eagle*, Luther Standing Bear, a member of the Lakota Sioux tribe of American Indians, offers a remarkably detailed account of his childhood and the education he received at the hands of his parents. Although the traditional Indian way of life was in decline by the time he was born in the 1860s, Standing Bear or Ota K'te (Plenty Kill) as his parents called him, was trained to be a hunter, a warrior, and a respectful member of his tribe. For the first six years of his life, Standing Bear, like all the other Lakota children, was cared for solely by his mother. It was her duty to do all in her power to ensure that her child would develop into "a future protector of the tribe."[10] To this end, no-one, not even her husband, was allowed to distract her attention. "A weak or puny baby was a disgrace to a Lakota mother. It would be evidence to the tribe that she was not giving her child proper time and attention and not fulfilling her duty to the tribe…A fine, healthy child was therefore a badge of pride and respect."[11] According to Standing Bear, Lakota law even decreed that there should be no other children born within that initial six-year period, and parents who disregarded the rule lost the respect of the other members of the tribe.[12] As soon as a Lakota child was old enough to walk, parents and grandparents spent time teaching through example and play. Respect for elders, obedience, truthfulness, and kindness were all virtues with which the children were surrounded. Grandmothers were greatly involved in the care of the little ones, and routinely acted as cooks, teachers, and advisors. Lakota fathers were generally very proud of their sons and Standing Bear remembered fondly the times he and his father worked and played together. Everything which the mother taught, the father reinforced, but included in this training were the skills which would transform the boy into a Lakota warrior.[13]

Just as in white societies, many of the games played by the Lakota children helped to prepare them for adult life. In *My Indian Boyhood*, Standing Bear describes constructing and playing with bows and arrows. Although smaller than those used by the hunters, and made from whatever wood was available at the time, they were "just like the large bows, perfect in workmanship, and though small were just the thing with which to practice both the art of making and shooting."[14] By the time the children had mastered all the stages of the craft, they had learned many useful skills which would be vital to them as they prepared "for the tasks and duties of manhood."[15] It must also be remembered that the bow and arrow served as both a means of supplying food and defending the tribe from enemies: "It was the one weapon that preserved us from starvation or defeat, so it would have been unpardonable for a Sioux boy to grow up without knowledge of this useful article. Without it he could not face life."[16]

According to Standing Bear, every boy in the tribe had his own pony and became an expert in horsemanship. Yet again, the vast amount of time spent on and with his pony was vital to later success as a hunter and warrior. The hunter who lost his horse during a buffalo hunt, or the warrior who was unseated in the midst of battle was in an extremely dangerous situation. Thus the children practiced many maneuvers and took many falls: "it was part of a good rider to keep his seat ...No matter if the pony fell and we were thrown clear of his body, we were supposed to be up and on his back by the time he had regained his feet."[17] Standing Bear explained that this type of training was necessary because theirs "was a life that called for strength, quick wit, and skill."[18]

Learning to hunt did not, however, only comprise skill in the use of the bow and arrow, and horsemanship. The Lakota boy needed to be brave if he was to become a successful and useful member of his tribe. Standing Bear recalls that throughout his boyhood he wanted to be brave like his father:

> Dangers and responsibilities were bound to come, and I wanted to meet them like a man. I looked forward to the days of the warpath, not as a calling nor for the purpose of slaying my fellowman, but solely to prove my worth to myself and my people.[19]

Standing Bear was given the first opportunity to demonstrate his bravery at the age of ten when his father invited him to join a war party. His only regret about the occasion was that they returned home without encountering the enemy! All of the activities, games, crafts, and skills which the Lakota boys undertook prepared them for the task of ensuring that their families had enough to eat. The traditional main source of food had been the buffalo but, by the time Standing Bear was growing up, the buffalo were rapidly disappearing from the prairies. Much to his delight and pride, however, he did take part in one buffalo hunt and successfully made a kill.

The education and training of Lakota children was an ongoing process which started at birth and continued throughout life:

> True Indian education was based on the development of individual qualities and recognition of rights. ... Native education was not a class education but one that strengthened and encouraged the individual to grow.[20]

Although Standing Bear concentrates throughout his books on the education of Lakota boys, he does point out that the girls were also trained for their adult duties; "[a]s the girls grew toward young womanhood, they were taught to imitate their mothers in everything. They were taught to tan buckskin and sew it together to make a tipi. ... In our play the girls would usually decide where the village was to be pitched."[21] This mimicked the adult practice in which the women selected the site for the family tipi. The only teachers in this Indian education system were the children's parents and the extended tribal family. The children did not leave home to attend school, neither were they awarded diplomas to prove that they had completed their course of training. But when the childhood phase of their education was over, they were ready to take their place in the adult Lakota society.

Gregory Cajete, a Tewa academic who explains science from a native perspective, grounds his narratives firmly with stories of his childhood and early education at the hands of his closest relatives. Cajete's first memories are "of swinging through the air wrapped up in something that [he] later came to know was a traditional cradle."[22] Although these memories do not constitute education per se, Cajete explains that they conjure ideas of being surrounded by people; an educational process that is profoundly indigenous. Cajete always felt "warm and safe…it was a good feeling."[23] Learning for the young Cajete did not constitute classrooms and drills. On the contrary, he learned about plants and animals on walks with his grandmother, and about the importance of community to the Pueblo people.[24] These lessons were not like those of Western schools which are learned for examinations and promptly forgotten. Cajete describes them as instilling in him a "sense of rootedness to place and people"[25] that has stayed with him throughout his life.

That same sense of connection to the land, community involvement, and care for all aspects of life can be found in personal narratives of indigenous people who lived through the turmoil inflicted upon them by colonialism. In the book, *Native Heritage: Personal Accounts by American Indians 1790 to the Present*, Arlene Hirschfelder has brought together over one hundred such voices to show the rich array of cultures, stories, experiences, and tragedies that together give some insight into the varied communities that comprise the indigenous people of the United States. One section of the book is devoted to indigenous education, and in its introduction, Hirschfelder provides an overview of recurring narratives:

> Tribal educators taught tribal history, what would now be called earth or physical sciences, physical education, codes of social behavior, religious training, health care, and many other subjects. And when relatives were not exposing them to these things, children played "tipi," "potlatch," and "family," trying on grown-up roles and preparing themselves for the time they would become adults with work responsibilities. Girls helped their mothers and grandmothers; boys assisted fathers and grandfathers. While they helped, they observed and listened to the words adults spoke.[26]

This was native education that was genuine; that was designed to secure the continuance of the community; that taught children their place in the circle of life; that modeled respect for all living beings; and that did not have to worry about assimilation into a society that treated them as if they were lesser beings. This was native education before the arrival of the white man.

In pre-contact days, the Mahican way of living was, according to Hendrick Aupaumut, communicated to children in much the same way as today's children are taught right from wrong; through God's commandments. In Mahican society, these rules, which were believed to have come from the Supreme Being, were passed down from one generation to the next and offered a prescription for a good life. They comprised the following list:

- My Children – …love all men, and be kind to all people
- My little Children – you must be kind to strangers
- My Children – …You must be honest in all your ways
- My Children – you much never steal anything from your fellow men
- My Children – you must always avoid bad company
- My Children – you must be very industrious
- And further my Children – when you grown [sic] up, you must not take wife or husband without the consent of your parents and relations.[27]

While many accounts of indigenous education concentrate on boys, Hirschfelder offers several stories of girls playing "mother." Crow medicine woman, Pretty Shield, tells of how she and her friends imitated their mothers and prepared for adult life through their play:

> I tried to be like my mother, and like another woman, besides…I carried my doll on my back just as mothers carry their babies; and besides this, I had a little teepee [lodge] that I pitched whenever my aunt pitched hers. It was made exactly like my aunt's, had the same number of poles, only of course my teepee was very small.[28]

Through play and imitation, Pretty Shield learned the ways of the women of her community and, by the time she was old enough to take her place as an adult, she would know all the intricacies of building her lodge and creating a home for her own children. Play was a vital part of Pretty Shield's education and as she aged, her playthings became more and more like the real thing. Why is it that Western children are allowed to play until they go to school, but once they enter the classroom, the notion of play is more than often left outside the door? Play and learning were one and the same thing for Pretty Shield and should be for all children.

Play was also an important part of childhood for Eastern White Mountain Apache woman, Anna Price. In an interview given when she was close to one hundred years old, she recounted the detailed role-playing games that she and her friends played, including keeping house, getting married, having children, providing food, and negotiating family relations. These games, that often lasted a whole day, were imitations of real life to the last detail:

> When we played at marriage, we were always careful not to marry some child who was of our own clan, just as big people were….We played at marriage

negotiations…We used to use the polite form of the third person in talking between son-in-law and parent-in-law, just like the grown people.[29]

Just as Anna and her friends pretended to be grown-up, so too did Kwakiutl, Charles James Nowell and his group of young male playmates. Learning about the importance of potlatch ceremonies, these boys enacted their version of the adult event by making canoes that were identical in everything but size from those made by the adults, giving ceremonial speeches and distributing the potlatch of canoes (gifts) to other boys. Often the boys would compete to see who could make the largest potlatch, because as in the adult world, size denoted place in the clan. Just as in Western society, adults sometimes waded into the boys' quarrels and helped to make larger and better potlatches.[30] It is hard not to think about father and son cub scout teams preparing for their Pinewood Derby races – not many boy-made cars ever win.

One of the reasons that fathers feel obliged to "help" their sons win the Pinewood Derby is that white society celebrates success over effort, and production over process. In its purest form, the lessons of the Pinewood Derby would be creativity, trial and error, and self-satisfaction for making something with minimal assistance. The reality is that fathers, not sons, compete to see who can make the sleekest vehicle to travel fastest over the course on race day. This is competition at its worst when grown men are celebrating victory over ten-year-old children and showing no mercy whatsoever. Terry Tafoya, a consultant on native and bilingual education, warns indigenous people to stay true to native educational methods that emphasize process over product:

> Life itself is the journeying, not the destination. The things that have traditionally been done within the tribes are a training process (the sweat lodge, old-fashioned methods of hunting and fishing, storytelling, Indian dancing) all these teach discipline, teach an attitude towards the Mother Earth, and an understanding of what our place is with all our relations. In short, the old ways teach us our purpose for being.[31]

Today's Western education model, which concentrates on standardized tests and grades, places little emphasis on process. And as technology advances the opportunity to amass information without knowledge or wisdom, to solve problems without knowing or showing the working, and to have virtual "friends" that are strangers in reality, Western society is becoming so product oriented that all of the aspects of life that Tafoya warned his people to protect will be lost.

Almost all indigenous people whose lives have been affected by colonialism mourn the loss of at least some part of their traditional way of life; none more so than the Hawaiian people. In the preface to *Ancient Hawaiian Civilization*, a series of lectures delivered to students at The Kamehameha Schools, the President of the schools points out that many modern Hawaiian people are not aware of the long history of Hawaiian civilization. While those communities had neither the natural resources, nor a written language with which to progress in the way that people in other parts of the world could, "they had rules of living, modes, and customs which permitted them to live happily and healthfully in these islands in very large numbers.[32] It is clear from the lecture given by E. S. C. Handy that religion and education went hand in hand. The young child was dedicated to a god and was taught the prayers associated with that deity. That aside, the young child's education was very like the experiences recounted earlier in this chapter; learning was generally accomplished through watching, listening, and imitating. In the early stages of life, children were seldom actively taught; they learned "customs, manners, ways of doing things in the home, not so much by direct teaching, as by direct learning through living and taking part in the life of the home."[33] One area of Hawaiian traditional education that does seem different from other accounts is the practice of sending older boys to work as apprentices to experts. Handy stresses that the main benefit of this practice over today's schools is the practical aspects of the tasks and the instruction. These jobs were real, the apprentice worked under the expert for a long time, sometimes years, until he had earned the right to be called an expert himself. For the Polynesian wayfarers, it is understandable that canoe-building was one such area of expertise. It is important to note that the expert did not only work in his discipline, but also committed to teach the next generation, thus ensuring the continuation of the community's skill base. And it is here that we can see the traditional and the modern combining in a way that should offer hope to all those who are involved in indigenous education. The Pacific Voyaging Society, of which we wrote in Chapter 3, is a vibrant organization dedicated to preserving the ancient art and science of Polynesian voyaging, and to educating young Polynesians to continue the legacy of their ancestors.

One of the most important and most telling points made by Handy is his comparison between traditional and modern education:

> ...the most successful of modern schools scarcely bring about the quality of learning which was achieved in the old days in Hawaii, when the whole situation was real and every man, woman, and child had his definite part to play in the life work for which he must be educated.[34]

It is true that one of the most difficult aspects of modern schools is the perception that students are learning for the sake of learning. There is little done in the classroom that seems relevant to the students' lives, and so they often resent the time spent there. This is most frequently the case for students who do not see themselves moving on from high school to institutions of higher education.

Pre-contact indigenous people had, and some still have, a vibrant, useful, meaningful education system for their children aimed toward enhancing the knowledge-base of the whole child and ensuring the security and future of the community. Children educated in this way were not only geared for a position of value, but they also understood that value.

It is clear from the accounts of traditional indigenous education retold here, that Western education practices are not only alien to indigenous children's way of life, but they also devastate cultural continuity. Everything about Western styles of education - confinement to classrooms, adherence to daily schedules which are divided into hours, minutes, and seconds, subjects that seem irrelevant to their lives; and the alien division between learning and play - are anathema to children who had been educated by their parents in accordance with traditional indigenous methods and ideology. Thus, it is the duty of educators involved in the learning processes of indigenous children to work toward a system that can somehow allow these young people to learn all that they will need to survive in today's world while at the same time developing the cultural skills and awareness that will ensure their adult place in their community.

In 1990, the Federation of Saskatchewan Indian Nations described the relationship between indigenous people and their children:

> Children of the First Nations are special gifts from the Creator. Their lives and thoughts have special meaning and significance and they are to be treated with care, love and respect. Children of First Nations have a right to understand and interact with the world in their own First Nations' language, to be nurtured by their parents, grandparents, and communities, and to the teaching and guidance of their Elders.[35]

In the next chapter we will examine Western educational practices and then, in chapter 6, we will discuss the profound harm caused to the indigenous people of the United States and Canada by separating native children from their parents and communities in the name of assimilation into Western society.

THE RIGHT OF MAN – SEEK AND DESTROY?

Even though I had natural advantages as I was growing up, I was also the product of a culture that assigned worth to production and profit. I was basically raised to follow the ethical code of the early 20th century generation of Americans who believed that nature was something that was to be conquered and exploited for wealth. Perhaps having survived the Great Depression, my parents and many other Americans of this era believed that they had a God-given right to harvest from nature whatever they needed or wanted. Thus, a culture developed in North America that promoted the idea that the natural world existed to be bought, sold, used, and abused for personal gain and social prestige. Any thoughts of a biocentric connection to the earth or of conservation were summarily dismissed as naïve. Within my community, and many others like it, people were admired for the number and size of fish or game that they brought home. Thus, I hunted, fished, and even trapped to acquire wealth and in doing so achieved an elevated social standing among my family and friends.

Now that I am older, I have evolved into a person who no longer hunts for the thrill of the kill. In fact, I no longer hunt game, and I take only the fish my wife and I can eat fresh. But I now recognize the difference between hunting and killing and also understand why some of the great hunters I have known don't shoot much these days. They still go hunting, but they are content to wait for the perfect shot that never comes or release all that they catch. I fish much less than I used to, but will I ever give up fishing? I think not, because I feel that much of my identity is linked with my ability to hunt – fishing is hunting. Both Joseph Campbell[1] and Robert Bly[2] argue that many of the problems experienced by contemporary human males stem from their inability to recognize and constructively facilitate their need to hunt, and its inextricably linked mentoring and companionship. I agree. My faithful deer rifle has not been sold, nor has it been relegated to a closet: it adorns a wall as a reminder of who I am and from where I came.

CHAPTER 5

INDIGENOUS AND WESTERN WAYS OF KNOWING: A CONFLICT OF INTERESTS

Neither the uneducated and uninformed of the truth, nor yet those who never make an end of their education, will be able ministers of State.

Plato, *The Republic*

Western philosophers have suggested that it is teleology[1] along with ontology[2] and axiology[3] that make human beings different from other animals. But what does that actually mean, and how does it affect everyday people? Basically, we see ourselves as apart from other living beings because we think about the end product or result of our pursuits, we consider the meaning of our existence, we pose questions with regard to value, morals, aesthetics, and we are creative. Unfortunately, Western culture has come to overvalue or misunderstand purpose and instead focuses on goals to the point where there is no alternative but progress. And when personal ambition is at its strongest, it can cause people to lose their sense of self, and to abandon their fundamental value system. The latter is particularly evident in minority groups where members are often compelled to leave or abandon their families, neighborhoods, and even their culture as a way of gaining social standing in contemporary society.

In his autobiography, *Hunger of Memory*, Richard Rodriguez[4] describes precisely this type of dilemma; one that many minorities have had to face. Education in a white dominated system leads to assimilation, which in turn leads to alienation from their heritage. Rodriguez, the son of immigrant Mexican workers, entered school in the United States knowing very little English. As he became familiar with the language, he equated success with knowledge, but that knowledge was in no way experiential: it was purely didactic. Rodriguez became what he describes as a "scholarship boy,"[5] reading books and regurgitating the thoughts and ideas of the authors and of his teachers. Throughout his academic years, he was aware that he was distancing himself from his parents, whose English was lacking, but his drive to assimilate and to progress up the ladder of success was stronger than his cultural ties. It was not until his adult years that Rodriguez realized all that he had lost.

Gloria Anzaldúa describes a similar situation when she writes about the way her culture has been subjected to the power differential between white society and that of Chicanos:

We need to say to white society: We need you to accept the fact that Chicanos are different, to acknowledge your rejection and negation of us. We need you to own the fact that you looked upon us as less than human, that you stole our lands, our personhood, our self-respect...you strive for power over us, you erase our history and our experience because it makes you feel guilty....[6]

Anzaldúa's *Borderlands* is reminiscent of the writings of Rodriguez and others who have straddled the "borderlands" of society, and who have written to an English-speaking audience in an attempt to right the wrongs of colonialism. Another such writer is Chinua Achebe[7] who published *Things Fall Apart* in 1954 as an answer to what he perceived as racism in Joseph Conrad's *Heart of Darkness*. Importantly, both Achebe and Anzaldúa insert passages of their native tongue into their work in an attempt to show white people that they do have a language, a civilization, and that, yes, they are just as human as those who are born with white skin. We see this same technique in the work of many Native American authors, such as Diné poet Laura Tohe, the title of whose book of poetry, *No Parole Today*, suggests that while prisoners usually have a set length of sentence, often with a chance of parole, many indigenous people are permanently imprisoned within the confines of subjugation, segregation, and discrimination.

Leon Tikly brings the idea of colonialism right into the heart of modern Western culture when he writes that,

[w]e are currently witnessing on a global scale...a new form of Western imperialism that has as its purpose the incorporation of populations within the formerly so-called 'Second' and 'Third worlds' into a regime of global government. Central to the new imperialism is education, which has become for the World Bank and the multilateral development agencies a key aspect of their vision of 'development'.[8]

Tikly supports his thesis by indicating the way in which people in developing nations are being educated to think of themselves as members of a global community. And he goes on to say that such education dehumanizes by reducing people to "the necessary human capital [required] to kick-start the industrialization process."[9] It also works to negate or devalue indigenous ways of knowing in favor of an assimilation of ideas, practices, and mindsets that promote the goals of those in power. But dehumanizing behavior and treatment are not confined to the developing world. Closer to home, a system that seems to force minorities and immigrants to choose either family and culture or assimilation with increased financial security, wreaks havoc within communities in our inner cities, in rural areas, and on reservations.

Historically, ghettos, barrios, and reservations have retained the highest level of ethnic purity, and to some extent still do. That purity, however, is often linked to poverty. When a person aspires to, and achieves, a higher level of economic security, he or she earns the opportunity to move out of the neighborhood into the surrounding community. The population there is more ethnically mixed, so there are opportunities for ethnic assimilation, and yet more economic and educational advancement. Beyond the middle circle resides a group with yet higher social economic status and education. In the United States, this group predominantly comprises the majority white population which is often less than welcoming to minorities. Thus, the darkest people live in the inner circle, the mixed in the middle, and the lightest are on the outside. Besides social class, economic and educational advantages follow this same migration pattern. People from ethnic minorities do have opportunities to become mainstream Americans but, more often than not, if they take advantage of those opportunities, they pay the price of losing their cultural heritage and identity.

It is especially distressing to realize that today's education system is still following, and thus reinforcing, the concentric ring pattern. Traditionally, the least successful schools are in the ghettos while educational resources and opportunities increase proportionately with distance from the center. For some, that may serve as an incentive to move away in search of a better life, but any advantages that they gain are paid for dearly in lost connections with their roots. Moreover, many who do not have the will or the ability to move away become trapped in a cycle of ignorance, poverty, and hopelessness.

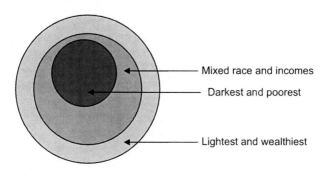

It is difficult to resist the attraction of assimilation, because it is both beneficial and necessary. Assimilation has always existed among humans as populations have moved from one area to another, have adapted to their new geography, and have inculcated the thoughts and experiences of previous settlers. It is, therefore, important to realize that assimilation affects everyone, not only indigenous people and immigrants. For example, the whites who settled the Pacific Northwest and relegated its native cultures (that is, those who survived the onslaught) to reservations have, after only a couple of hundred years, adapted to their native surroundings. The physical dominance of the land, and the natural essence that sustained its native people and determined their way of life, found their way into the psyche of the newcomers, to such an extent that many of the whites now living in the area have adopted a lifestyle that is remarkably similar to that of their indigenous predecessors. Ectopia,[10] as the area is now commonly known, is the bastion of "Earth First!"[11] an environmental advocacy movement that, according to its website, "…was named in 1979 in response to a lethargic, compromising, and increasingly corporate environmental community."[12] Earth First! advocates stress the differences between themselves and other environmental groups. There are no members, only Earth First!ers who share "a belief in biocentrism."[13] Thus, for Earth First!ers, consideration of the Earth is paramount and, while their interests and lifestyles are diverse, "...there is agreement on one thing, the need for action!"[14] The most important point here, however, is that the population of this area has not just "gone native" but has gone back to embrace as best they can, a way of life that is most natural to their surroundings. David Abram[15] described the phenomenon succinctly when he said, "They rejuvenate their senses by entering into reciprocity with the sensuous surroundings."[16] But the experience of the people living in this area is not shared throughout the country. Indeed, most people have little or no connection to their natural surroundings, and live lives that are motivated solely by technological and economic progress.

The societies in which most people live have them striving toward some self-determined, or worse still, society-determined goal—think about the number of university students who are stressed more by the need to declare a chosen career path than they are about successfully completing the course in which they are currently enrolled. A recent conversation between a Canadian native and an American tourist illustrates this point very well. When the tourist politely asked the native what he did all day long, the latter thought long and hard before replying "I live." The tourist did not understand the profound nature of the answer, and the agreeable native didn't even try to explain. Having a sense of purpose is important and creates meaning in our lives. When, however, that sense of purpose is taken to the extreme, the resulting anxiety and stress brings us further away from all that is natural in the world. In the wilderness where there are few, if any, of the conveniences of modern living, everyday chores and tasks offer a natural and physical purpose but, more importantly, the proximity to nature creates an environment in which people find themselves to be more intuitive, creative, and closer to their idea of a Creator than they are when surrounded by concrete, incessant noise, and intense pressure to keep climbing that ladder of success. In the city, success is usually defined by material wealth, but character reigns in the natural world. Under certain circumstances, especially when people are distanced from the distractions of "civilization," all that is important is to live: that is, to exist in harmony with their surroundings. But while people are caught up in the whirlwind of modern life, especially in large cities, it is difficult for them to escape the driving force of cultural expectations that constantly urge them to seek new ways to progress.

The seemingly unstoppable pressure to progress stems from a Euro-American worldview that has assimilated the values of evolution, particularly social evolution, into its culture. Meaning is therefore achieved from purpose, which is in turn derived from development and technology. But what effect, if any, does that have on the population at large? When the pursuit of progress encompasses a society, its education policies place technological know-how, and the ability to measure attainment of prescribed standards, above any and all needs of the individual. One fundamental result is that valuable knowledge and skills become defined in technological terms, and people's worth defined in their ability to manipulate technological tools. Thus, artistic and intuitive abilities are marginalized. That is not, of course, to say that all artists struggle to earn a living in today's technological society. American society has more than its fair share of exceptionally wealthy actors, musicians, and other performers, but the reality is that for every success story, there are hundreds of thousands of artistic hopefuls who might be making a reasonable living, but for an inner drive to progress—to become a 'star.' Many of these would-be celebrities, despite having the talents necessary for a successful life, are often doomed to feel like failures.

In the educational world, it is easy to see evidence of this obsession with progress. When students are asked about career choices, many respond that their parents would like them to choose university majors and professions that can be identified as having good earning potential. Thus, English, philosophy, and history majors often find themselves having to defend their choice, and explaining that they are, most certainly, not restricting themselves to *just* teaching. The same type of stereotypical thinking is evident at university open house events and orientation. So now, not only are traditional indigenous subjects devalued and scorned, but so too are many of the liberal arts that are considered by some to be the foundation of Western classical education. In today's global economy, science, engineering, and technology are deemed to be the most lucrative career choices, so resources are being poured into those areas, while others that teach critical thinking and communication skills are feeling the pinch. It would appear that it is acceptable to produce scientists, engineers, and computer specialists who are unable to read or to write at a professional level.

So why are parents trying to steer their young people away from the arts? In a word—fear. They want their children to succeed and to enjoy the fruits of their labor, but that labor must conform to society's needs and emphases; and those focus on science and technology. So parents fear that their artistically-inclined children, if not prodded into a scientific or technological field, will be condemned to a lower standard of living than their counterparts, and be permanently dependent on their parents, all because their knowledge and skills are not valued in today's society as much as skills in subjects such as mathematics, science, and technology. Success is, of course, never guaranteed; although some have a much greater chance of educational satisfaction and career choice than others. Choosing a career path purely for its financial opportunities will rarely lead to job satisfaction, and the average worker spends far too long at work to settle for nothing but financial reward.

American educator Michael Apple[17] is an important voice in contemporary progressive education; he is a teacher, a critical thinker, and a political activist who has written extensively about the need for democratic schools. In *Official Knowledge* he suggests that for some people,

> ...schooling is seen as a vast engine of democracy: opening horizons, ensuring mobility, and so on. For others, the reality of schooling is strikingly different. It is seen as a form of social control, or, perhaps, as the embodiment of cultural dangers, institutions whose curricula and teaching practices threaten the moral universe of the students who attend them.[18]

Furthermore, Apple sees the education system acting in much the same way as Michel Foucault's description of Bentham's Panopticon in which the students, just like the inmates, are controlled by a "power relation independent of the person who exercises it; in short, [they are] caught up in a power situation of which they are themselves the bearers."[19] Close analysis of Foucault's body of work shows an overriding recurring theme—the relationship between power and knowledge in social settings and its effect on discourse. Nowhere is that relationship more visible and more critical to the development of future generations of citizens than in schools. According to Foucault, schools are not politically neutral institutions in which young people are free to accept and reject information through inquiry and evidence; and so he states:

> Although education may well be, by right, the instrument thanks to which any individual in a society like ours can have access to any kind of discourse whatever…Any system of education is a political way of maintaining or modifying the appropriation of discourses, along with the knowledges and powers which they carry.[20]

While Foucault's theories may not have received due recognition by educators in the past, it is important that those in the field today accept that power and knowledge are linked to every aspect of society, and that people acquire the knowledge and learn the relationship between power and knowledge through the education system.

Most young people strive to conform to their peer group, and so in a system that isolates the individual - the one who transgresses the 'norm' - its members will monitor their own behaviors to ensure that they are aligned with societal (peer) expectations. Apple also argues that defining "some groups' knowledge as the most legitimate, as official knowledge, while other groups' knowledge hardly sees the light of day, says something extremely important about who has power in society."[21] Within mainstream society in the United States, the power lies mainly with those of European descent, and in particular white men. Thus, when Apple talks about "official knowledge," he is warning against a body of knowledge that is government decreed, politically motivated, and designed to keep power in the hands of those white males.

In *Educating the "Right" Way*, Apple voices his concern about "pastoral power" when he discusses "the growing influence of authoritarian populist religious conservatism on education…."[22] But not only does the religious right promote fundamental Christian beliefs, it also relegates to "other" anyone who does not fit into its structure of power, which favors white males. Thus, women, people of color, and those who do not follow the fundamental Christian way of life are deemed inferior and are denied, whenever possible, the opportunities afforded the white male population.[23] Apple calls on all educators to be cognizant of the power/knowledge relationship that is being promoted in schools, and to be open to discussions about ways to "loosen the grip of the narrow concepts of 'reality' and 'democracy' that have been circulated by neoliberals and neoconservatives in education…."[24] Much of Apple's work echoes that of Brazilian thinker Paulo Freire[25] who, in *Pedagogy of the Oppressed*, promoted the idea of liberatory education in which the curriculum is an agent of freedom. He coined the term "banking system" to describe the Western educational model in which central government decrees the curriculum, and students have no choice but to buy into it. The main advantages of such an agenda lean totally toward maintaining the nation's *status quo*, and thus the power basis for the dominant culture. It offers very little possibility for minority students to grasp a higher rung on the ladder of economic or political opportunity. According to Freire, students "have the opportunity to become collectors or cataloguers of the things they store. But in the last analysis, it is the people themselves who are filed away through the lack of creativity, transformation, and knowledge in this (at best) misguided system."[26] In short, children are trained to accept the establishment's version of truth.

Ronald David Glass, while criticizing some of Freire's reasoning, points out just how much Freirian pedagogy is needed today. "Low-income Americans face an increasing education gap as the testing stakes get raised and as public school resources are more broadly privatized."[27] Freire's model offers children the opportunity to learn in an unbiased environment that promotes equality. Carl Herndl, however, poses a pedagogical problem to Freirean-styled teacher activism;

> [A] pedagogy which sets up a stark confrontation between the repressive ideology of the dominant discourse and the teacher's emancipatory ideology structures the classroom as an opposition between teacher and student...The more this opposition structures the classroom, the less chance the students have of exploring their own discourse and cultural position. Ironically, students will become once again the objects of what Freire calls the banking model of education.[28]

In *The Politics of the Interface: Power and Its Exercise in Electronic Contact Zones*, Cynthia and Richard Selfe point out the problems that minority students face when attempting to navigate their way through today's technology-laden educational environment. Throughout their paper, the authors suggest that computer interfaces, which they describe as "linguistic contact zones," reinforce the colonial power divide that marginalizes and oppresses people on the basis of race or gender.[29] The solution, in their eyes, lies with the classroom teachers who must "recognize computer interfaces as non-innocent physical borders (between the regular world and the virtual world), cultural borders (between the haves and the have-nots), and linguistic borders."[30] Selfe and Selfe report that recent scholarship has painted an overly optimistic picture of "the positive contributions that technology can make ...."[31] Of course technology is extremely useful for those who have access to it, but for others it is an impenetrable barrier to equal opportunity in school and in the workforce. For this reason, technology can be described as an instrument of oppression that enlarges the gap between those in power and those who are kept on the margins of society by an education system that is historically designed to enforce that divide.

Andrew Feenberg makes strong connections between possible misuses of technology and Foucault's power/knowledge theory when he states,

> Technologies are selected…from among many possible configurations. Guiding the selection process are social codes established by the cultural and political struggles that define the horizon under which the technology will fall. Once introduced, technology offers a material validation of the cultural horizon to which it has been preformed. I call this the "bias" of technology: apparently neutral, functional rationality is enlisted in support of a hegemony.[32]

As online educational platforms become increasingly popular, programs that are accessed through technology, for example, online and hybrid courses, are only available to students who are already computer literate. Minority students are disadvantaged, not because of racially-biased interfaces, but because their lack of access to technology robs them of the choices afforded to their wealthier, generally white, counterparts. A short article in the Winter 1999–2000 edition of *The Journal of Blacks in Higher Education* reported that a then-recent census found that "27 percent of black high school students had a computer in their home [while] more than two thirds of all white high school students had a computer in their home."[33] The unnamed author, however, noted that Gateway computers and America Online were donating respectively a large number of computers and Internet services to inner-city children in an attempt to close "the racial gap in computer ownership."[34] Although such altruism is laudable, it can only help to alleviate the problem if both white students and minority students are taught to use the technology in the same way. That, according to Sheingold, Martin, and Endreweit, is not always the case. They suggest that even when minority students do have access to computers, the devices are used in different ways and for different purposes. Different purposes often result in restrictions:

> Such restrictions may work against the best educational interests of students in at least two ways. First, where uses are limited to remedial tasks or to drill, emphasis in mastery of basic skills becomes the central academic goal for students. In contrast, students in suburban schools are more often using computers in the service of more comprehensive literacy and reasoning goals.[35]

Virtually all public and private universities in the United States require their students to complete a set of core classes designed to ensure that they are well prepared to succeed in the workplace; thus, emphasis is placed on rhetoric or communications skills, mathematics, natural sciences, behavioral and social sciences, humanities, and fine arts. Private schools that are faith based usually add theology to the list. The core curriculum indicates the strong link between the liberal arts foundation of United States higher education and the thinking of Plato. Yet, as we mentioned earlier in this chapter, many of these liberal arts subjects are under threat from the heavy emphasis on and funding of science, technology, and business agendas. Instead of removing opportunities to hone critical thinking skills from the curriculum, we would like to see additions that would help our young people to appreciate knowledge derived from diverse sources (ancient and modern, intuitive and scientific, artistic and inartistic). Such a curriculum would, we believe, allow these same students to both compete in modern society and maintain a healthy connection to the natural world.

NOT SO GREAT EXPECTATIONS

A number of years ago I attended an all-school reunion, though my school closed many years ago. The school, which housed grades one through twelve, had been situated in a geographically isolated region of Minnesota. Because of its location and the number of American Indian students within the student body, this was not a place to find good teachers. Those who did join the faculty tended to be new teachers who stayed for just a year or so before moving on to greener pastures. At the secondary level, particularly, most of the long-standing teachers tended to be social misfits or simply poor teachers. I do not remember much of my primary schooling, but with regard to the requisite knowledge and skills required for promotion to the middle and high school grades, I suspect that it was adequate at best.

I recall a few good teachers who cared that we learned, but I remember more who did not. It was not, I believe, a case of poor teaching as much as no teaching at all. As long as we behaved, we would be promoted, and I'm sure that seemed fine to us at the time. Looking back, however, it is clear that we were robbed of the opportunity to excel. These thoughts are, of course, those of an adult reflecting on days long past, but students seldom recognize poor teaching while they are actually in the class. Furthermore, students rarely mind if their teachers' expectations are low and the requirements minimal. It is only once the student has graduated, and has joined the working society, that he or she realizes that those who have attended other schools in other districts are better prepared for college or employment. Very few who graduated from my school continued on to higher education, and even fewer graduated. It is fair to say that we were not expected to further our education beyond high school, and most of us lived up to that.

During the school reunion, after the usual catching up, the very first topic of conversation turned to the quality of our shared educational experience. Given my professional interest in the subject, I decided to sit back and listen to the views of my former schoolmates. They universally agreed that our education had been poor, and that any efforts toward post secondary education were either doomed from the outset or were torturously labored. There was even talk of a class-action suit, but I doubt that we could ever prove that most of us had been summarily robbed of our potential.

THE WESTERN EDUCATION SYSTEM

In Indian civilization I am a Baptist, because I believe in immersing the Indians in our civilization and when we get them under holding them there until they are thoroughly soaked.

Richard Henry Pratt, *Battlefield and Classroom*

There are various methods of pedagogy that address the accepted range of differences among learners but these are, on the whole, convergent; that is, they require the learner to internalize and then to articulate the knowledge prescribed by the curriculum offered by the teacher. Very little teaching and learning foster divergence among learners, partly because of the difficulty brought about by the government's recent insistence on standardized testing. Standardization has always implied convergent ways of knowing and learning, and has adhered strictly to a canon of knowledge that is valued by those in authority. The authoritative source has the power to decide what knowledge will be included in the canon.

Constructivist methods of education, in which the teacher provides the learner with the tools and the environment to build up his or her own knowledge through personal inquiry, is well known, but the obsession with standardization has caused a decline in its popularity. It must be said, however, that even when they are promoted and supported, neither divergent nor constructivist ways of learning address or value the collective cognitive experience but rather focus on the individual.

When we talk about "others," people usually think about strangers from distant lands, but indigenous people in this country and elsewhere have, since the days of colonialism, found themselves labeled thus. It is also true that indigenous people have been grudgingly recognized at times as perhaps having some separate knowledge, but it is most often summarily dismissed as not *the* knowledge. Thus, the Western educational model, with its focus on convergent methodology and standardized testing, has been able to marginalize indigenous students, and student success rates among this population are far from stellar. But are there different ways of promoting learning among indigenous students of which mainstream educators are unaware? And can pairing indigenous teachers with indigenous students help to increase learner outcomes? Not necessarily. Research undertaken in northern Saskatchewan by Katsuo Tamaoka in 1986 concluded that teacher education programs required by native preservice teacher candidates preclude them from being any more effective among native K-12 students than non-native teachers, and that they are more alike than different in their use of instructional methods and strategies.[1] Other studies have mirrored Tamaoka's findings.[2] Thus, answers to these core questions are not easy to come by. Indeed, a review of the literature and discussions with native teachers and learners do not reveal any radically unique methods that differ widely from those of Western pedagogy, so the emphasis should be on creating teacher education programs that help preservice teachers to learn about and utilize methods that take advantage of indigenous ways of knowing and learning.

Of much more importance, however, is the relationship between teacher and student. Modern teachers have been taught, albeit slowly, to recognize their responsibility for establishing and maintaining a strong partnership between themselves and parents, and to foster close connections between communities and schools. And this relationship can be strongest when the teacher hails from and resides in the same community as the learners. In such a situation, both parties approach their work from the same framework and understand each other's language. There is an old Indian saying, "it is never the arrow, but always the Indian," and that perhaps holds true here. It is the teacher and his or her relationship with the students and their community that is most important. As far as indigenous educational communities are concerned, a teaching philosophy and delivery system as suggested by Paulo Freire could be the starting point for a relevant program for their students.

It has been over a quarter of a century since Freire launched his ideas of liberatory education in his highly acclaimed *Pedagogy of the Oppressed*, and they have since interested many educators in multiple fields and educational settings. Liberatory pedagogy is an educational philosophy that especially facilitates aims, methods, and content of education toward all who have been educationally disenfranchised. But Freire's main goal for all students is critical consciousness, which promotes the idea of social action or mobility. Students reach this optimum state through, but not necessarily linearly, three stages: semi-intransitive consciousness, naïve transitivity, and critical transitivity. According to Tom Heaney in his 1995 document *Issues in Freirean Pedagogy*, "Freirean programs in [the United States] have 'raised consciousness,' but seldom directly influenced social change."[3] Perhaps this is because they are not seen as meaningful in a "banking" education system or, even more to the point, that Freirean educational programs are considered to be dangerous to the status quo. As discussed in Chapter 5, Freire coined the term "banking system" to describe the Western educational model in which government decrees the curriculum, and students have no choice but to buy into it. The main advantage of the "banking system" is that it is a major factor in maintaining the base of power for the historically dominant culture. It offers very little, if any, possibility for those with a non-Western worldview, or indeed for disenfranchised whites, to grasp a higher rung on the ladder of economic, social, or political opportunity.

Freire's model of pedagogy, which first motivated Brazilian peasants to forge a social revolution, is most effective among populations that are clearly oppressed, such as indigenous people who are striving to re-establish community structures and values. The Western model of education, consciously or unconsciously, remains patronizingly paternalistic and cognitively imperialistic, and thus discourages teachers with a sincere desire to teach critical consciousness. Consequently, too many students are left to accommodate and then regurgitate information that is deemed necessary to fit into today's society.

The rationale behind Freire's paradigm is to have students who are active learners and who think. The idea of having students who reflect and act on social constraint is revolutionary and appealing to some, but many in positions of authority fear that this type of education could cause unrest among the socially, educationally, economically, and politically under-privileged, thus threatening a country's balance of power. But the Freirean model would help not only the historically oppressed, but also all students to become more active in their own communities by allowing them to see optimum ways to work for the betterment of their society.

Universities are now realizing that people acquire knowledge in multiple ways; some learn best by seeing, some by feeling and manipulating, some by hearing, and even some by intuiting. Howard Gardner's popular theory of multiple intelligences posits that everyone has many faculties for learning (linguistic, logical-mathematical, musical, bodily-kinesthetic, spatial, interpersonal, and intrapersonal); but that some lie undeveloped because the Western education system does not recognize them let alone foster them.[4] Gardner has recently added naturalist and existentialist to his list. The latter was rife with difficulties since existential intelligence, that is, an intelligence that deals with issues of existence, inherently must include spiritual and religious issues. Existential intelligence has little empirical evidence to support its inclusion, while naturalist intelligence has not been criticized as much, but rather simply ignored. Gardner, although widely accepted by many educators, has been viewed critically within the academic world, and the criticism has increased since the additions.[5] Gardner is not a radical environmentalist nor is he promoting religion—he is recognizing innate human characteristics that reside in all of us. Thus, Gardner's critics put him in the same camp as Isaac Newton who not only believed that there was ancient knowledge we needed to know, but also that the day would come when science and religion merge. We recognize the contributions of Gardner and Newton and Einstein, and many others, as long as what they say fits within our ideology, but we are quick to reject that which we don't like.

Developmental psychologists have recognized that young people develop in stages, and that everyone progresses through these stages at different rates. Gardner suggests that within these stages of development there are "windows of opportunities" for each intelligence.[6] Linguistics is a familiar example, because it is accepted that it is easier for a six-year-old child to learn another language than it is for an adult. Virtually all of the "windows" for these intelligences occur during the primary and secondary school years. Thus, a student's ability to learn material to his or her optimal potential is diminished if it is not achieved during the time that the "window" is open. Similarly, despite an adult's motivation to remediate for an earlier educational deficiency, his or her chance of reaching full potential is minimal. It is possible that a 16-year-old student has enough of an external locus of control[7] to survive poor secondary teaching, but primary grade students are much more vulnerable and harmed by inadequate teaching. These children quickly lose their intrinsic motivation to learn, often suffer from low self-esteem, and retreat into silence. Many feel that this situation is criminal; more so because it is most often committed against the children of the powerless.

Western education has historically used aural methods to teach, and because that has for so long been the norm, that it is the only real means of academic teaching and learning. Western students have become proficient at learning through hearing, but at the expense of fully developing their other skills. Western schools' preference for oral (speech-based) delivery of information, the lecture, is neither ineffective nor bad as such, but it has retarded the development of other learning methods, disadvantaged those who have difficulty learning aurally, and advantaged those who do not. People's potential to learn is only partially fulfilled if only one style of teaching and learning is used.

Using the oral tradition as a way of transmitting information is both understandable and obvious. The Mexica (Aztecs) teachers and students developed their oral skills through poetry and prose, along with developing their memory, which ensured that knowledge was passed along accurately. Before the advent of written language, it was *the* way that stories were passed from one generation to the next. Ancient people used a diversity of teaching methods, more than we use today, as there were fewer political or economic reasons to favor any one method over another.

With compulsory education as we know it, it is not surprising that students learn to devalue intuition, and lose the magic and delight in learning that we knew as children. Compulsory education and its prescribed curriculum and standards ensure that children learn only that which is measurable. The hugely popular scientific method with its reliance on quantification, coupled with a "banking" system as described by Freire, was the perfect epistemological engine and educational delivery system to drive the European Industrial Revolution and to import to the colonies. When the Europeans arrived in this country and discovered the presence of an indigenous population, they set out to diminish any possibility of threat to their settlement plans, and to trample the native cultures with traditional colonial dominance. This was achieved through education.

The determination of Europeans to "educate" the indigenous people of the Americas has been unyielding ever since the first settlers arrived. Indeed, the main aim of the French and Spanish missionaries in the early 1600s was to neutralize native resistance. According to Jorge Noriega:

> The Spanish Jesuits, who had pioneered a system of some thirty mission schools in Paraguay and Uruguay from 1609 onward—these were termed "Reductions," an entirely appropriate description given their intended role in diminishing indigenous cultural integrity to the point of nonexistence—passed along the benefits of their experience to the Dominicans and Franciscans, who were quick to attempt to duplicate such feats in North America.[8]

Throughout the following centuries, education was used as a weapon to disrupt native societies by creating an educated elite that would adopt and promote European ideals. This system has been, and still is being, used in many countries, and employs schools "to ensure, as much as possible and apparently with some success, that those in the worst economic positions do not rebel against the system which represses them and identify with leaders who would work within the framework of action set by the dominating ruling class."[9]

The success of this type of program depends upon the belief in the superiority of the colonizer in the eyes of both the oppressed and the oppressor. This is achieved by teaching history from the colonial point of view. A good example of the above can be found in Freire's homeland of Brazil. Charles Mann, in his highly acclaimed text, *1491: New Revelations of the Americas Before Columbus*, cites evidence that suggests that much of pre-contact Amazonia was a managed agricultural environment which only went wild because of European colonists. The agricultural knowledge and contributions of Mesoamericans is well documented with regard to cotton and maize, but the agricultural knowledge necessary to manage and farm the Amazon is probably lost forever.[10] But we are taught, and virtually all textual materials would have us believe, that Amazonia is an untouched laboratory of Darwinian evolution, while objective evidence tells us that it is a large ancient abandoned farm interwoven with vibrant communities. Knowledge of this little known and unpopular theory was first brought to the scientific community by Betty Meggers in 1971 in her *Amazonia: Man and Culture in a Counterfeit Paradise*, but was promptly ignored for a variety of reasons, not least that it did not support a Western worldview. Indeed, Meggers attempted to open our eyes to an indigenous world that did not include slavery and patriarchy in its agricultural societies but which included communal ownership of land. This concept contrasts strongly with the worldview of Plato and Aristotle who both believed in male superiority, and considered slaves to be necessary and to be little more than living, breathing tools.[11]

Yet the native student is made to feel that everything of importance or worth that has happened has come from elsewhere, and that assimilation is the only road to success. When the results of colonialism are seen to leave the indigenous people in a worse state than before, the natives are educated and "invited" to lay the blame on deficiencies within their own cultures. The solution to this perceived problem "*must* lie in an ever closer embrace of the very entity which placed them in such dire straits in the first place."[12]

In the years following the American Revolutionary War, colonizers were obsessed with the idea of expanding their territorial holdings. The main obstacles in their way were the natives whose lives and livelihoods were inextricably connected to the land the Europeans wished to confiscate. Armed with preconceptions of Indian savagery and inferiority, the white settlers offered the Indians two choices: "civilization" or extinction. There were many short-term attempts to teach the natives how to farm and adopt sedentary lifestyles, but most of these failed not only because of a lack of funds, skilled teachers, and Indian compliance, but also because of the oppressors' greed and hatred of the indigenous people. As an attempt to avoid violence as much as possible, government officials made funds available to offer "educational services" to the Indians in return for treaties and alliances. The following are two examples, one in the United States and the other in Canada, of how education can be used for evil and oppression.

For several decades, the missionary teachers tried many educational methods to transform the Indians while keeping the tribal family units intact, but as J. D. C. Atkins, the then U.S. Commissioner of Indian Affairs, said in his 1886 annual report:

> The greatest difficulty is experienced in freeing the children attending day schools from the language and habits of their untutored and often savage parents. When they return to their homes at night, and on Saturdays and Sundays, and are among their own surroundings, they relapse more or less into their former moral and mental stupor.[13]

In light of Atkins' findings, the U.S. Commissioner of Education at the time, John Eaton Jr., suggested that a boarding-school environment, although much more expensive to operate, would afford better results by removing the native children from the cultural contamination of their families and homes completely. Moreover, government policymakers decided that the schools would adopt "penal procedures developed to break the wills of some of the most 'recalcitrant' of the indigenous resistance leaders."[14]

And so, in November 1897, the Carlisle Indian Boarding School, in Carlisle, Pennsylvania, was opened with Captain Richard Henry Pratt, who had been commandant of Fort Marion Prison in Florida, appointed as its superintendent. Pratt was not new to Indian education. Indeed, he had piloted a scheme at Fort Marion that transformed Indian inmates into students. There, adopting the role of a father figure, Pratt treated his charges as children, teaching them that obedience to his rules could result in some degree of freedom. Pratt dealt with infringements of the rules as a parent would with children. As the system began to take effect, Pratt extended his experiment to include lectures, which were intended to provide the Indians with the necessary knowledge to participate in the white man's world, and excursions into nearby Saint Augustine to let them see "civilization" in action.

Next, the Indian inmates were given the skills needed to earn money. They began by polishing and stringing beads, which were collected from the nearby seashore, and then selling them to local merchants. Soon some were selling traditional Indian crafts, while others worked as laborers for local farmers.[15] Pratt kept a separate financial account for each Indian to create an awareness of the European economic system.

The final phase of Pratt's work with these Indian prisoners was to teach them to speak and understand English: "Promoting English speech was among the earliest and most persistent of our efforts in order to bring the Indians into best understanding and relations with our people."[16] With the help of local volunteer teachers, the Indians were taught to read and write, and instructed in the white man's values and beliefs. Christianity was a major topic at this Indian prison school, and Bible stories were especially popular. There were even some converts to Christianity. According to David Wallace Adams, "[t]o all who visited the fort, it appeared that Pratt, the stern

Christian soldier, had wrought a near miracle. The Indians had arrived as savages; now they were decent Christian men walking the path of civilization."[17] Pratt's experiment was considered a resounding success, but it was just the first step in a long process. Pratt persuaded the government to allow the older prisoners to return to their homes, but asked permission to continue to educate the younger Indians. But a prison was not the correct environment to educate young people: a school needed to be found and funding secured.

Richard Pratt established the Carlisle Indian Boarding School on the principle that total assimilation into white society was the only way that Native American Indians could survive amid the ever-increasing number of white immigrants. Indeed, the Carlisle school slogan was, "To civilize the Indian, get him into civilization. To keep him civilized, let him stay."[18] According to Pratt, some of the Indians actually admired and looked for ways to benefit from the technological advances of white society. During one of the solemn winter councils, he was asked to advise the Indians on their future progress, "and [he] used the opportunity to suggest to them that their only safe future was to be found in merging their interests with ours . . . quit being tribal Indians, go out and live among us as individual men, adopt our language, our industries and become a part of the power."[19]

The idea of educating Indian children away from home was not entirely novel. Nor was the Indian reaction. When, at the 1744 Treaty of Lancaster, six young Indian men were invited to attend the College of William and Mary, the offer was refused. Chief Canasatego, speaking on behalf of the Iroquois, explained the reasons behind the Indian decision:

> We know you highly esteem the kind of learning taught in these Colleges, and the maintenance of our young Men, while with you, would be very expensive to you. We are convinced therefore, that you mean to do us Good by your Proposal; and we thank you heartily. But you who are so wise must know that different Nations have different Conceptions of things; and you will not therefore take it amiss if our Ideas of this kind of Education happens not to be the same with yours. We have had some experience of it. Several of our young People were formerly brought up in the Colleges of the Northern Provinces; they were instructed in all your Sciences; but, when they came back to us, they were bad Runners, ignorant of every means of living in the woods, unable to bear either Cold or Hunger, knew neither how to build a cabin, take a deer, or kill an enemy, spoke our language imperfectly, were therefore neither fit for Hunters, Warriors, nor Counsellors; they were totally good for nothing. We are however not the less obliged for your kind Offer, tho' we decline accepting it; and to show our grateful Sense of it, if the Gentlemen of Virginia shall send us a Dozen of their Sons, we will take great care of their Education, instruct them in all we know, and make Men of them.[20]

The success of the off-reservation boarding schools depended initially, of course, upon attracting the requisite number of students. While some parents voluntarily sent their children away to be educated in the ways of the white man, feeling that assimilation was the only way that their children could survive in this "new" America, others, according to annual reports of the Commissioner of Indian Affairs, had to be persuaded or forced to give up their offspring. Persuasion came in the form of withholding food and clothing, and sometimes even imprisonment.[21] The Indians had great difficulty trusting the welfare of their children to the same people who had deceived them over land rights and had broken treaty after treaty. Pratt's answer to this charge was to suggest that the problem lay in the Indians' lack of understanding of the English language, and that if they had been able to read English they would have understood treaties. "Under the laws of my government, one white man with education and intelligence can own all the Black Hills and hold them as his own against everybody. If you, yourself, had had education you might be owning the Black Hills and be able to hold them."[22] He thus reasoned that the Indian children would be in a much better position to look after their own interests if they were educated at the boarding schools and learned to speak English. But it was not always possible to fill the boarding schools with willing volunteers. During "round-up" days, the agents on the reservations had to cope with all forms of resistance, ranging from total tribal opposition to individual children hidden by their parents. When quotas had to be filled, the adults often persuaded the authorities to take orphans, or children of tribal outcasts.[23]

The terror and heartache of the Indian children and their relatives is described in detail by Plenty Kill (who we first introduced in chapter 4 and was later renamed Luther Standing Bear by the teachers at Carlisle) in his autobiographical works *Land of the Spotted Eagle* and *My People, the Sioux*. He explains that, although the idea of leaving the reservation to attend school was daunting, he left on a voluntary basis:

> When I had reached young manhood the warpath for the Lakota was a thing of the past. The hunter had disappeared with the buffalo, the war scout had lost his calling, and the warrior had taken his shield to the mountain-top and given it back to the elements. . . . I could only meet the challenge as life's events came to me. When I went East to Carlisle School . . . I could think of white people wanting little Lakota children for no other possible reason than to kill them, but I thought here is my chance to prove that I can die bravely. So I went East to show my father and my people that I was brave and willing to die for them.[24]

For most of the journey, Luther Standing Bear and his companions, accompanied by Richard Pratt, traveled on what was described as a "long row of little houses standing on long pieces of iron."[25] The movement of the train and the sight of the rapidly passing countryside terrified the children, and reaffirmed their belief that they were soon to die. It did not help matters that, whenever they stopped for food, large numbers of white spectators came out to stare at them. The farther East the train traveled the more densely populated the landscape became. In Chicago, there were so many people and houses that the older Indian boys commented that "the white people are like ants; they are all over – everywhere."[26]

The first part of Pratt's agenda was underway. Upon their arrival at Carlisle, Indian children were given haircuts and uniform-style clothing to make them look like their white counterparts. It was now time to go beyond the visible changes and to start working to sever the Indians' mental connection to their homeland and heritage. It is important to understand at this point that Pratt based his educational philosophies on the theories of British philosopher, John Locke, who espoused that the mind of a baby was like a blank slate, thus suggesting that racial collective memory was not a viable concept.

One of the first assignments on the academic schedule was the allocation of English names to the new students. There was, as always, more than one reason behind this practice. First, many of the Indian names were very difficult for the teachers to pronounce, and second, land allocation and the promise of citizenship necessitated a clear family lineage which could be understood by government agencies. There were, according to David Wallace Adams, several methods used to select names for the students. Some original names, which were easy to pronounce, remained unchanged, some were translated literally, while other students, received totally new names.[27] In *My People, the Sioux*, Luther Standing Bear recounts his naming experience at Carlisle.

> . . . our interpreter came into the room and said, 'Do you see all these marks on the blackboard? Well, each word is a white man's name. They are going to give each one of you one of these names by which you will hereafter be known.' None of the names were read or explained to us, so of course we did not know the sound or meaning of any of them. . . . When my turn came, I took the pointer and acted as if I were about to touch an enemy.[28]

Although the rules for naming were relaxed a little in later years, there is no mention of any of these first students having been allowed to keep an original name, or even to adopt a translation.

The next academic objective of the curriculum was to instruct the children in the English language. This posed many problems for both students and teachers, and was a source of immense frustration because each classroom contained students of different tribes, speaking different languages. This, combined with teachers most of whom had no knowledge of, or inclination to learn these languages, made it almost impossible to overcome linguistic barriers. But if the proponents of the boarding-school system were going to succeed in their mission to prepare Indian children for a life of assimilation into white culture, a way had to be found to encourage the use and mastery of English. To that end, school officials announced that students were forbidden to speak any languages other than English, and that the punishment for infringement of this rule would be severe.[29] But the English language was not the only alien concept that the whites forced upon the native children. For example, the Indians could not understand the white man's obsession with time, and found it hard to correlate talk of hours and minutes with the movement of a clock. They considered hours and minutes too short a time to be of any concern: "When the sun rose, when it was high in the sky, and when it set were all the divisions of the day that we had ever found necessary when we followed the old Arapaho road. When we went on a hunting trip or to a sun dance, we counted time by sleeps."[30]

By 1900, the Indian boarding school program was, on paper, a tremendous success with over 21,000 students in residence. But one of the most visible results of Pratt's Carlisle experiment was the disastrous effect that his educational program had on Indian children and their families. Although most students spent several years learning English, their command of the language was often not proficient enough to secure employment away from the schools. The young people were not ready for life in white communities but at the same time, they had lost fluency in their native languages. These young adults, after serving their time in government boarding schools, were totally unprepared either for the white world or for their own.

As a result of the perceived success of the U.S. Indian boarding school experiment, similar schools spread throughout Canada and, although the Carlisle Indian Boarding School closed its doors in 1918 and the Indian New Deal of the 1930s caused the remaining government boarding schools in the United States to cease operating, the McIntosh Indian Boarding School in Ontario, Canada remained fully operational until the late 1960s. While there is still interest and many references to the Carlisle School, very little evidence remains of its Canadian counterpart. It is almost as if the people who were involved with the school are, or were, trying to erase all thought of it from their memories.

The McIntosh Indian Boarding School was built in 1925 by the Oblate Catholic Missionaries to convert and assimilate the educationally neglected children living in remote reserves that until then had little or no contact with whites. Within just four years, however, the school had to be expanded to accommodate students from most parts of Northwestern Ontario.[31] Much like Carlisle's superintendent, Richard Henry Pratt, the principal of the McIntosh School, Father Perrault, found himself in constant conflict with the Department of Indian Affairs, especially when the policy of forced assimilation conflicted with the sparse resources and economic state of Canada in the 1930s, a situation which caused desperate Indian parents to abandon their children at the school, and resulted in an exponential increase in its population and serious overcrowding. When criticized about the cramped conditions in the school, Father Perrault retorted that the children were better off there than at home. Even when the country began to recover from the ravages of the depression, the school was assured of a constant supply of students because the Canadian government withheld family allowance payments from parents who refused to enroll their children or who shielded runaways from the authorities. The enforced separation of children from their families and their culture destroyed many native families, and remains one of the darkest periods of institutional racism within Canada.

Cultural separation was reinforced within the school by alienating the children from their native ways of life. Most of the Canadian students identified their fathers' occupation as "trapper," but by the time they were ready to leave the school, they either had no native skills or felt no inclination to adopt a traditional lifestyle: they had been taught to be ashamed of their heritage. Meanwhile the assimilation of the students continued. The females were taught to cook, sew, and weave, while the boys learned manual shop skills and tended the school's livestock.

The initial primary mission of the McIntosh school was the conversion of the students to Catholicism, with a lesser concentration on schooling them for assimilation into white society. In the early days of the school, the students were referred to as "scholars,"[32] but it soon became clear to the administration that because of their traditional native background, the students' Western-style education had to begin at a pre-school level. Furthermore, it is probable that few, if any, of the teachers had any experience in speaking native languages, teaching English as a second language, or had any pedagogical skills whatsoever. These factors alone would have made learning extremely difficult, but the students were further hampered by having to carry out the inordinate number of manual chores that running a school of that size engendered. Thus the study of academic subjects was increasingly marginalized.

After World War II and on the recommendation of the District Indian Agent, the school administrator introduced sport and leisure activities to the curriculum, as well as woodwork using locally found native swamp ash. Among the many wooden items that the boys produced, hockey sticks were considered to be second to none and so the school went into full production.[33] Indeed, as the hockey stick industry expanded, the sport became the main activity at the school, and the sport and the school became synonymous in much the same way as did the Carlisle Indian Boarding School and football. The administrators of both schools seemed to share ideology when it came to the activities of their students, and the potential favorable publicity that could be derived from their participation in a seemingly white sport. When Richard Pratt agreed to allow the Carlisle boys to play football it was under the following condition, "That, in the course of two, three, or four years you will develop your strength and ability to such a degree that you will whip the biggest football team in the country."[34] Similarly, the McIntosh Indian School became a "hockey camp" in which almost all the boys participated. From the early 1950s until the school closed, The McIntosh Indian School enjoyed the title of one of the best hockey clubs in Ontario, if not in the whole of Canada. The hockey program was strictly organized with boys entering at kindergarten age and progressing through the ranks by age. The very threat of being deprived of his hockey stick for infringements of school rules kept even the most unruly boy on the straight and narrow.

Although the McIntosh Indian School continued to expand until around 1962, inspectors continually criticized its concentration on recreation and religious training at the expense of academic progress. At the same time, the Canadian government began to lose its faith in the Indian boarding school program and consequently native day schools began to spring up on the reserves. The Canadians, like their United States neighbors thirty years earlier, were losing interest in the idea of forced assimilation. A former student, Tim A. Giago Jr. wrote the following poem to describe his missionary boarding school experience:

> You probably remember differently.
> Or do you?
> You had Senior proms, hot rods,
> Soda shops and pinball machines,
> And nights at home
> With the family
> At white schools.
>
> We had the three R's,
> Reading, Riting, and Rithmetic.
> Taught to the tune
> Of the Principal's belt.
> Separation from our mothers,
> Fathers, brothers and sisters.
> And indoctrination
> By our new
> Fathers, Brothers, Sisters and Mothers Superior.
>
> But it wasn't all bad.
> We made friends.
> We shared secrets.
> We gained strength,
> From each other.
> And most important,
> We gained knowledge.
>
> No, it wasn't all bad.
> But I never learned to like it.
> And I ran away again.
> I never returned.
> I never stopped running
> Until now.
>
> I lost something at the Mission,
> And this summer,
> Many years later,
> With trepidation,
> I came back to retrieve it,
> So that I could
> Stop running, stop reaching,
> Stop fearing.
> And there it was,

Waiting where I had left it
On the steps of the church.

I found my spirit.[35]

It is interesting to note that residents of the area surrounding the school claim to have seen adult natives walking among the ruins of the school.[36]

Boarding schools for native people were ruinous—a cancer for all indigenous people who have had to endure their legacy. The Carlisle and McIntosh schools represent prime examples of the unholy alliance of government and religious hegemony for the purpose of destroying culture and knowledge. Nevertheless, government and missionary boarding schools for indigenous students still exist throughout the Americas, including the United States and Canada.

The boarding school era has passed but that does not mean that policies for educational opportunities and equity have significantly improved. Despite some positive aspects of No Child Left Behind (NCLB), its overall legacy may prove to be as reprehensible as the boarding schools. NCLB's narrow-minded and rabid adherence to standardized tests (which rely too much on word recognition - vocabulary words being about 85% of the content and have been the sole means of determining grade promotion and graduation[37]), has created an underclass that for the most part is destined to fuel the service industries and to fill the welfare rolls for the next generations. Between NCLB and the "Great Recession," numerous states are seriously considering closing schools. Michigan, New Jersey, Pennsylvania, and California have already "boarded up" schools, effectively withholding reasonable access to education from untold numbers of students. In Texas high schools it is estimated that 50% of all minority students are in the 9th grade. This is commonly referred to by educators as the *9th grade hump*. The drop-out rate in Texas schools for Hispanics is approximately 50%, now roughly equal to that of American Indians nationwide. Although never as low as white students, in 2004 the high school attrition rate for Hispanic students was in the mid to lower 30%, but with the implementation of the requirement of course retention and the inability to score high enough on the examination, the dropout rate for students of color is now nearing all-time highs.[38] Indeed, parents within many communities are so embittered by the ruinous effects of this educational policy which has further disadvantaged minority children that they commonly refer to the program as "No White Child Left Behind." Maria Robledo Montecel, President of the Texas-based Intercultural Development Research Association, claims the reason is simple, "One of the most fundamental reasons for which students leave school is that they feel disconnected."[39] It must be assumed that similar conclusions can be found in other states that require a single passing score on a standardized examination in order to graduate. This is not to say that state examinations should be abandoned, but rather to require that multiple criteria be used to determine whether a student has passed a course, and whether he or she has learned enough to graduate.

It is true that standardized tests have been used since 2200 B.C.E. in China and in other authoritarian regimes.[40] The policy of mandatory standardized testing ensures that government determines what knowledge is, which inherently reflects what government wants us to know. This not only favors convergent thinking, but also ensures privilege among the higher socioeconomic classes, and creates a byproduct of human economic fuel for the service industries, so keeping wages down and profits up. It is perhaps unfair to say that this result of NCLB was predictable and intended for economic purposes, but there were many who did predict the failure of this policy, which raises the question: how was it that the government did not? And if the government was aware (which it should have been), and instituted it anyway, it was a crime—a crime against children which over time will be seen as odious as that of the Indian boarding school era.

THANK GOODNESS FOR COMIC BOOKS
AND SOCIAL PROMOTION: THE IMPOSITION
OF A LANGUAGE

When I was 5 years old, I entered the first grade. Our school didn't have a kindergarten; therefore I knew nothing about reading or language. My family spoke mostly English along with some Finnish, and my grandparents, who lived next door, spoke English and French and Mitchif (French, Indian, and English). I could understand enough Finnish to follow a conversation and could speak some, and I knew some French words and I thought I communicated well enough. In school I recall being taught to read using phonics—dreary stuff, and the stories I had to read were totally alien to my way of life and experiences. Thank goodness for comic books; "*The Deerslayer*" was my favorite.

I was raised in a hunting society. When together, my father and my male mentors spoke Finnish and English, and when I was with my Grandfather he spoke English and French. Between them all, they taught me what I needed to know to ensure that I could hunt, fish, and trap. Knowledge was passed orally and was rich with meaning. Vowels and such were not required, nor were they relevant to my world. Besides comic books I eventually included the *National Geographic* with its wonderful pictures and later I started to read the articles that told of the natural world, which included my own. I also added outdoor magazines. And so I learned to read despite what I had to read in school. Had I not gone to school, there is no telling where my personal reading might have taken me.

It should come as no surprise that I earned poor grades. I thought I might be dumb, so I also didn't say much either. I was, however, a good hunter and fisher for my age, and I knew a lot about those things. Moreover, the people whose opinions mattered most to me valued my behavior and actions, not what I was learning in school. One day my high school English teacher, Mr. Lindquist, became upset with me for not reading *Silas Marner*. To my knowledge I had never angered a teacher before. He said that he was angry at me because he felt that I was one of the smartest kids in my class, but was barely graduating. I was shocked, not about my class ranking, but that a teacher thought I wasn't dumb. That got me thinking that maybe I was smart enough to join the Navy, and to my surprise they accepted me. And somewhere on the South China Sea, I read my first book. I am, however, still under-confident about my use of language and will always wonder how much better I could have been had the curriculum and methods of teaching remotely interested me and reflected my community environment.

CHAPTER 7

LANGUAGE AND POWER

Of the over 300 pre-contact tribal languages, slightly more than 200 remain, and only 11 percent (20) of those are still being learned by children the old way, from parents and others.

Linda Cleary & Thomas Peacock, *Collected Wisdom:*
American Indian Education

In most parts of today's world, the written word is trusted as the primary means of communicating human ideas, and indeed, it is often seen as a society's validation of a person's acumen with language, in other words his or her ability to tell a story, or to communicate information. Indeed, when people want to look for the definition of a word that they have read or heard, the most trusted source of choice is nearly always some type of text, such as a dictionary or a glossary. Written language is unique to humans, and the development of the printing press heralded a monumental advance in human history. Yet for all the obvious social benefits that are realized through written communication, it is beset with shortcomings that can bring, and has brought, the utmost harm to some communities.

When two people communicate, the information transmitted is always subject to a certain degree of distortion, the extent of which depends upon multiple variables that can limit the effectiveness of both the sender and the receiver. Less distortion is present when they are of a similar age, of the same sex, have acquired knowledge in the same pedagogical manner, and have grown up in the same community speaking the same language. It is also extremely important that cultural differences are addressed to minimize communication difficulties.

It is evident from the study of indigenous knowledge and language that a major variable between many languages and the Western way of transmitting knowledge is that of noun and verb consciousness. Traditional Western schools are based on Plato's idealism and Aristotle's realist taxonomies, and are noun-based, meaning that concepts are concrete, such as names, colors, and numbers. The theory behind this teaching is that students must learn to name these concrete nouns to help them make the connections between their prior knowledge and new information. When whites began their programs of assimilation through education in the United States, one of the most problematic issues for native children revolved around language.

Because language is culturally based, Indian children who were educated in white schools found it very difficult to correlate the words that they were learning with the world with which they were familiar; as David Wallace Adams explains:

> Unlike the German-or French-speaking student, to whom similar linguistic patterns would be readily recognizable, the Indian student struggled with a language that was entirely outside his native morphological and syntactical frame of reference. Many Indian languages place little emphasis on time or verb tense; others make little differentiation between nouns and verbs or separate linguistic units; still others build into a single word thoughts that in English can only be expressed in an entire sentence.[1]

Thus, primary age Indian boarding school students found themselves with many things to name and categorize that in no way matched their prior experience. In *My People the Sioux*, Luther Standing Bear describes the confusion:

> [S]everal of us had an idea that some morning we would awaken and discover that we could talk English as readily as we could our own. As for myself, I thought . . . I would wake up some morning with a full knowledge of the English language. We did not realize that we must learn one word at a time.[2]

In the first section of *The Man Made of Words*, Kiowa novelist and poet, N. Scott Momaday, explains the connection between Indian people and language. Momaday, in describing the oral tradition of storytelling, points out that without written documentation, the stories, histories, and traditions are always "but one generation removed from extinction."[3] This puts a great responsibility upon both the storyteller and the listener. The former must choose the precise words to convey accurate meaning, while the latter must concentrate fully to ensure that nothing is lost. The telling of stories was more formal than it is today. The storytellers (teachers) had to be precise with their words and speech. The receivers (students) had not only to hear, but they also had to consciously listen and concentrate on processing the information they were learning from their short-term memory into their long-term memory by retelling (re-teaching). But as Momaday states,

> One does not necessarily speak in order to be heard. It is sometimes enough that one places one's voice on the silence, for that in itself is a whole and appropriate expression of the spirit. In the native American oral tradition, expression, rather than communication, is often first in importance.[4]

Hence there is a moral responsibility between teacher and student, which is not just cognitive, but also affective. The storytellers are role models and the students have expectations not only with regard to the content, but also to inculcate the behavior of the teachers into themselves. Most cultures, especially those without a written language, use the telling of stories as a means of transmitting knowledge. And storytelling remains popular in the folk culture of virtually all societies today. Only now do we recognize this teaching and learning style as *recurrent*. In addition, it is actually better than most

Western learning and teaching styles for developing students' upper-level cognitive skills such as analysis, synthesis, and evaluation (higher order thinking).[5] The ancient Hawaiian tale of the war between Pele and her sister offers a good example of how ancient storytellers employed higher order thinking to explain Continental Drift Theory:

> Pele, the goddess of volcanoes, once lived in Kauai. But then she was attacked by her older sister, Namakaokahai, the goddess of the sea. And so she fled, southeast, to Oahu. Namakaokahai attacked again, and Pele moved southeast once more, to Maui. And then a third time, whereupon Pele moved yet again, this time to the Halemaumau Crater of Kilauea, on the summit of Hawaii itself. She had moved three hundred miles southeastward, hopping from island to island, and one volcano after another exploded and died behind her.[6]

The relationship between storytelling and higher order thinking is, however, totally dependent upon the listeners' abilities to understand the story. And when that cultural connection is lost, the effect is loss of self-esteem, misunderstanding, and alienation. When Western society imposed the "English only" rule at off-reservation boarding schools, all-important generational and cultural bonds were broken. Momaday recounts the story of a former Carlisle Indian Boarding School student, Plenty Horses, who found himself in a cultural and linguistic no-man's land after his Western education. He shot an army officer who was attempting to initiate peace talks in the aftermath of the massacre at Wounded Knee. While awaiting sentence, Plenty Horses spoke of how his school days had estranged him from his people, and how he hoped that his actions would make them proud of him. Momaday explains what the loss of language meant to Plenty Horses:

> At Carlisle he had been made to speak English, and his native Lakota was forbidden—thrown away, to use a term that indicates particular misfortune in the plains oral tradition. To be "thrown away" is to be negated, excluded, eliminated. After five years Plenty Horses had not only failed to master the English language, he had lost some critical possession of his native tongue as well. He was therefore crippled in his speech, wounded in his intelligence. In him was a terrible urgency to express himself—his anger and hurt, his sorrow and loneliness. But his voice was broken. In terms of his culture and all it held most sacred, Plenty Horses himself was thrown away.[7]

The main problem was that while Indian parents and elders still had the ability to pass on their stories and knowledge, the children had difficulty understanding the message; the oral tradition was in grave danger of extinction. This takes on an even greater significance when the relationship between language and religion is considered. According to Indian oral tradition, "The telling of the story is a spiritual act, and the storyteller has a profound conviction of the religious dimension in which the act is accomplished."[8] "Every word spoken, every word heard, is the utterance of a prayer."[9] So when indigenous children were schooled exclusively in the Western tradition, not only did their native verbal skills diminish, but they also lost touch with their native religions. Thus, the oral tradition was attacked on both the linguistic and religious fronts. Western teachers also undermined the important significance of the power of speech by their concentration upon writing. The written word has, according to Momaday, created an attitude of complacency toward the power and beauty of spoken language. Words can be stored and retrieved so easily that "we have developed a kind of false security where language is concerned, and our sensitivity to language has deteriorated."[10] The importance of silence has also been forgotten. For cultures steeped in the oral tradition, the loss of language represents the loss of meaning of life itself. Since the arrival of the first white settlers, many of the problems suffered by the Indians have been caused by cultural and linguistic differences, and consequent misunderstandings. The facets of life that were of fundamental importance to American Indians, such as their relationship with the land and their oral traditions, had little or no significance for the settlers. Yet the involuntary loss of their language was devastating to the native people and, in many ways, dehumanizing.

In retrospect, while many might regard the loss of language by indigenous people via assimilation over hundreds of years as normal and harmless, in the United States it worked to define English as the language of power and, when children were removed from their homes to be educated to assimilate into white society, it often created a rift between the student and his or her family. The problems were not, however, always instantly recognizable. Sun Elk, or Tulto as he was also called at home, was the first boy from the Taos Pueblo to attend the Carlisle Indian Boarding School. Unlike many of his fellow students who did everything in their power to avoid attending school, or the other boys in the Pueblo who were eager to learn the Indian rituals, Sun Elk favored the white man's way of life, thinking that "he had better magic than the Indian."[11] In a 1933 interview with historian Edwin Embree, which is reprinted in *Native American Testimony*, Sun Elk described his eagerness to go to school, despite his father's sadness. Thinking that his son would soon outgrow this obsession, Sun Elk's father agreed to allow him to attend Carlisle: "There was plenty of time to go into the kiva."[12]

Sun Elk spent seven years in Carlisle working at his academic studies and on his technical skills; "I set little letters together in the printing shop and we printed papers."[13] Clearly, much of Sun Elk's education centered around learning how to be a white man, and to reject his native way of life. For those seven years, Sun Elk and his fellow students lived like white boys: "We all wore white man's clothes and ate white man's food and went to white man's churches and spoke white man's talk."[14] After a while, the boys began to believe that Indian ways were bad and then started to scorn their own people.

When Sun Elk returned to his home, he had forgotten much of his native language and initially had trouble communicating with his family. There was, however, jubilation at his return: "We chattered and cried, and I began to remember many Indian words."[15] The celebration was, however, short-lived. The governor and chiefs of the Pueblo neither celebrated nor welcomed the return of this boarding-school educated boy. They rejected him and treated him as an outcast, who had neither training nor the skills to be accepted as an Indian child. Everything about him was different; his hair, his name, his religion, and his language. He had been educated in the ways of the white man, and therefore could not be considered as a useful member of the community. Just as he had been taught to scorn his own people by the teachers at Carlisle, members of his own community were turning their backs on him. While his father was once again saddened because of his son, Sun Elk himself was furious. He left the Pueblo and did not return for many years.[16]

During his time away from the Pueblo, Sun Elk lived as a white man working first as a printer and later in farms and blacksmith shops. But he was not happy. "I made money and I kept a little of it and after many years I came back to Taos."[17] On land given to him by his father, which was situated just outside the Pueblo, Sun Elk built a house "bigger than the Pueblo houses."[18] But it was not until he married an Indian girl who his father brought to him that Sun Elk began to feel like an Indian again. "I let my hair grow, I put on blankets, and I cut the seat out of my pants."[19]

Sun Elk's experiences of alienation were caused, at least partly, by Carlisle's English-only policy. Colin Baker of the University of Wales uses the term *subtractive bilingualism* to describe the phenomenon. According to Baker,

When the second language and culture are acquired ... with pressure to replace or demote the first language, a subtractive form of bilingualism may occur. This may relate to a less positive self-concept, loss of cultural or ethnic identity, with a possible alienation or marginalization...

When the second language is prestigious and powerful, used in mainstream education and in the jobs market, and when the minority language is perceived as of low status and value, minority languages may be threatened. Instead of addition, there is subtraction; division instead of multiplication.[20]

Many parents of non-native speakers feel pressured into forcing their children to abandon their native language in order to succeed in school. On the contrary, the following advice is offered based on the research of Jim Cummins, a leading authority in second language acquisition and bilingual education:

It is very important that students be encouraged to continue their native language development. When parents ask about the best ways they can help their child at home, you can reply that the child should have the opportunity to read extensively in her own language. You could suggest that parents make some time every evening to discuss with their child, *in their native language*, what she has done in school that day: ask her to talk about the science experiment she did, question her about her understanding of primary and secondary sources of historical information, have her explain how she has solved a math problem etc.[21]

One of the main difficulties faced by non-native speakers in any part of the world is that native speakers often deem them illiterate. Indeed, language classes are commonly known as literacy classes, even if the students are literate in their own language. Does that mean, therefore, that people who lived before the days of written language were unable to communicate other than by voice? Absolutely not. Paleolithic drawings have tended to be considered art at best or just graffiti by all but a few dedicated scholars. There are, however, excellent examples of this type of communication throughout North America, and indeed throughout the world. These drawings may conjure some wonder, but most often they are seen as just the doodling of uneducated ancients. But if one thinks of *place,* the drawings are not graffiti but rather ancient way-signs, a sort of global positioning system, that told early travelers which way to go: directions that were painted for all to see and use. Of course, we don't know much about how to read ancient forms of pictographs with any degree of accuracy, but it is almost certain that they had real communicative meaning – meaning that is now lost to modern man, not that he has, until relatively recently at least, really cared too much about pictures. In much the same way that the written word signaled what almost became a death knell for the oral tradition, so too was the fate of early forms of visual communication. The art of creating pictures was either left to specialist artists or relegated to the realm of children's means of expression – a form of communication that was expected to be abandoned in favor of the written word as the child matured and learned. It is only in the past few years that visual communication has gained a level of respect, but it is still generally considered to be subordinate to written language.

Many scholars have argued about the value of the visual image in communication; while some see visuals as nothing more than decorative or illustrative enhancements to verbal text, others feel that they have unique attributes that have, in modern times, yet to be fully recognized and realized. One of the most important points emphasized by social semiologists[22] Gunter Kress and Theo van Leeuwen is the range of meaning-making expressions available to sign-makers. Children, for example, "have both more and less freedom of expression" than adults.[23] Kress and van Leeuwen explain that because children have yet to be constrained by social and cultural conventions, they are not restricted in their choice of signs; on the other hand, their lack of semiotic resources limits their range of expression. Children do not, however, recognize these limitations; they use whatever means are available to them to create meaning. Kress and van Leeuwen describe this ability to adapt and use any sign available to them as "semiotic potential [which] is defined by the semiotic resources available to a specific individual in a specific social context."[24] Because children are limited to the semiotic resources available to them to create their signs, it is understandable that adults, especially those who are not familiar with children's environments, might have difficulty interpreting them. And while Kress and van Leeuwen appreciate children's communicative talents, M.A.K. Halliday[25] describes infant speech as "pure signs, content-expression pairs analogous to a cat's miaow or the danger warnings signaled by an ape."[26] Halliday explains that "because it has no grammar," this type of utterance cannot be considered language. It is a "proto-language in the sense that it is there they first learn how to mean; but they then replace it in the second year of life, by the higher-order semiotic system which we call "language" And language, unlike the protolanguage, has a grammar in it."[27] When Halliday likens infant communication to the sounds of animals he finds it necessary to assure his readers that he means no offense; "I am not belittling these creatures, or their abilities; I am simply locating them in an evolutionary perspective."[28] Clearly Halliday not only sees language development in children as a sign of their humanness, but also that language development per se is a sign of evolutionary process. Conversely, Kress and van Leeuwen view children's adeptness with visuals as special and feel that this ability "should be understood better and developed further, rather than being cut off prematurely as is, too often, the case at present; and an ability that should also be available to adults"[29] Kress and van Leeuwen diverge from Halliday's linguistic theories because they recognize that literacy does not refer solely to verbal and written language, yet "literate cultures have systematically suppressed means of analysis of the visual forms of representation."[30] According to Halliday, "knowledge is prototypically made of language. Once you have language – whether 'you' as species or 'you' as individual – then you have the power of transforming experience into meaning."[31] This attitude is classically colonial and not only devalues, but totally dismisses the power of non-linguistic communication. It was this belief in the superiority of language over image, and written language over the oral tradition that formed the basis of Western notions of superiority. Now that we know better, it is time to reexamine cave art and hieroglyphics in a different light as some of these caverns and rock walls were *intentional* libraries and a means of preserving knowledge. While we are still out of touch with the ancients' modes of communication, perhaps we can at least try to understand what they were saying.

Most archaeologists argue that Paleolithic drawings were not just signposts, but also an effort to depict the spirits of animals. David Lewis-Williams of the University of the Witwatersrand in Johannesburg, South Africa, spent his professional life studying San rock art[32], and is convincing in his belief that Paleolithic paintings led to the birth of imagination among early humans. Lewis-Williams further states that art was not just a depiction of everyday life but rather had other worldly, spiritual, and symbolic meaning.[33] This form of art was not only again intentional but also facilitated formal operational thought which allowed the San to acquire a degree of knowledge of their environment even beyond our ability today.[34] For example, our understanding of the worldview of the San and of the Australian aborigine is so restricted by the Western definition of consciousness, that we cannot begin to grasp their beliefs about the universe, their place in it, and the natural laws that maintain order. Perhaps we could learn more if we were prepared to remove our cultural lens and use the technology available to us to help us to look back now and again instead of constantly (often blindly) forging forward. Although technology is seen as a tool of progression, there are times when new ways of doing things are not always the best. And in communication, new modes should certainly not be seen as automatic replacements for the old.

It is clear in today's technological world that the printed word provides more opportunities for the transmission of worldviews than the oral tradition, but it can be considered in some ways more restrictive, in that a concept as broad and meaningful as a worldview should not be confined to the literal definition of a word or series of words (we may, for example, read into ancient art, meanings that are nowhere close to those understood or intended by their creators). Languages, both written and oral, carry inherent restrictions that can foster or hinder the way in which people make sense of their world. Momaday warns us that a comparison of written and oral languages is complex, but we need to be aware that any comparison is usually undertaken by those committed to favor the written form and thus are inherently biased.[35] Not only does oral knowledge become distorted during translation to written language, but also it is further restricted in meaning by the modern day desire to record traditional knowledge systems digitally.[36] Linguist and educator Michael Christie argues that efforts to digitize traditional knowledge leads to filtering and assimilatory effects. Further, he points out, for example, that Australian aboriginal knowledge resides and originates from within the ground, and that it reflects the relationship between the people and the earth.[37] That established, he then questions how that can be put into a computer, and also argues that the motive for and intent to digitize indigenous knowledge should not be to allow easy access and use by non-aboriginal people for whatever reason.[37] Thus it would be best if it were "to remain small and local."[38] The concerns voiced by Christie on behalf of aboriginal people are neither new nor restricted to Australia; a number of tribes in the United States and Canada have strict research restrictions that go beyond the traditional institutional review boards of universities. Moreover, worldviews are not static; words change meaning over time, and even the same words can have totally different meanings for different cultures. Thus, if access were granted to all regardless of heritage, the data, that is, "the traditional knowledge practices,"[39] of indigenous people could be used by Westerners to promote their own agendas.

In ancient times, as permanent settlements grew, so too did the need for governance and the spread of linguistic recording. Special people were needed to read and record these written utterances, and thus the shaman (the spiritual leader) became the priest, and the chief became the king. Charles Mann agrees when he says that shamans were the gatekeepers to the supernatural and, with the establishment of permanent settlements, they evolved into a hereditary priesthood, restricting access to the temples, and counselors to the kings.[40] The tome replaced the petroglyphs. And herein is the shift away from sacred places to sacred texts. But as earthly places were replaced by local temples, their importance diminished. Anyone could travel to earthly places, but temples were most often restricted to only those who were worthy. The advent of the written word facilitated the separation of the natural world from those who resided in and around population centers. David Abram argues:

In indigenous, oral cultures, … language seems to encourage and augment the participatory life of the senses, while in Western civilization language seems to deny or deaden that life, promoting a massive distrust of sensorial experience while valorizing an abstract realm of ideas hidden behind or beyond the sensory appearances.[41]

Furthermore, natural senses were dulled by urban living—a dulling of senses was replaced by constructs which in turn led to ideology. The natural world also gave way to the abstraction of time and space. The here and now was replaced by yesterday and tomorrow. Abram posits that it was the ancient Hebrews who made this first transition.

They were perhaps the first nation to so thoroughly shift their sensory participation away from the forms of surrounding nature to a purely phonetic set of signs, and so to experience the profound epistemological independence from the natural environment that was made possible by this potent new technology. To actively participate with the visible forms of nature came to be considered *idolatry* by the ancient Hebrew; *it was not the land but the written letters that now carried the ancestral wisdom.*[42]

The written text became a "portable homeland" for the wandering Jews. Hence, "for the first time, the prophets placed a value on history, succeeded in transcending the traditional vision of the cycle (the conception that ensures all things will be repeated forever), and discovered a one-way time."[43] And with it came the birth of linearity.

When people think of where they have been and what they have learned, they should think in terms of where they are going, that is, they should relate the future to the past. Those who live in Western society, however, have been taught to consider the future as something ahead that they cannot see, but which they can anticipate, and the past as behind them and of limited value; that time has gone and is therefore beyond their control or sphere of influence. Western students are encouraged to write in linear prose in the present and future tenses, and to avoid the past tense. Western students are also taught to value the present and future over the past, and they do. They are encouraged to plan ahead more than to reflect on their past actions and achievements, and to learn that any such reflection will often incite criticism and even ridicule. Today's society values producers over thinkers. Students are not taught even to consider another paradigm, such as the past is actually in front of us and we can see it, whereas the future is behind us since we can't see it. There are people, such as the Sng'oi of Malaysia, who have this worldview. The Sng'oi's worldview seems irrational to us only because of the way we have been taught to think. And it is troubling to have to conclude that as difficult it is for us to comprehend such a model, it is even more so to admit that it is logical. Yet it is intuitively obvious that the reflective practitioner will improve by examining and learning from past practices, and then avoid future mistakes. Performance outcomes are increased when people are encouraged to visualize past successes and failures, and to work in a circular instead of a purely linear mode. To many of us, linearity seems natural and logical, but to many others it is not.

An advantage of the oral tradition over the written word is that spoken stories are not restricted to pre-set linear patterns and they can easily adapt to changes that are required to reflect cultural transitions. But because written words have physical, social, and political anchors that restrict change, they are far more permanent and unyielding. Unfortunately, the early Western colonizers used the indigenous people's lack of a written language as a sign of inferiority. The first contact indigenous people had with Europeans, especially in the Americas, often included priests who were literate, recorded their travels, and wrote about the native people they met. Encounters such as these are described in *Jesuit Relations: Natives and Missionaries in Seventeenth-Century North America*. Given the radical differences in language and cosmology, not to mention the sheer arrogance of the invaders, little of the native worldview was valued. Ironically, the Western worldview is often credited to classical Greece where the oral heritage of preliterate Greece shaped Greek culture. But once the Greeks developed a written language, they wrote down their oral poems and stories – the literary folklore then became an important character of the culture. Not surprisingly, Plato considered poems and stories to be the principal obstruction to his new society. Idealism, the core of his fledgling social order, was based on an authoritative source; therefore, the veracity of the oral tradition could not be reconciled with the new order. Plato's world of ideas took precedent over anything sensory-derived and eventually led the way for the monotheistic oppression of nature. The oral creation stories and myths of the Greeks evolved into poems, theatre, and literature, which also became more androcentric and paternal, and led to the further demise of the shaman and his or her gods. The priest finally replaced the shaman, the king over the chief, Plato the writer over Socrates the orator, the *Essential Form of Goodness* over all things having a spirit, and the Greek alphabet over the sensible world. Yet perhaps in the political spirit of compromise, Plato kept Greek oral traditions alive by including poetry and literature in his definition of art as detailed in chapter IX of *The Republic*, "Primary Education of the Guardian." And today, as in Plato's time, many educators still consider the liberal arts as classical and therefore required to be taught, but as we mentioned earlier, today's obsession with science and technology has placed their future role in North American education in jeopardy.

EMBRACING IDENTITY

I was about 30 years old when my mother announced at a family gathering that my sister and I were part Indian. My mother's announcement came during the time of the civil rights movement and the reemergence of Indian Pride. I recall feeling more curious than surprised by the revelation. I had always thought that my grandparents were French Canadian, but it seems that my grandmother was mostly Indian. My grandparents had left the North Dakota plains so that my grandfather could take a railroad job in Knife River, Minnesota, which would provide a better standard of living for his family. The move took my grandmother away from her culture, but it also spared her family from the overt racism that Indians were forced to endure on the northern plains. While my grandmother had chosen to cloak herself in a new identity as a French Canadian, my mother, once her secret was out, embraced her Indian heritage.

My new knowledge of Indian ancestry led to a greater curiosity in my heritage. Several years of research brought to light a typical example of forced assimilation. My great-grandparents on my mother's side were members of the Devil's Lake Agency (reservation) in eastern North Dakota. This reservation, with its proximity to the Red River Valley, happened to comprise some of the most fertile land on the North American continent, so the government simply claimed the land under the Federal General Allotment Act of 1887 and sold it to white farmers. My grandmother moved to Pembina, North Dakota where she married my grandfather, a newly immigrated French Canadian, and they then moved to Minnesota. And that's really how assimilation works; an Indian becomes a French Canadian or a Hispanic becomes white, and although some may suspect she has Indian or Mexican in her, she is married to a hard-working, respected non-minority. In my case, my grandparents become part of the community of Swedes, Finns, and Norwegians that had also just arrived from Scandinavia. My mother married a Finn, but the irony here is that he was a dark, blue-eyed northern Finn of Sami descent and looked more Indian than my mother.

Although we did, at times, visit "friends" at both Fond du Lac and Grand Portage Indian Reservations in northern Minnesota, we did not participate in tribal activities. I suspect my mother would have liked to, but I think she also wanted to protect my sister and me. My mother was still in the closet.

Being an Indian with no tribe is an issue. When tribal Indians meet you for the first time, it isn't long before you are seemingly innocently asked, "Where are you from?" What they are really asking about is your tribal affiliation or lack thereof.

I have come to realize that I need not be embarrassed about being just part Indian nor having tribal status. I do not need to be more Indian, or less white. I am American.

NEITHER WOLF NOR DOG

> The question of my "identity" often comes up. I think I must be mixed-blood.
> I claim to be male, although only one of my parents was male.
>
> Jimmie Durham, In *Real Indians: Identity and the Survival of*
> *Native America*

The quotation above suggests that Jimmie Durham, who is of Cherokee heritage, is able to make light of his cultural background, but many feel no humor about their mixed heritage. The title of this chapter, which captures the struggle and pain of a cloudy sense of being, is taken from Kent Nerburn's 1994 book *Neither Wolf Nor Dog: On Forgotten Roads with an Indian*, in which he describes the issues of living between two worlds. Many people, especially in the United States, are neither "wolf nor dog."

People who live between two cultures often feel disconnected both from the colonial-based mainstream society in which they live, and from their cultural heritage. Thoughts about murky identity can often lead to confusion and alienation. Canadian newspaper columnist and Ojibway, Richard Wagamese, writes in his award winning book, *Keeper'n Me*, that "Not knowing who you are is like the wind whistling through your gut."[1] This anxiety is particularly prevalent when new ethnic groups with their own unique identities are created through ethnogenesis.[2] One contemporary example of this process can be seen in the *Tejano* culture of South Texas. There were many Indians in Texas, but one of the first acts of the new Republic of Texas in 1835 was the establishment of the Texas Rangers. And the first charge of the Rangers was to make the new nation safe from Indians. Bands of Comanches fled to the wilds of West Texas and the coastal Indians, the Karankawa, fled into Mexico, where they were hunted down and killed by the Mexican Federales. What often happened, however, was instant assimilation as many Indians simply abandoned their traditional Indian names, adopted titles such as "Jose" or "Maria," and overnight *became* Mexicans—who for the most part were Indians from northern Mexico anyway. In the new Texas, it was better to be beaten up as a Mexican than killed as an Indian. It is important to note that a large section of the Hispanic population comprised, and indeed still comprises, people of Mexican/Indian descent who lost the language and cultural practices of their indigenous ancestors. They are the progeny of ancient people and cultures who were colonized by Europeans—first in the south and then further north. (Spanish is just as much a colonial language of imposition as English.) Yet in their psyche remain vestiges of their ancient indigenous heritage; the Mexican American link to the earth, favoring place over events, and strong family/clan ties are but a few signs of their indigenous past.

When people share a common heritage and experiences, a collective consciousness is created and, according to Thomas Overholt and J. Baird Callicott in their 1982 *Clothed-in-Fur and Other Tales*, historical experiences, voices, language, and heroes provide a distinct worldview that "may be understood as a set of conceptual presuppositions, both conscious and unconscious, articulate and inarticulate shared by members of a culture."[3] If a worldview becomes distinct enough, it may even create a discrete epistemology, that is, a unique way in which those within the culture acquire knowledge.

It is patently obvious that the population of immigrant nations, such as the United States, is comprised of many different cultures. But in the early days of European settlement, those cultures tended to stay separate. Today, as cultures are integrating more and more, the mixed population in the United States is becoming prevalent. Consequently, the mixed K-12 student population is an increasing one that has specific educational needs because of the students' bicultural or even multicultural heritages. Developmental psychologist Erik Erikson[4] argues that all normal adolescents pass through a tumultuous time of identity versus role confusion on their way to young adulthood, and while this passage may be more challenging for a student with a mixed heritage it can, when joined with low self-esteem, become toxic for anyone, especially mixed-race students.

Throughout Latin and South America, the Caribbean Basin, and Canada, there is recognition and acceptance of mixed populations, and in many regions and islands mixed populations are the majority and the dominant culture. The people of the United States, however, have been slow to accept the legitimacy of this type of mixing, nor is it even recognized that ethnogenesis has taken place. The word ethnogenesis is rarely heard or found in print in the United States. Thus, people of mixed race often seek to align themselves solely with just one of their blood identities; commonly with the one that is most physically apparent. Often mixed race students *pass* themselves off as members of a single ethnic or cultural group, depending upon their skin color or where they live. It has been more difficult, however, for students of mixed African American and white ancestry to *pass* exclusively as white, and even today no matter how a person looks, talks, behaves, or how educated he or she may be, people of just a small degree of Black heritage still primarily self-identify as African American. This is best summed up by the light-skinned Colin Powell when he said, "In America, which I love from the depths of my heart and soul, when you look like me, you're black."[5] The old "One-Drop Rule"[6] is seemingly still applicable for many mixed Blacks and whites, but that is far from the case with Indians and whites. So therein lies another problem; mixed individuals are not always welcomed, because minority groups are often reluctant to recognize the level of assimilation that has taken place throughout the United States.

Mixed American Indians tend not to define themselves so rigidly with one culture; they are more apt to blend in with the common culture of their surroundings. More troubling is that some mixed American Indians and whites do not self-identify as being of both populations. This may not be much of an issue for adults but as students, this identity denial or confusion may contribute to poor academic performance. Under the best of circumstances, a student with parents from different cultures (and different identities) can face unique problems in school. It is normal for all children, especially in adolescence, to question their identity. Identity issues are particularly problematic for a student who attends a school which fails to value one or both cultures, let alone a combination thereof. Yet, children have no choice when it comes to heritage; they cannot select their parents before birth. Thus, caregivers, especially educators, should reject neither culture, for if they do, the young will often fail to take the best from their cultural milieu. In the case of mixed children's heritage, it is important to recognize both their cultures, specifically for those children who live on or around reservations or ghettos. Cultural identity crises are not, however, restricted to children of mixed culture. All children, regardless of heritage, have to go through the painful stages of adolescence with all of the inherent worries and questions that growing up brings.

Identity versus role confusion is Erikson's fifth stage of young people's march to adulthood and, importantly, the first that they must do alone. Each stage is important, but all the previous stages are inherited, and their passage through these is navigated with the guidance of others. As if early adolescence is not difficult enough, with all its emotional, social, and physical changes, it is also where young people must travel through the swamp of cultural identity and determine where they fit within it—and it must be done alone. No one can tell them any longer who they are, they must discover that for themselves. It is a time of turmoil and confusion that is further confounded for indigenous young people by the difficulties surrounding their cultural designation – are they Native Americans, American Indians or should they have some other, perhaps more meaningful title?

The terms Native American and American Indian have historically been used to refer to the indigenous people of the United States. Neither term, however, is without difficulty and controversy. The first was intended to designate people who were the original inhabitants of the country, and to escape the colonial misguided term "Indian," but the name did not engender much support from the very people it was designed to serve. The word "Indian," when used to describe a native of the Americas, has often been thought of as a pejorative, colonial term that harps back to the geographically-challenged Columbus and his encounters with the indigenous people he met. Moreover, this title has often been linked with stereotyping by evoking thoughts of the noble savage, or the fierce warrior. Many of the United States' indigenous people today prefer to use the term American Indian, but it too has problems, because it has the national term "American," as well as the problematic "Indian." Clyde Tucker, Brian Kojetin, and Roderick Harrison in their analysis of the *Bureau of Labor Statistics 1995 Measurement of Race and Ethnicity* found that there was little consensus on the favored term for the indigenous people of the United States. Indeed, surveys revealed that:

Persons identifying as American Indians were asked which of the following terms they preferred to describe themselves: American Indian, Alaska Native,

Native American, Some other term, or No preference. Over 50% chose the term American Indian or Alaska Native as the one they preferred, but a sizable number preferred Native American.[7]

It would be easy for people to read the sentiments exhibited in the census survey as indicative that indigenous people have no consensus on the issue of what to be called, but that conclusion would be erroneous. Many indigenous people of the United States favor neither term because both are seen as stemming from colonialism and having been foisted upon them by whites. Lakota activist and actor, Russell Means, in a July 1980 speech given at the Black Hills International Survival Gathering in South Dakota, made clear his views on the matter:

> You notice I use the term American Indian rather than Native American or Native indigenous people or Amerindian when referring to my people. There has been some controversy about such terms, and frankly, at this point, I find it absurd. Primarily it seems that American Indian is being rejected as European in origin-which is true. But all the above terms are European in origin; the only non-European way is to speak of Lakota-or, more precisely, of Oglala, Brule, etc.-and of the Dineh, the Miccousukee, and all the rest of the several hundred correct tribal names.[8]

Indigenous or aboriginal is the worldwide designator for native people. An indigenous person from the continents of North and South America is more correctly known as a native. However, this term is unclear, as anyone born in the Americas is in fact also a native thereof. For all practical purposes the term aboriginal and indigenous are the same, and they can legitimately be used interchangeably. The term mixed race is, however, a construct. Biologists have stated for over 100 years that race does not exist. DNA tests have determined that our physical differences are less than 1% among all people, but we still label people based on skin color and use the term race because we do not know or choose not to know anything better, and thus accept these vestiges of an archaic past. Nevertheless, indigenes, in full or in part, regardless of whether or not they adhere to a native worldview, still have aboriginal heritage and probably will experience periods of a cultural disconnect if they live outside an indigenous culture.

Anyone can acquire an indigenous worldview and essentially "go" native, and history is full of them. But can someone *become* native? The answer has to be a resounding no. A person can *become* an "other," but that is more an indication of a political stance, or a lack of acceptance by the resident majority, than a statement of identity. If it was possible to *become* native, then all constructs surrounding national or group birthrights would be voided. Anyone willing to go through the necessary procedures for native status could earn the right to call himself or herself a native of anywhere and, thus, demand all the benefits that go with the title. Native status would also surely incorporate citizenship, a topic that is vehemently argued and defended in discussions of legal and illegal immigration, so it is unlikely that a law allowing a person to become native would receive much, if any, backing. One can, of course, be raised native, with a respect for all aspects of existence that is inherent in indigenous people, and not be conscious of it. Indeed, when people talk about "going native," they are not generally discussing heritage. The ideas behind these discussions usually center around environmental and planet stewardship issues.

Most would agree that a primary component of the indigenous worldview is an environmental ethic that instils in people an inclination to value a sense of place versus time. Geography and a person's relationship to it provides a propensity toward valuing non-human life, and ultimately may even lead toward associating life or spirits with the non-living aspects of his or her geographical environment. Virtually all members of indigenous cultures agree that all things animate and inanimate have a spirit, and that humans have a relationship with all things. Conversely, Western science holds that only things that are animate are alive; a rationale that is used to place dogma over geography. The Eurocentric worldview instills the belief that the environment can and should be manipulated, and that the four most sacred spirits of indigenous people – earth, sun, water, and moon – are inanimate, and thus are to be controlled.

No one ever questions the *Indianness* of Crazy Horse. Yet he is thought by many to have been of mixed heritage. Although no pictures were taken of him, he is described as being of light skin with fair, curly hair. Crazy Horse biographers Larry McMurtry[9] and Mari Sandoz[10] suggest that Crazy Horse's self-consciousness about his mixed heritage was a significant reason behind his need to prove himself as a warrior. Crazy Horse lived in the Dakotas, an area that in his time already had at least two hundred years of contact with white fur traders and explorers. Most of the contact between these Indians and white males was hospitable, and often included providing Indian female companionship to the white males. Considering the evidence, it is probable that one of the most famous of all American Indians was a product of his people's goodwill toward strangers.

As for modern-day American Indians, their mixed heritage can be a critical factor in how they identify themselves. The French post-impressionist, Paul Gauguin[11], prophesied critical and relevant questions for the new millennium: Who are we? Where do we come from? And, where are we going? Much of Gauguin's angst, including his suicide attempt, stemmed from his understanding of the importance of being able to answer these questions, and his inability to do so. These answers were, in Gauguin's eyes, simple and straight-forward for the natives of Tahiti. These people did not seem to share the anxiety and doubt experienced by Europeans and they showed Gauguin a way of life that was both exotic and real. Gauguin was certainly not the first from a "highly civilized" society to "go" native, and to find that there was much more to the meaning of life than could be learned in schools. Moreover, he realized that his formal education was of little use in his adoptive environment. But what of those, and there are many, who are part white and part indigenous, or a part of any other non-white group? Gauguin was a visitor who chose to live in Tahiti, but children do not choose to leave one culture for another, although when they become aware of being culturally mixed, they very often feel the push and pull that can lead to angst similar to Gauguin's. Children of a homogenous culture are not exposed to such a dichotomy.

Those of mixed heritage often have a foot in both cultures, but are then educated in schools that only recognize or value the attributes of the dominant one. Kent Nerburn suggests that mixed-blood Indian children in the United States who live on reservations and are educated in white schools suffer between being marginalized in school, and teased and harassed at home.[12] The uncertainty surrounding their self-identity often gives cause for concern; life is certainly easier if you know who you are. Motivational theorist Abraham Maslow, in his *Hierarchy of Needs*, identified a sense of belonging as a deficiency need that must be fulfilled before someone has a desire for learning, aesthetics, and self-actualization. It is therefore inevitable that the ambiguity of identity of students hinders learning outcomes.

The majority of people have ready answers to these questions of identity. They may not like their answers and may harbor resentment regarding their heritage, but the fact remains that they *do* know. This is not so with mixed heritage students, as they often exist in a schizophrenic-type cultural identity. Their identity is often more a function of geography or, in the case where there is only one custodial parent, the cultural or racial identity of that parent. This can lead to a devaluation of the other ethnicity or culture, because of acrimony often associated with divorce or desertion, or of simple ignorance of the other culture on the part of the custodial parent. A single parent may also avoid or deny his or her previous partner's culture because of the negative experience of that union, and may force the child also to deny the other culture—and in so doing deny part of his or her own existence.

Historically, issues surrounding Indian identity were moot because the language spoken or even body art identified tribal affiliation. Tattoos identified the obvious such as clan and tribe, a woman's village, or valor in battle. Perhaps even more important was the spiritual aspect of tattooing to assist the soul in achieving harmony with the spirit world, and to help in entering the afterlife. The ritualized use of tattoos was a means of identification, much like a passport, enabling the soul to join its family after physical death. Tattoos then were much more than an identity card, but rather an integration of belonging and belief. Identity and spirituality were one and the same. It is not surprising then that Christian missionaries banned tattooing on religious grounds[13] and in so doing stripped Indians of their identity and sense of being.

All cultures have membership that comes with rights. But membership and rights are neither standard nor static, and myriad variables affect status within a cultural group. There is no ethnic group within the Americas that has been, and remains, as complex and stratified as the Indian. A critical issue among indigenous people in the United States and Canada is tribal affiliation. If people have tribal affiliation they are deemed Indian; if they do not, then they have to prove that they are Indian. How can they do this? To prove they are Indian, most people ultimately must provide documents that identify their descendants as Indian, since from these "authoritative sources" the percentage of Indian blood running through their veins can be calculated. So people of mixed-blood, without their names on a current tribal roster, must prove their right to claim Indian identity, thus it is no surprise that such people have self-identity issues. Equally, people who don't know for sure where they come from will always have trouble answering Gauguin's core question: Who am I?

But even Indians who are confident about who they are must still answer questions about their Indian identity, and demonstrate their eligibility for tribal affiliation. Tribal affiliation is now likened to membership of a select country club, where committees arbitrarily determine eligibility. Recently, the Cherokee tribe voted to revoke tribal membership to African Americans whose forefathers had been owned as slaves by members of the tribe, despite those slaves being listed on the Dawes Rolls.[14] According to Jodie Fishinghawk, a leading member of the group who campaigned for the exclusion, "It's an Indian thing, we do not want non-Indians in the tribe, our Indian blood is what binds us together."[15] In the United States, tribal membership can come with a variety of benefits depending on whether a person lives on or off a reservation. Membership of some tribes in the United States, such as the "Casino Tribes," comes with significant financial benefit, and consequently their exclusiveness is religiously guarded (in order for a tribe to have a casino, it must be recognized by the federal government). The primary criterion used for recognition of a tribe is documentation that the tribe has or had a form of written language. Many non-indigenous people today see advertisements for tribal-owned casinos and believe that this is the modern way for Indians to make a living. Not all recognized tribes, however, have casinos, and nor do they want them.

Blood quantum level is still a common term used among native people and is used to describe the degree to which a person is an Indian. Is there a percentage above which a person can be considered Indian or, if below, then what? Those who are less than 25% Indian are often referred to as "thin bloods," or "blooded out." But when is a person no longer an Indian? No other United State's population uses blood quantum levels to determine identity, and many indigenous people denounce the system as dehumanizing and "othering." Interestingly though, in the 1940s, the Nazis used blood quantum levels to create their *Judenfrei* society.[16] Today's research in genetics provides an even more accurate means of determining racial heritage and, although it was said at the outset that researchers would never use it for human taxonomical purposes, it has become popular among anthropologists and genealogists. To demonstrate the "slippery slope" of blood quantum levels and genetics research, insurance companies are seriously looking at its use with regard to applications for health insurance and pre-existing conditions. But someone still has to determine what percentage equals what. Many scholarship programs and tribal councils use 25%, while others use 50% for membership.

Bias aside, given the "premium" of being full or near full blood Indian, it is understandable that many who can claim that status may resent or question the authenticity of mixed bloods. And it is reasonable to assume that someone may be offended by seeing a tribal ceremony in which a white person is on the drums, or mixed bloods are dancing. In addition, not to partake in such activities, or to be reticent to do so for fear that someone *more* Indian may be offended, is to deny one's heritage. We are imprisoned by the stereotype of what an Indian is, and by how Indians are supposed to look. Are we more comfortable being around more traditional looking Indians who live where Indians are supposed to live, than being among Indians who do not look Indian and who live in cities? More Indians live off reservations than on, and the majority of Indians *do* live in cities. Personal identity and *Indianness* is not diluted by blue eyes or non-tribal membership. *Indianness* may be enhanced by living on a reservation, living within a jungle, or the subarctic, but how someone was raised is far more important. The sad reality is, however, that for Indians, looks and lifestyle do tend to matter in ways that they don't for other populations. Anglos, Hispanics, and African Americans, for example, do not have to apply for membership for their cultural group; but good luck to the Indian who wants to get into the tribal country club. Unless he or she is a member of a "Casino Tribe," there is no advantage to being labeled an Indian unless it is personally important. That personal need will, however, need to be satisfied if it, as is generally the case, revolves around identity. The cultural identity issue, while important to many people living in the United States, is not limited to that population; it is applicable in part to any culturally distinct group. If, however, globalization and increased assimilation continues, and who can doubt that it will, cultural distinctness must eventually be absorbed into a global melting pot[17] for better or for worse.

Until that point, however, universities are mostly happy to mark people down as Native American or whatever they say they are. With only a few exceptions, no verification is necessary; just as with the federal government, they are what they say are. The University of Minnesota Morris campus in central Minnesota was originally an Indian boarding school, but now that it has become a university, qualified Indian students can attend tuition free. Identified Indian students are asked to apply for the tuition remission, and to provide documentary evidence of their Indian heritage. The policy states that if a student has tribal membership, his or her application does not have to go through a committee, but all other applicants must go before a committee, and documents must be provided. Most students provide documentation, but sometimes the source is just a statement from parents claiming they are Indian. The most heated debate involves the criterion surrounding the blood quantum level needed to receive the tuition remission. Historically, these discussions were often so acrimonious that the committee membership was kept secret, and eventually the decision was made that any percentage of Indian blood qualified a student for tuition remission. One student qualified with 1/64%.[18] The Morris campus policy has caused much debate among Indian students, and has created a caste system of tribal versus non-tribal students. Non-tribal students often resent the burden of proof to the point that some of them refuse to participate in any of the Native student organizations or in minority student activities on campus. Unsurprisingly, if a student looks Indian, it is usually easier for him or her to be accepted into the Indian student community. Nevertheless, no other student groups have to justify their identity, or worse have it questioned; nor is membership in any other group determined by a student's level of blood purity, and by his or her ability to prove it. This is a source of discontent on campus and causes, in some instances, more worry than perhaps the tuition remission is worth. In this case, being an Indian has financial advantages but, ironically, relegating non-tribal Indian students to the common culture denies them opportunities for increased self-identity. There was a particularly troubling case of an Indian student adopted by Indian parents; no records were available to prove that the student had an Indian blood line, although she was raised by parents who had tribal membership. The young woman was fair skinned and had blue eyes and blond hair (not unusual among northern plains Indians), and was raised with strong cultural links to an Indian community. Fortunately the young woman (and her adoptive parents) firmly believed she was Indian, and they were able to convince university authorities that she was eligible for the tuition waiver. She did participate within the minority student program, but the situation created resentment among some Indians and non-Indians alike.

So, when does the child of a union between a Norwegian and Swede become an American, and thus perhaps not recognized by some from Norway and Sweden as being either Norwegian or Swedish? When people relate more to mainstream American culture instead of their Hispanic heritage, are they no longer Hispanic? When are people's physical and cultural blood homogenized to the point that they are simply American? Questions of identity are not unique to the United States; the process of assimilation and ethnogenesis has always been the same worldwide, and ethnogenesis is but a step closer to that great melting pot.

The debate over blood quantum levels being used to determine Indian heritage, let alone tribal membership, is one of the most serious issues facing indigenous people on this continent, although if there were not some standard, then it follows that anyone could claim to be Indian. That might solve the identity problem for some, but it would raise legal questions. Given the legal status of reservations[19], the governments of those territories clearly have the right to determine citizenship as does any other sovereign nation. A person cannot go to Italy or Iceland declare himself or herself Italian or Icelandic and expect citizenship.

Of course, marriage is a means of entry, and it works amongst most nations, but not necessarily so with Indians. Marriage to a non-native lowers the blood quantum level of any children. Thus, in order to maintain a blood level in a tribe that quantifies its membership on that criterion, there is a *de facto* restriction on who members can marry if they want their children to be members. Although Canada (in the Canadian Indian Act of 1985[20]) recognized the Métis[21], and accorded them certain rights, these rights, and those of their children, can be lost if they marry a non-Indian. But the Act is much more complicated than the issue of who a Métis can marry. The Canadian government still has a policy that will eventually eliminate all tribal (status) natives in Canada. Albeit a slower form, it is still ethnic cleansing. The issue is legally called an "extinguishment" clause in the Act, because in order to keep their rights and to pass them on to their children, Métis are legally obliged to marry their own kind; otherwise they are classed as having "outmarried." In theory, this protects the blood quantum level, but in reality the population that qualifies will become fewer and fewer until they are no more. Membership based on a degree of ethnic purity is, however, arguably racist and doomed anyway. The Métis have had the practice imposed upon them by the Canadian government, while in the United States the "Casino Tribes" have imposed it upon themselves in order to ensure short-term wealth for the privileged membership at the expense of cultural wealth.

In the United States there are no governmental rights accorded to mixed populations unless they have tribal membership, but not to have some limiting criteria invites certain assimilation to the point where, after a few generations, the cultural identity of the tribe will diminish and reflect mainstream norms. What is necessary to ensure a group's survival is to promote and instill a rich cultural heritage, and to determine membership informally and (if necessary) formally based upon multiple criteria, not the least being how behaviors and lifestyle are congruent with the cultural community in which someone lives. Assimilation is not bad. A thorough discussion of assimilation will show that it is not only natural, but biologically necessary for any group's survival. Forced assimilation, such as that described in Chapter 6, however, led to multigenerational trauma. The history of the indigenous people on this continent has been one of genocide and forced assimilation. That, together with the cognitive imperialism that still affects society and educational systems today, causes many of the identity problems evident in contemporary classrooms. So it is understandable that indigenous people and other minorities are reluctant to see the positive side of assimilation.

No one should be embarrassed about being an "urban" Indian, or just "part" Indian, or part any other group for that matter. No one needs to be more *physically* Indian. It is, however, imperative that all people know who they are, and that should not be and indeed cannot be measured in blood percentages. Equally, those who participate in indigenous cultural events are not necessarily more native than their neighbors who follow a more Western lifestyle; dancing at Pow Wows or participating in sweat lodges does not make a person any more Indian. Today, in the United States, Indians are asked to prove heritage by blood quantum levels, but there is more to being Indian than having Indian blood; true Indians must remain true to native values that will keep their feet firmly on the spiritual *Red Road*.[22] The same can be said for any cultural group, large or small, membership card-carrying or not. Assimilation is inevitable, and our common culture is enriched and made stronger by diverse contributions. If divergent cognitive and cultural contributions diminish, we will become so common and so convergent that we will eventually live in the culture void in which Kurt Vonnegut's *Harrison Bergeron* died.[23]

IN SEARCH OF UTOPIA

Being raised on the shores of Lake Superior it was natural for me to become a fisherman. I eventually concentrated on the elusive and notoriously difficult to catch steelhead. Steelhead fishing became a passion. Over the years I have fished with many different men, and many years ago I occasionally fished with a younger fellow who seemed to be even more passionate than me; we would walk to the river together, but he had a habit of then moving rapidly ahead of me from pool to pool.

Looking back, I can remember a time when I was much like the young man; when my passion was more like an obsession over the number of fish I caught. As I got older, I came to realize that if I slowed down, read the river, and concentrated my efforts on my delivery and environment, I could catch as many and larger fish without exhausting myself.

I recall one particular day with my younger partner in a wilderness area noted for its excellent fishing. The conditions were perfect and the river we had chosen was showing distinct promise because we were both catching fish. True to his nature and despite his success where he was fishing, my companion decided to move upstream in search of even better fishing—I did not see him for several hours. Meanwhile, fishing in but a few pools near where we had started, I experienced the best day's fishing of my life. The area proved to be a steelhead fisherman's paradise the likes of which I had never experienced before or since.

My partner did not fare as well, and at the end of the day, he had little to show for his efforts. Reflecting on the occasion now, I think that this young man was always searching for the end of the rainbow—for that something better, yet he failed to recognize it when it was right in front of him.

CHAPTER 9

A UNIFIED THEORY

It is when one reaches down into the dark realms of the past that creative ideas surge forth.

Sigrud F. Olson, *Reflections from the North Country*

People who have been educated in the Western educational system have been taught to accept that science offers them irrefutable facts about the world in which they live, and that those facts confirm and build upon already established knowledge. Findings that lie outside these parameters are often deemed erroneous and tend to be systematically ignored. In the late 1950s, a young Harvard University PhD student, Thomas Kuhn, called this practice into question when he suggested that, contrary to popular belief, science experiences times of radical change; occurrences which he termed "paradigm shifts." He published his theories in 1962 in a book entitled *The Structure of Scientific Revolution*. Kuhn's idea of paradigm shifts disputed the accepted understanding of science's "development-by-accumulation"[1] and described a process wherein scientists "begin the extraordinary investigations that lead the profession at last to a new set of commitments, a new basis for the practice of science."[2] These "science revolutions" are, according to Kuhn, "the tradition-shattering complements to the tradition-bound activity of normal science."[3] One consequence of these processes is that knowledge that was once deemed meaningful is rendered no longer relevant to the society of the day and is thus discarded. Equally, it is reasonable to suggest that a "paradigm shift" does not always produce new knowledge, but simply revives and reworks theories that were considered to be scientific anomalies and, therefore, abandoned or ignored. Perhaps some of these so-called anomalies were competing theories that did not attract enough popular support to gain momentum, while others may have simply been before their time. Today, university receptions and cocktail parties swoon around the few who can articulate "new" knowledge that may have been considered common knowledge around campfires 10,000 years ago. Kuhn's theory seems to suggest that he recognized that there is ancient knowledge waiting to be brought forth that will benefit future civilizations.

Both Plato and Aristotle, despite their differences, were both dualists[4] and thus argued that knowledge comprises intelligible essences, but that it is also, in and of itself, dangerous and can be used to the detriment of society. Understanding the meaning of knowledge is at least as important, if not more important, than the knowledge itself. Examine the two circles overleaf.

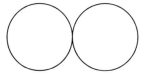

Knowledge   Understanding

One circle represents knowledge and the other understanding. Westerners live by the premise that success is measured by the amount of knowledge a person is able to accumulate, while aboriginal people believe that awareness of the meaning of life, which is housed within the circle of understanding, offers the key to happiness and success. There is significant agreement among scholars of indigenous epistemology that native philosophy is still evolving; yet many believe that it is equally important to search the past as it is to look forward for answers for the future. But for the sake of the future, knowledge and understanding must amalgamate. The knowledge of the past should not be dismissed as no longer valid but instead used with the new ideas that come with scientific discovery. Accordingly, Western society requires a new theory; one that acknowledges that a life that harmonizes people's desire for progress with an understanding of, and respect for, their surroundings (the planet on which they live, their spirituality, and their reason for being) and finds the answers to questions, is not in the center of the knowledge circle, but at the point where the two circles meet. It is time for a paradigm shift.

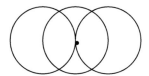

It would, of course, be foolhardy to think that those who live exclusively within the Western worldview are ready to abandon their way of life for something that might at first seem to take them backward. They have, after all, been brought up to venerate progress as the index of a successful life. Re-searching the past for knowledge towards a successful life, however, will be more fruitful than economic progression. What knowledge, insight, and cures will be found from the honest study of the codices, hieroglyphs, Amazonia and other advanced cultures thought inferior? How much more would modern medicine know if it built upon what the ancient Egyptians knew about the subject instead of destroying or ignoring it? What wonders and how would the worldviews of most everyone change from the ancient knowledge once held in the Library of Alexandria? Given, for example, the knowledge the Egyptians and the Incas had of tumors, perhaps Western science would be further along toward a cancer-free world if more respect and attention were given to ancient medical knowledge.

Combining the Western way of life with an indigenous worldview will provide a course-correction that fosters less materialism and a desire to live a life that is grounded in a healthy sense of place. Yet many will say that the two are incompatible and the concept inconceivable. But are the two really so alien to each other that they are mutually exclusive? And is an indigenous worldview and lifestyle even possible for Westerners, or is it accessible only to indigenous people? The colonial invasion of many parts of the world brought myriad indigenous people into contact with Europeans who imposed their Western practices and rituals on the natives. As a consequence, the indigenous traditional worldview was subjugated by many aspects of Western philosophical thought. With that in mind, it should not be too unreasonable to think that it might be possible for the reverse to have taken place or, easier yet, for a union between the two worldviews to have been established. But the Western fundamentalist might argue that the indigenous worldview is in no way compatible with a profit-driven regime; less productivity is anti-capitalist and socialistic. The indigenous, on the other hand, could worry about the effects of introducing a capitalist trait into their lifestyle, and both would most likely see a movement toward the center as abandoning their traditional values and, like many before them, they would use all forms of resistance when faced with change. One clear victim of the present Western lifestyle is the ecosystem. Developed countries have become so used to their technology-supplied comforts and a way of life that is placing undue pressure on natural resources, that there is a clear danger that the planet will not be able to sustain life as we know it indefinitely. Moreover, the rapid increase in human population is adding exponentially to the problem; rainforests are cleared at ever-increasing rates, fresh water and food become scarcer, plant and animal species are threatened with loss of habitat, and fisheries are depleted. There is also clear evidence that the present global climate changes are at least partly due to human activities. As the present consumer-driven, individualistic lifestyle continues to put pressure on the planet, it is becoming clear that the status quo will soon be untenable.

The effects of rising non-renewable energy costs and climate change will eventually be compelled to fuel a movement toward biocentrism. Those who support the Green Movement will then have the opportunity to create jobs, stockholders who invest in those companies will make a profit, and people will eventually see how this benefits everyone. Capitalists in over-developed countries that have large populations of citizens who have been privileged and accustomed to taking from nature and making a product for profit will, of course, resist. "Takers"[5] may not change, but they do eventually die, and it will then be through education that future generations will be able to see further than their parents. Children must be educated to be sustainers, and eventually leavers versus takers. Many people have enthusiastically adopted the environmentally sound idea of taking only pictures and leaving only footprints when they vacation in "natural" areas, but asking them to take that philosophy home and live it on a day-to-day basis is usually a difficult sell. They are happy to be leavers for a week or two each year, but not all the time; that takes too much effort and sacrifice.

Too many people are infected with the virus that creates a proclivity to amass and covet more and more "stuff" which has, in turn, made too many of them be *in* the world, but not *of* it. Having much more than they need has dehumanizing effects. We seem to put more effort into acquiring living and non-living things as objects rather than establishing and maintaining relationships with our fellow humans. The danger is that in the pursuit to have more we can lose ourselves among our possessions. We no longer are, but merely have. We need a conceptual framework or philosophy to make sense of the changes that are happening around us. But neither term seems appropriate. Conceptual framework sounds immature, and philosophy sounds old. But eventually we will come up with a new meaningful and more descriptive phrase. This movement toward a new philosophy may sound radical but it will be gradual unless some cataclysmic environmental event provides us with an avalanche situation. There is common ground between the leaver worldview of indigenous people and the progress-centered worldview of Westerners, and this middle ground has been articulated before—but it has not been heard because the message has come from people who have been deemed "outliers," and generally ignored. Those who do listen, however, soon realize that these people can share wisdom and knowledge that is rarely found in schools.

Georges E. Sioui[6] believes that all people, including Europeans and Euro-Americans, once shared the spiritual gifts that are now considered the domain of indigenous people, but that industrialization and technology have dimmed most of us to the point where we are outside our consciousness. In his 1992 book, *For an Amerindian Autohistory*, Sioui recounts the story of a little-known French philosopher, Louis-Armand de Lom d'Arce, better known by his Indian name, Lahontan. Lahontan had traveled to New France in the late 1600s and quickly assimilated into the native lifestyle. Although his important work, *Dialogues Avec Un Sauvage*, influenced the thinking of Jean-Jacques Rousseau, Voltaire and other philosophers during the Age of Enlightenment, the French government, the Church, and traditional historians of his time considered his ideas and his writing to be a severe threat—he was declared an *outlier*!

Lahontan posited, even using the logic of Aristotle, that the New World native people and their cultures were *more* advanced and desirable than those of their European invaders, which lead a contemporary Jesuit to write, "it would be not so grave were he but a bad Writer, but he is also a dangerous author."[7] Lahontan disputed much of the Jesuits' writings in their *Relations,* dismissing the authors as nothing more than self-serving missionaries. When Lahontan wrote about Kondiaronk of the Wendat, whom he called the "naked philosopher,"[8] he commented favorably on his purity of spirit, and his physical, moral, and intellectual superiority. Kondiaronk, paraphrased by Sioui, stated that "the language of nature is the sole authentic message from God, because of its dazzling, universal clarity. It alone can rally all humans, if only they will listen."[9] Kondiaronk through Lahontan and Sioui articulated a view of human nature that has resurfaced in the new millennium as a means of salvation from uncertainty and the misery of meaninglessness. It is not surprising to learn that little is known of Lahontan and even less of Kondiaronk. Sioui suggests that they lived ahead of their time, stating that the two "had already foreseen the need for a world government and may be said to have helped lay the intellectual foundations for the great social revolutions of our own time."[10]

Age of Enlightenment thinkers recognized something uniquely different when they read the writings of Lahontan. Rousseau's philosophical emphasis on *naturalism* certainly stemmed from his boyhood experiences, but it is also possible that at least some came from New World indigenous thought. European born American, anthropologist Paul Radin, provided rich field work research among both American and Canadian natives for which he became famous. Radin's work is important because he not only was a peer of John Dewey, but he also influenced Dewey's belief in experimentalism. His writings also validated the high level of Native American cognitive development. Radin was an accomplished linguist who found a unity of schema among indigenous language, and he came to realize that although indigenous mentality is different, it is not different in sophistication or depth. In 1927, Radin published *Primitive Man as Philosopher*, in which he concludes that progress and moral awareness have been conflicted. Although an anthropologist and not a philosopher, Radin's work was considered so important to John Dewey, that Dewey wrote the foreword to *Primitive Man as Philosopher* in which he suggests that Radin's work on the historical speculation about "primitive" thought demands serious reconsideration. Dewey claims that crude conclusions have been reached because of a limitation of subject matter, and also suggests that the bias interpretations of the small Western intellectual class are self-serving.[11]

In this regard, Sioui writes that native people share a common ideological philosophy that transcends tribal differences and that their combined misfortunes are relatively minor when compared with the tragic loss of human existence and the divorce from nature that has befallen their white brethren: such words are shocking and scary. Sioui also states the big difference between the two societies is that the indigenes follow a circular, non-evolutionist vision, while the Euro-Americans adhere to a linear, evolutionist paradigm that has led to a loss of conscience and spirit resulting in dismissal of the laws of nature.[12] The indigenous worldview does adapt and change, but the change is not predicated on progress, whereas the Western worldview believes that progress is not simply an option but a necessity and a right; a viewpoint that is greatly facilitated by a linear mindset.

A linear worldview creates an historical timeline through which events and experiences from the past are examined and used to make sense of the present, and then to make decisions with regard to the future. Paulo Freire, in his *Pedagogy of the Oppressed*, provides a significant critique of the political purpose of linearity. Humans can construct tridimensional time, which is: to reflect, to do, and then by doing (*praxis*) to transform reality, but it can also create a sense of societal normality upon which behavior patterns are set. Plato and Aristotle constructed a definitive reality using tridimentional time that elevated some humans over others, and created a privileged and androcentric worldview. Paulo Freire provides an example of the destructiveness of this worldview when he writes:

> Proposing as a problem, to a European peasant, the fact that he or she is a person might strike them as strange. This is not true of Latin-American peasants, whose world usually ends at the boundaries of the latifundium, whose gestures to some extent simulate those of the animals and the trees, and who often consider themselves equal to the latter.[13]

Freire agrees with the Swiss educationist, Pierre Furter,[14] who stated in his *Educação e Vida*: "The universe is revealed to me not as space, imposing a massive presence to which I can but adapt, but as a scope, a domain which takes shape as I act upon it."[15] In his text, *Pedagogy of the Oppressed*, Freire not only demonstrates agreement with Furter, but also goes as far as to quote his views on the differences between naïve thinking and critical thinking, wherein naïve thinking sees "historical time as a weight, a stratification of the acquisitions and experiences of the past."[16] A naïve thinker will always try to accommodate the status quo and be threatened by change. Furter's and Freire's words describe and emphasize the vast gulf between Western and indigenous ways of seeing and interacting with the physical world

Non-indigenous Western educated people can, and often do, reach non-Western philosophical conclusions, but reaching that state of knowing requires not only thinking, but also acting upon that thought. The acting or doing may not be as overt as quitting an investment banker job, joining Greenpeace, and shipping out to save the whales, but it may involve activities such as volunteering for an organization like Habitat for Humanity, or making efforts to conserve natural resources. The acting and doing may not even be conscious. As we noted in chapter 2, Laurens van der Post initially wrote about the Bushmen through a thick cultural lens. But as he travelled, and especially after he had made contact with the Bushmen, his worldview seemed to change as he wrote about his journey and his experiences, and reflected upon them through his narrative. Perhaps this was purely his style of writing, but more likely the change came through self-discovery. Van der Post's attitude toward the relationship between thinking and doing is clear to see in these words:

> Today we overrate the rational values and behave as if thinking were a substitute for living. We have forgotten that thought and the intuition that feeds it only become whole if the deed grows out of it as fruit grows from the pollen on a tree, and so everywhere in our civilized world there tends to be a terrible cleavage between thinking and doing.[17]

If that were not evidence enough, van der Post's philosophical conversion is defined absolutely on the last page of his book where he writes about finally seeing the "timeless" Kalahari and discovering his "aboriginal heart."[18] Van der Post's journey was transformative in that his thinking and doing were, through his writings, intended to affect not just himself but also his readers.

The lesson that van der Post learned was that the Western model of time is based upon an historical construct, while the indigenous model focuses on the here and now, and the individual's interaction with the present. Paulo Freire concurred with Furter and van der Post when he said:

> Because—in contrast to animals—people can tridimensionalize time into the past, the present, and the future, their history, in function of their own creations, develops as a constant process of transformation within which epochal units materialize. These epochal units are not closed periods of time, static compartments within which people are confined.[19]

Freire argues that when we become trapped in epochal time, we create a reality that becomes mythicized, and that not only separates humans from nature but also creates divisions among people and dehumanizes everyone. For example, to be considered educated by the standards of the Western model, people are encouraged to study time periods, such as the Renaissance. But thematically categorizing content knowledge within a number of years is *periodization,* a by-product of linearity, which is, as we stated earlier, a construct. John Dewey was also critical of linear measurement as it lends itself to standards, and he would argue that our present day reliance on standards is neither better than, nor even relevant to, what is real. Uniformity of thought is aided by standards, which can only exist in a linear worldview. But much within that worldview is not real; rather it is a product of someone's imagination. Anyone who rejects dualism as Dewey did would reject standards. Dewey understood that the ancients and indigenous people did not need duality and that critical and spiritual consciousness is predicated on experiences. Thus his experientialism is not dualistic since he understood that dualism is too self-serving and not democratic. This is why Dewey has enjoyed resurgence among critical theorists: he was far ahead of his time, which may help explain why he may be recognized as the first American philosopher, yet sadly few of his educational principles and practices found their way into American schools. Dewey was an experimentalist, and thus, espoused process over product, which he described in his book, *Art as Experience.* The wealthy power brokers would not accept this emphasis, since it was the antithesis of mass production. Dewey was indeed a visionary and provides us with a model to use in educational restructuring. In fact, all stakeholders and change agents in today's educational arena would do well to study Dewey as he articulates a strong rationale for where schools need to go, and provides a significant argument and foundational pillar for educational change.

Linearity is also the root of yet another malady of Western society, albeit, perhaps a more recent one, but cancerous nonetheless. We term this ailment time-sickness. Time-sickness is a fear of not having enough time to do what needs to be done within a given period. That may not bother some who simply do a task when it comes around, but for those who have time-related responsibilities and deadlines, the associated fear of not meeting those obligations can cause anxiety and increased stress. Some stress can be considered beneficial and even welcome, because it is an indicator of separation between humans and lower order living beings; the higher the intellect, the higher the potential stress. As with all things, however, too much of anything can be bad. Most modern city dwellers, whose lives revolve around working, commuting and simply trying to survive, may not realize or articulate that they are overly stressed, but many will be. Nevertheless, most agree that they do not have enough time to do what they want or need to do. For example, it is not unusual for graduate students, especially women, to attend an evening class after working all day, having started the day by getting their family off to work or school or day care. After work, they rush to class often arriving tired and frazzled. Yet they are also relieved, because now time no longer exists. They have no responsibility other than to sit, listen to their professor, and participate in class activities. After class, their anxiety returns to the fore as their smartphones tells them that the clock has started, *time* is now moving again, and they must begin to prepare for the next day; and so the cycle continues. Time-sickness is an insidious source of stress and depression, and a steady dose radiates from Western society.

Even more worrisome than time-sickness afflicting adults is the realization that it is spreading to children. *Hurried Child Syndrome* results when parents of young children unnecessarily overemphasize early childhood education attainment. This often happens at the expense of allowing the child to experience the wonderment and creativity associated with the outdoors and nature, and the socialization that comes with healthy sessions of unorganized play. It is well documented that children are maturing earlier than previous generations. Better health care and nutrition, and increased societal expectations, are making children grow up faster. Yet, children who grow up faster are not really better off than their predecessors. They might, however, be better able to purchase and consume products and use technology, so that will make them very attractive in a consumer-driven capitalist society. There is significant concern that technology is consuming children at an alarming rate. A recent survey by the Henry J. Kaiser Family Foundation reported in 2010 that children ages 8–18 spend 7 hours and 38 minutes a day on average using some form of technology for fun.[20] There is a fine line between fun and addiction and more than 7.5 hours doing anything beyond being in school and sleeping is excessive and addictive. It is concern enough that increased media use now correlates to lower grades in school, yet there may be an even a greater concern. A long childhood where children play with other children is considered one of the most important attributes that separates humans from other animals, most of which must and do grow to adult size very rapidly so they are less vulnerable to predation. Our most recent ancestors, Neanderthals, reached sexual maturity, for instance, much younger than modern humans. A long childhood has, until now, been considered an evolutionary attribute. If a long playful childhood defines our humanness, it is a cause for concern that growing up too fast is yet another form of time-sickness that is facilitated and enhanced by long periods of isolation away from other children because of increasing use of technology. Instead of escaping reality by entering virtual worlds, children should be outside playing and being a part of the real, natural world.

Arguably there may have been a time when the Western philosophical scheme was appropriate and perhaps even necessary. But those days are long past. Western society needs a new enlightened framework for the health of all those who live within it. And with this new and vibrant model there needs to be a new educational delivery system that fosters societal and individual health. But like most reform movements, it will not sustain itself unless it is built upon a solid foundation.

Since the time when Plato legitimized the social construction of knowledge, and Aristotle dictated that only knowledge deduced from inquiry could be real, Western scholars have looked at the trees and not the forest; these people can be defined as field independent. Field independent individuals are able, and are conditioned from a young age, to look at discrete points or parts of a whole, whereas field dependent individuals tend to see the whole and relate it to a social context. Indigenous people generally look at the world in a more field dependent way, and consider themselves part of that complete entity. The Western (field independent) worldview, based on Platonic Idealism and Aristotelian Realism, became central to all aspects of life as Western civilization matured and increased its range of influence. As a result of the overwhelming success of colonialism, Western customs supplanted indigenous traditions, including their relationship to the world around them. Thus the indigenous field dependent worldviews, considered irrelevant by Western colonists, were dismissed and ignored. The Western worldview, based on Idealism and Realism, allowed the colonists to gain dominance and to set up a regional hegemony wherever they wished to settle. And so began the system that continues today, in which those who derive knowledge and the associated meaning of that knowledge in a field dependent manner have long been ignored and undervalued. Even before the global expanse of Western influence, many human communities had begun to turn from a field dependent to a field independent lifestyle. As people moved from the nomadic tradition to a more static community-based existence, some began to abandon their holistic ways of making sense of the world to concentrate more on their own lives and needs—the individual apart from the clan, and accumulation of individual wealth versus their needs and those of the clan. Thus began the march toward field independent thinking.

People living and learning in Western society are taught to learn not only words, but also specific concepts, parts, and usages. This ultimately results in "the barbarism of specialization,"[21] a term created by Jose Ortega y Gasset, and later articulated by educational philosopher Mortimer Adler. Linear thinking forces us to see one thing at a time, and to progress to whatever is next, which will in turn lead to more. However, if instead of taking this field independent, one tree at a time, viewpoint, and rather studying the forest as a whole, people would glean not only some discrete knowledge, but also, and more importantly, the meaning associated with it; thus they would see an interconnected, holistic, more humane, and biocentric picture. It is less sexist because, despite modern thinking about equality of the sexes, men and women are still hardwired to behave in different ways. Men still have the urges that makes them want to hunt, and consequently they have an over-developed propensity to look for the discrete signs and paths of an animal that will make them more successful hunters. Men are thus more field independent; they look and see things that are a small part of the field—the tree versus the forest. Women, on the other hand, are conditioned to be gatherers, and are more successful if they look at complete scenario patterns that will benefit their community. Thus, women are more field dependent. Western education and knowledge favors the part over the whole, men over women. Many students today find it difficult to see meaning in the knowledge they are directed to acquire, as that meaning is often derived through seeing the interconnectedness of the various parts that make up a whole. Because the whole is not always visible, it is difficult to comprehend the meaning, and if we cannot comprehend the meaning, we cannot see the spiritualism of the interconnectedness. Meaning and spiritualism are closely linked. When students are not required, or are unable, to make the necessary connections between the knowledge they are asked to learn and its meaning, they fail to learn at a higher level and are thus not fulfilling their cognitive potential. The fable of the men who were blindfolded and then told to touch a part of an elephant and try to identify it via deduction illustrates this concept; they all erred in their conclusions. It was only when they removed their blindfolds did they see more and understand the truth. Too much of our teaching is telling, and too much of our learning takes place in the dark.

It would be both naïve and, indeed, totally wrong to suggest that the secret to successful living and saving the planet is to reject the Euro-American way of life and return to native ways or to the wild. The parting scenes from Hollywood's *Dances With Wolves* and *Instinct*, and more recently *Avatar*, romanticizes that if things don't work out in mainstream society, people can move in with the natives or relocate to the jungle and live with other animals. That romanticized and idyllic world portrayed in books and movies never actually existed. The lives of indigenous people past and present were, and are, far from utopian. There have always been problems with societies regardless of their makeup—human societies are inherently messy and will always be subject to criticism. But to have a bad society is profoundly better than to have none at all. A move toward tribalism as an answer to societal ills is an ignorant goal. Furthermore, Western society has brought great advancements and has increased the standard of living and life span for more humans than the world has ever seen. The introduction of non-native species in agriculture and livestock has supplanted and altered native grains and animals to such an extent that it would be impossible to feed the present world population without them. If it were not for Europeans and Euro-Americans, the world would be in a far different place. For the most part Western society can be proud of its accomplishments. But those accomplishments have come at great expense to other people and the environment. Peace and harmony has not been the by-product of Western civilization. While the Euro-American way of life compels people to strive continuously for power and material wealth, culturally-imposed upon indigenous people have tended to yearn for days past; but living for or in the past is not a solution for the future. The road toward a unified way of living and knowing needs to be traveled by all people.

Those who follow the ways of Western society should examine the lifestyles of indigenous people and adopt practices that will allow them to reconnect with the spiritual side of nature—to understand what is meant by the necessity to reflect on beauty, and the peacefulness of "forest time."[22] As Albert Schweitzer said, "[u]ntil he extends his circle of compassion to include all living things, man will not himself find peace."[23] Equally, indigenous people have a responsibility to reach out to others. They should not always look to the past or they will remain bitter and isolated, and doomed to extinction like so many of their ancestors. There is no static or past-centered indigenous philosophy; indigenous philosophy has been constantly evolving as has the natural world upon which it is based. With a more unified way of living, people from all cultures can use their complex and different thinking abilities to create a way of life that encompasses scientific methods of inquiry and other means of acquiring knowledge, which includes searching our past to try and restore more healthy and natural ways of living. As it seems with most things, balance is important. A good many of us are finally coming to realize that our development has had a deleterious effect on the environment and other creatures, and that to ensure our existence we must make changes. The stress and snarl of rush hour traffic is not something that any of us value. Yet it is representative of human development—a byproduct of human intelligence and creativity. Anti-development and radical environmentalists are a reaction to environmental degradation, yet they too are extremists. As the sensible conservationist Sigrud Olson[24] came to realize, as important as natural places are (and much more so than we realize), we cannot make a living staring at them. We too often just hear the extremists, when we need to listen and learn from the words of Aldo Leopold, Rachel Carson, the not so well known Olson and other conservationists whose approach to compromising the natural world with technological progress is balanced and considered.

A nature-based spirituality and self-sustaining environment is not new to American thought. Ralph Waldo Emerson's writings on a distinct American characteristic of self-reliance launched many pioneers west, and along with it the concept of the rugged individualist. He was very popular in American schools in the 19th century and was considered by many as the father of the *transcendentalist* movement. Once a Unitarian minister, he came to realize that nature was the only source of truth. Emerson believed in intellectualism and scholarship within an educational setting, but that setting must also include nature. He believed that intuition was a critical ingredient, alongside science, in learning what is true.

The transcendental movement provided Americans with an intellectual precursor to environmentalism and conservation, if not praxis. We may think of the present day "Green" movement as only a recent radical reaction, but that is not true. Along with Emerson, Henry David Thoreau provided us with at least the idea that nature should not be exploited, but that our rich natural resources were a means for us to transcend our own experiences within nature toward a higher level of consciousness. Thoreau believed that we were not only a part of nature, but that nature was critical for our being human. He also believed that intuition was enhanced by nature and that there is an interconnectedness of all living things, which have since been validated by both chaos and string theory. But the human desire to have far in excess of what is actually needed, not only destroys nature but creates privilege. Paulo Freire agrees when he argues that *having more,* is destructive not only to nature, but also to ourselves, as it dehumanizes us and replaces who we *are* with what we *have.* The great danger in valuing inanimate things is that it dehumanizes, and encourages sadism, slavery, and genocide.[25]

Many theologians have concluded that the world's major religions share many more beliefs than not, and this is particularly relevant within the monotheistic religions. Yet one must wonder if in the Western world, the big three: Christianity, Islam, and Judaism provide humans the spiritual vision that best serves the future. Just like dancing around Stonehenge faded away and became a "primitive" religion that was cruelly replaced with a new one, so too might be the fate of today's major religions. The priests, pastors, rabbis, and mullahs need not fear each other, but they might want to be wary of those who seek solutions for the future, and who view them all as primitive and archaic vestiges of the past. Western religion hasn't evolved. If anything it has regressed; too often motivated and seduced by economic and political power that in turn fuels fundamentalist ideology. Fundamentalist ideology can become addictive, and ideological addictions are even more dangerous than personal addictions such as drugs, alcohol, or tobacco, since they afflict entire groups of individuals or communities. Surely, there are monotheistic religious groups within Christianity, Islam, and Judaism who are futurists and want to avoid becoming religious relics. Organizations such as Blessed Earth are prime examples. Blessed Earth is a nonprofit environmental ministry that works with churches and other community organizations to promote the earth as a living and spiritual entity. Blessed Earth has seven guiding beliefs, of which the following two exemplify a philosophical shift from androcentric to biocentric:

- *Blessed Earth* is motivated by the biblical mandate to care for creation. We recognize that mountains, trees, oceans and wildlife are our inheritance and that they have meaning beyond merely supplying the raw material for human commerce. The earth exists to meet an unknown number of generations' needs. We must not destroy it to meet this generation's wants.
- *Blessed Earth* believes that science without humanity leads to great harm, and that faith without works is dead.[26]

Environmentalism and its developing spiritualism will preach an emergent God as prophesized by the fourteenth-century German mystic Meister Eckhart.[27] Eckhart wrote that God "becomes and disbecomes," and so too religions when they no longer serve our needs, and fight selfishly and constantly among themselves. Humans must move beyond religious *tradition.* The French paleontologist, Pierre Teilhard de Chardin[28] in his *Phenomenon of Man* theorizes that the evolution of the biosphere ultimately leads to a global psychosocial unification, and a convergence with the natural world. Having a sense of belonging and meaning and oneness with nature is not an indigenous thing; it is a human thing. It just seems as if indigenous people relate to nature more, and that many Westerners don't see it, nor seek it, and thus do not value it. Western society has over-steered its people in the wrong direction, and now needs to make a course correction. Just because progress has translated into a move away from nature does not mean that nature is not needed, nor that it does not need us—the exact opposite is true. Perhaps motivated more by global environmental degradation than religion, the ecology movement will foster biocentrism and its byproduct, biospiritualism. There are already signs of a diminution of the social constructs of androcentrism, and a disappointment in religions that support it. If we consider that God did not create the universe, but is rather emerging through a long process and becoming unified with all earthly things, then the historically fixed, human interpretation of an omnipotent God will devolve and be replaced by an emergent God much as Eckhart envisioned. Because the monotheistic God in today's terms sustains a belief of man over nature, earth and its human inhabitants are disconnected and are in a state of disequilibrium.

Aldous Huxley, more contemporary and better known than Eckhart, also professed an emergent God rather than an omnipotent Being that created the universe. Huxley was best known as the author of the novel *Brave New World*, published in 1932. He was a futurist and considered by many as a leader of modern thought. Although he originated from England, Huxley spent much of his time in the United States and grew to be afraid of the growth of technology as a means of controlling people and their ideas. Huxley spent many years studying ways to expand consciousness outside the human social constructions which he feared, opposed any form of religious dogma, and ultimately abandoned Western religion.

David Abram also agrees that the supernatural and hence psychological preferences within monotheistic religions are followed at the expense of the natural world. Abram writes,

> For it is likely that the "inner world" of our Western psychological experience, like the supernatural heaven of Christian belief, originates in the loss of our ancestral reciprocity with the animate earth. When the animate powers that surround us are suddenly construed as having less significance than ourselves, when the generative earth is abruptly defined as a determinate object devoid of its own sensations and feelings, then the sense of a wild and multiplicitous otherness . . . must migrate, either into a supersensory heaven beyond the natural world, or else into the human skull itself—the only allowable refuge, in this world, for what is ineffable and unfathomable.[29]

Philosophically, Islam and Judaism fare no better than Christianity; all three are monotheistic theologies woven from Idealism. However, while establishing a mutual relationship with nature is necessary to ensure our survival and to make us healthier and happier, we should not elevate Mother Nature to goddess status. To do so would be to create matriarchal and patriarchal dualism—Mother Earth and Father Sky as goddess and god. Clearly both women and nature have suffered from the worldview that created and favored dualism and a patriarchal god, but to create a matriarchal goddess is to sustain androcentrism. Many New Age religions and fundamental environmentalists see nature in god-like terms, and most indigenous people, as important as nature is to their cosmology, also look up as well as down for spiritual harmony. If Mother Earth, is at one end of the axis, then at the other extreme must be Father Sky. Between them, all things revolve and create harmony. A Great Spirit and mystery may reside in the heavens; but an equally Great Spirit and mystery resides in the earth. But this is dualism. It is between them, *on* earth that is most important; the atmosphere and the soil and water are critical for our survival, and it is among them that there must be balance. Ultimately that is where harmony is found, not within some mysterious construct.

This harmony or unification will not only serve to bring humans in tune with nature, but also will allow them to reconnect with their natural heritage, This type of holistic focus, if it became popular, could create a spiritual and sacred connection that hopefully would promote the necessary conservation mindset to save the planet from an ecological catastrophe. Nevertheless, whether humans believe in intelligent design or a lucky cosmic roll of the dice, a biocentric perspective will help them to remember what they have lost; that is, the creativity and sacredness of the universe. Regardless of design or lucky roll, *reflection* is necessary, and that is best undertaken in silence or solitude. That is why, for reasons that cannot be explained, people tend to feel closer to their spiritual center during a retreat or visit to a natural setting than in a city or any other built-up area. Wilderness areas are the least-altered terrains and offer a clear, authentic view where reflection is often better achieved. Yet an emergent God is accessible anywhere, whether it be in a forest, or a man-made cathedral. Sigrud Olson wrote that nature is more than lakes and rivers, "It is the sense of the primeval, of space, solitude, silence, and the *eternal mystery*."[30]

A profound sense of nature can and should exist, and be felt in our cities and urban areas. It is not, however, just nature but the critical concept of *wilderness* that must be restored and supplemented in our societies, religions, universities, and psyches as we move our worldviews from androcentric to biocentric, or our religions and universities as we know them will be left behind as footnotes to our spiritual and educational past. Nearly a century ago, John Dewey said that he was worried about society becoming too reliant upon technology and its rapid expansion. When he argued that all of us should remain in touch with our *primitive realities*, he meant that we must never lose the ability to provide food and shelter for ourselves, our families, and society as a whole.[31]

Hurricane Katrina demonstrated what many experts predicted: We have 60 hours. Given our present reliance on technology and fossil fuel to provide electricity to run our technology, unlike previous generations, we live only 60 hours away from chaos. Again, John Dewey warned us nearly 100 years ago that no matter how we progress as a society, and evolve, we must maintain a connection with the earth lest we lose the skills necessary to last longer than just 60 hours.

Instead of finding answers for our inadequacy in taking care of ourselves, people today tend to look to technology to distract them. Yet there is no meaning in technology; it is nothing more than a set of tools, and it will never reconnect us to the sensuous world. Dewey's warning was prophetic, for what he feared has come to pass; it is doubtful that many of us have the skills to build or maintain our homes, or to acquire and prepare foods without the local supermarket. These skills should not only be maintained, but also taught in curricula where the objectives are not only to be self-sufficient and self-sustaining, but also to protect the earth's natural wilderness and in so doing keep it alive within us.

It is telling when two of the most important philosophers of the last century in the Americas, Dewey and Freire, have warned us of the dangers of technology. Like Dewey, Freire warned that science and technology would reduce humans to objects or mere things, and he states on the very first page of his *Pedagogy of the Oppressed* that one's humanization can be increased, but so too is it possible to dehumanize others to the point where they believe they are incomplete.[32] Technology has been at the forefront of educational reform and economic development since at least the 1970s, but it is a cautionary tale indeed when these two philosophers warned us that it is soulless and dehumanizing. Of course, the use of technology is not the only area of education that requires a rethink. Many changes are needed to bring education onto the path of biocentric thinking.

Will making radical institutional change require a whole new philosophy and psychology of education? Not really. To find and make the changes posited more palatable all that is required is to cull from other philosophical models. The idea of a child being gently guided toward learning through personal inquiry is in no way new. Two hundred years ago a Swiss educator named Johann Pestalozzi established an educational philosophy simply based on love...*a mother's love.* Pestalozzi, who was influenced by the naturalism of Rousseau and others, felt that with her intuition, her moral superiority, and her power of observation, a mother was the most effective first teacher for her children. Home and community were, and still are, the first school. Pestalozzian methods, that were built upon these mother/child interactions, emphasized learning through the senses, manipulating objects, active learning, and learning for discovery. Pestalozzi's principles include:

- Begin with the senses.
- Never tell children things that they can discover for themselves.
- Activity is the law of childhood, so educate the hand. Train children not to merely listen, but to do.
- Love of variety is a law of childhood.
- Cultivate the faculties in their natural order. First form the mind and then furnish it.
- Reduce every subject to its elements, and present one difficulty at a time.[33]

Pestalozzi recognized and emphasized the close relationship between home, school, and the natural world to ensure a child's success. Central to this was the unselfish care by mothers of their children that Pestalozzi called their "fidelity."

This fidelity extends from the family into the community and then to the school where teachers have fidelity toward educating all students. But there has been little interest in developing Pestalozzi's philosophy beyond a child's early years. While it is true that Pestalozzi is not a household name in the United States, Maria Montessori, who was greatly influenced by his work, is. Montessori schools use methods closely akin to those of Pestalozzi listed above, and are a popular alternative to public school for many parents, especially for the early childhood to grade 5. Some high schools based on the Montessori method do exist, but most Montessori students move on to more traditional middle and high schools to complete their K through 12 education. It must also be noted that, while the vast majority of Montessori schools are private, there are some public Montessori programs. According to the American Montessori Society website, while there are some differences between private and public Montessori programs, all are expected to include:

- mixed-age classes,
- teachers with credentials from an accredited Montessori program,
- a full complement of developmentally appropriate Montessori learning materials, and
- a Montessori instructional approach throughout the program

When it comes to state and national standards, the public Montessori schools have strict guidelines:

> Montessori public schools must meet the same standards as other public schools: they receive a state "report card," are accountable for their students achieving adequate yearly progress, and comply with other federal education regulations.[34]

While most Montessori schools, because they are private, appeal only to the more affluent sector of society, the public initiative offers parents who cannot afford to send their children to private school a choice of educational program. The Pestalozzi and Montessori philosophies offer educational reformers a starting point toward a new student-focused initiative.

A new philosophical focus should also be congruent with the developmental needs of students. Again, a new psychology of education need not be looked for, but rather just adhered to. According to psychologist Abraham Maslow, the motivation to meet personal needs is predicated on fulfillment. Thus, before moving to a higher level, people must have their physiological needs fulfilled and feel safe. People must also feel that they belong and are respected before they are motivated to actually learn to their optimum potential. Schools must be safe and if necessary provide students with the food they need in order to learn optimally, but schools also must provide food for the soul. When all needs are addressed successfully, then young people will have the confidence to learn and to believe in themselves and in their potential. Importantly, each level of previous needs must remain fulfilled to ensure a person can function at their optimum level. Unknown by many, the peak of Maslow's Hierarchy of Needs is not self-actualization as most believe, but self-transcendence, the ultimate level that emphasizes intuition, altruism, creativity, compassion, and spirituality. Schools must create an integrated curriculum that focuses around students' total needs.

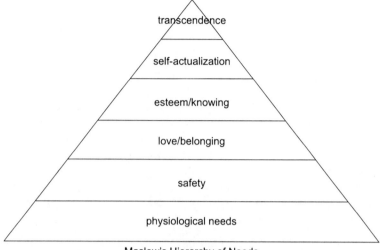

transcendence

self-actualization

esteem/knowing

love/belonging

safety

physiological needs

Maslow's Hierarchy of Needs

Most educators are well aware of Maslow's Hierarchy, and how crippling a lack of fulfillment is for many children. This is the primary reason behind the success of private and some charter schools. It is not that most of the teachers are "highly qualified," nor is the curriculum any different or better, but rather these schools and teachers are more vested in the holistic care and needs of each student, and are consequently treated well and valued in return. Of course, this is a lot easier to achieve in smaller schools, such as most private and charter establishments.

Given that all the great world religions believe in the existence of an immortal soul, let us assume there is at least a chance that something spiritual, a "soul," exists within us, and that that something makes us uniquely human. Let us also assume the "soul tank" is full when it has a healthy mixture of metaphysical fuel, such as purpose, self-identity, values, and love. And in the same way that low levels of vitamins C, D, A, or B_{12} can cause us to become ill, a low level or bad mixture in our soul tank can cause us to feel physically poorly, become mentally depressed, and bring disharmony to our well being. The symptoms of this *low soul* would probably include lack of purpose, loss of meaning, withdrawal, obsessions, addictions, and violence. Just as once we were ignorant about scurvy and the cure was in plain sight, so too might be the case with the sickness that plagues over-developed societies today: the cure is in plain sight but we just do not see it – or do not want to. Thomas Moore, a prominent author of archetypal psychology (collective subconscious) and philosophy claims "Tradition teaches that the soul lies midway between understanding and unconsciousness, and that its instrument is neither the mind nor the body, but imagination."[35] Moore lists the emotional complaints of our times:

- Emptiness
- Meaninglessness
- Vague depression
- Disillusionment with marriage, family and relationships
- Loss of values
- Yearning for personal fulfillment
- A hunger for spirituality[36]

Let us assume that Moore's list of contemporary maladies are just half accurate, yet neither alone nor together can science, technology, and the present educational system solve the problems of Western society; rather they further distance us from real solutions. Psychology and science are respectively egocentric and sterile, while philosophy and theology are respectively dry and rigid. Yet add imagination, creativity, spirituality, and the mysterious sacred to education, to science and technology, and together those disciplines produce a rich mixture of fuel for our souls. Moore writes,

> We yearn excessively for entertainment, power, intimacy, sexual fulfillment, and material things, and we think we can find these things if we discover the right relationship or job, the right church or therapy. But without soul, whatever we find will be unsatisfying, for what we truly long for is the soul in each of these areas.[37]

To *yearn excessively* for the distractions that Moore identifies leads to perversity and addiction, and away from the goal of providing depth and richness to our lives. Achieving this enriched soul does not mean that our lives will be trouble-free, but rather that we will have the strength to overcome the periods in our lives when we have difficult experiences. There was a time when our families, communities, and religion helped us with all this. But frankly, they do not do a very good job of it anymore. This is a problem, but also an opportunity for education to assist in reunifying our lives and communities. Having peace of mind and individual happiness is a positive personal attribute toward mental health. With all the world's major religions and most cultures believing in the existence of a soul, we should at least teach students to have a respect for spirituality, and establish a spiritual or community common area in each school that provides a quiet place for reflection. As opposed to "religion," a central part of a spiritual center should have a component featuring earth-based reflection that helps students to feel a sense of belonging, both within their local community and as integral members of earth's living creatures. Joseph Campbell in his book *The Power of Myth* says it is absolutely necessary for everyone to have a sacred place. For those students who have neither the means to travel outside their communities to find that sacred place, nor a sacred sanctuary within a local religious center, a spiritual place within their school is especially important.

Some will say this spiritual stuff is religious and has no place in schools, and if it is necessary, it should be dealt with by churches—yet the reverse is true. Just as education and schools are not synonymous, nor is spirituality and religion. We need to recognize that truth, and take spirituality back from the exclusive domain of organized religions—they don't own it. When religious organizations suggest that they own spirituality exclusively, history reminds us that many have used their mission and theological imperialism as an accelerant for cultural unrest and war. There is nothing wrong with religious literacy, but spiritualism is much more important. The mind can know spirit. However, the imposition of cultural and religious dogma upon people, especially indigenous people, threatens the very fabric of their existence. It threatens their past, present, and future knowledge gained through cultural diversity and experientialism.

In conjunction with families, communities, and spirituality, schools can be a bonding agent. Science and spirituality can easily be integrated to include an education of knowing how to be moral. Schools can facilitate this unification in teaching love over logic through the use of stories, which Moore claims is an excellent way to care and foster the development of the soul. This is perhaps the alchemy many have sought, the re-animation of all things: "It takes a broad vision to know that a piece of the sky and a chunk of the earth lie lodged in the heart of every human being, and that if we are going to care for that heart we will have to know the sky and earth as well as human behavior."[38] We know humanity as a social construct, but wilderness is the real heart of humanity, and is essential for being truly human. Only when nature becomes part of our lives can we find meaning and God. And even if this is a bit "pie in the sky," to some, it is a worthy effort to heal the emotional sickness and toxic afflictions that we have brought upon ourselves and the earth.

Robert Bly claims that in the mid 1900s Eric Hoffer was the "canary in the coal mine" when he saw modern society degrade and said,

> Drastic change [has produced] this social primitivism . . . a new identity is found by embracing a mass movement . . . [the] mass movement absorbs and assimilates the individual . . . [who] is thereby reduced to an infantile state, for this is what a new birth really means: to become like a child. And children are primitive beings—they are credulous, follow a leader, and readily become members of a pack. . . . Finally, primitivism also follows when people seek a new identity by plunging into ceaseless action and hustling. It takes leisure to mature. People in a hurry can neither grow nor decay; they are preserved in a state of perpetual puerility.[39]

The mass movement our society has embraced absorbs the individual and takes us further and further away from leisure and nature. When a physical adult rejects the responsibility of adulthood and remains a child in so many ways (called neoteny), and is aided in doing so by escapism, it portends, as Hoffer and Bly fear, a devolution toward "modern primitivism." Bly writes, "The extended family is gone for most;

playtime outdoors has been replaced by television and computers indoors. Grown-up people have no time and decline the hard work of parenting."[40]

Just as the lead-based glaze used in pots during Roman times unknowingly caused such massive infertility and retardation among its citizens that civilization slipped into an abyss; when our youth spend nearly half of their waking life indoors on a computer alone or watching television, they will enter a mentally infertile abyss. The world and universe is a great spinning engine and it is advisable to stay at the core, right in the hub of the wheel, and not out on the edges where all the frantic whirling takes place, where it can tear a person apart or make him or her crazy. The hub of calmness must be in both the head and the heart. It is then in that place where a person will find peace and happiness. According to many of those who have been privileged to work among isolated indigenous groups, laughter is employed in a way that is alien to Western understanding – laughter that, perhaps to us seems not altogether appropriate or with cause, such as the Mashco-Piro women, the Bushmen of the Kalahari, the Sng'oi, and many American Indians. How can we understand a worldview such as that of the Tasaday of the Philippines which revolves around one central tenet – happiness – when many can hardly remember being happy? Perhaps these people are hearing or seeing something that the rest of us cannot.

Every culture has knowledge and things that all people living in that culture or country should know. No one can know everything that is knowable. To have a repository of facts that we all should learn and know, and to be considered educated, preserves and renews past greatness and values. As we add to the list, however, new knowledge often diminishes or even repudiates traditional knowledge. The most conservative of us looking down from an orbiting spacecraft would have to admit that the earth is not flat. Thus the flat earth dogma, held as fact and worshipped for eons, is inevitably replaced with new knowledge. To hold to the belief that the earth is still flat, and that nothing new should be taught to protect and honor this ultra conservative idealistic worldview, is archaic and destined for the fundamentalist fringe. In this case, the conservative fundamentalist is inane. The other extreme is inept—to run around screaming that the sky is falling, to believe it can be shored up by more money and better social programs, and to scrap previous knowledge and replace it with fundamentalist-like liberal revisionism, because we can, is simply nonsensical.

Like the young man in the personal narrative that precedes this chapter racing from pool to pool in search of Utopia, many are prone to search for a new elixir to solve their woes. In much the same way as the ancient alchemist who is always adding a new ingredient, we are quick to pin our hopes on new math, new software and technology, a new teacher from a new certification program, or a superintendent with a new funding scheme. But instead of always adding, perhaps we should sometimes take away. It is necessary that we search for new things and better ways of doing what we do, but as is so often the case, as with the young fisherman, Utopia or the solution is right in front of us; it needs to be recognized. We don't have to run to the next pool—if we look, we will often find the answers right in front of us, the challenge is to take facets, old and modern, from the Western world, and from the ancient and indigenous worlds, and then to select components which construct a more efficient and effective way of living. As the environment changes, so too must the system. We must change the educational delivery system and apply it equitably to sustain everyone's means of living. Our present means of educating sustains those centuries old philosophical pillars that support the favored few over the majority, and humans over nature. To continue this bias keeps the status quo, and all of us remain mired in the teachings of the Greek philosophers.

And as long as we retain the consumer-driven economic system and a representative democracy, there are parents who will never send their children to public school. More than a few education professors have muttered that there will be no significant educational reform to public education until the wealthy send their children to public schools. This is a pessimistic view that has stifled meaningful reform, especially by higher education. However, in their defense, centuries of criticism have had little or no effect on the education of the masses. The Americas have always been about assimilation into the mainstream culture, but the education system has not kept pace—it has not evolved. Our education is not neutral, it is purposeful and requires conformity to succeed but by doing so favors the logic of sustaining a system that is inherently biased. Those who successfully navigate the system are rewarded, and thus will support it. Education professors should show more leadership than they have in the past—Dewey's and Freire's visions for public schools broke through the spell of idealism, but the former was generally ignored and the latter branded as communist. We all need to know and believe public schools should be, and can be, inherently better than any private school, and this needs to be the norm nationwide. There are excellent public schools; but all public schools need to change. No school should simply copy another, and one size does not fit all.

So are we calling for reform—no. Reform is but a Band-Aid to this country's broken educational system; it needs total restructuring. But what else can be done when all the money in the world won't fix it. It is perhaps true that educational reform has failed because those in power do not send their children to public schools; but it is also true that reform has failed because the reformers have simply replaced failed programs with new versions based on the old philosophy – a very old and flawed educational philosophy. It is also necessary to ask whether or not those in power really want the system changed. After all, the system as it is now does maintain the status quo, and protects not only the positions of power of the favored few, but also ensures it for their children. American schools need to be restructured, and not reformed, for two additional important reasons. First, the massive public school district systems are so expensive that tax payers can no longer support them; and second, too many schools are ecological disaster zones that consume too much energy and thus too much money. Energy financial costs may be the final straw for many, but even more important is the dehumanizing nature of the system. After Robert Wolff returned from his time of living with the Sng'oi in Malaysia, he confided that it was his Western education that alienated him from both his fellow humans and nature; his education was de-humanizing. Wolff's educational experience is shared by too many who don't even know why they feel alienated and unhappy. So the problem is not just money; nor is it that the schools are not educating optimally. The reality is that our schools are harming our students. We are painfully aware that it is easy to criticize, and we have done that in some of the previous chapters, but here we wanted to provide an even stronger rationale for why education needs to change. This chapter provided a theoretical foundation that is radically different than that of the past, and upon which we can build. The next chapter provides chilling reasons why that must happen.

HERB

I mentioned in chapter 5 the profound exchange between a representative of today's Western civilization, the Chicago dentist, and Herb, a Canadian Métis. Over several summers I rented a cabin near the place where Herb was born and raised and spent much of his life; although at times he lived elsewhere while working for the railroad. I got to know Herb pretty well and despite being in his 70's, he was active and always engaged in some project or another. Herb not only knew how to be happy and live life, he knew much more. One day he shared something special with me—he showed me the center of his universe. It was a small non-descript island toward the middle of the enormous Lake of the Woods, but on June 21st when we went out on the lake and pointed due west, we were able to watch the sun set directly over the middle of the island. On the island and away from the shoreline in the small woods, there sits a stone cairn. Hanging low on a tree next to the cairn were several strips of both old and new colored cloth. Close by a ledge of rock and other carefully placed stones made up a medicine wheel which served this ancient gathering place. Herb knew not only where he was from, and what his purpose was, but also where he was going. He was one of the happiest most purposeful human beings I have ever met.

CHAPTER 10

WHY A NEW PATHWAY

There is no such thing as neutral education…
Paulo Freire, Pedagogy of the Oppressed

Is it not reasonable to expect that both informal and formal education should help us to achieve a level of peace, purpose, and happiness that comes at least close to Herb's? Societal demands today are certainly different than they were during Herb's era, but he did not have it easy; very few, if any, indigenous people did. Yet his sense of geographical *place,* community, and system of belief were all intertwined and forged stronger by the racism and the abusive and poor education he had to endure. In Chapter 6 we documented education programs that were designed purely for oppressive purposes; they were but two examples of a system that was aptly described and detailed by Freire as actual pedagogy *for* the oppressed. Perhaps some of the people who implemented such programs in the United States and other Western countries may not have intended them to be oppressive (Richard Henry Pratt genuinely thought that he was saving indigenous children by killing the Indians within them), but then again perhaps they were fully aware of the implications of their action. Regardless of questions surrounding intentions, these schools were undoubtedly oppressive and, sad to say, many still are. This chapter provides a rationale for why we suggest that public education and schools, especially in the United States, are oppressive and need to be changed.

There is a difference between schooling and education; the two terms are not synonymous. Schooling tends to imply formal instruction or training, and is often associated with places of learning (for example schools, colleges, and universities), while education implies broader connotations that include the process of acquiring knowledge, and honing reasoning and critical thinking skills. The latter can, and indeed must, at least some of the time, take place outside the school, but today, unfortunately, it is usually formalized within a structured setting such as a school. If meaningful education is going to take place in a school, it must be the educational center of a community, and the education and school must meet the needs of both the community in which it is located and society at large. That is not happening, and so we need a new model for educating our children and, for that matter, re-educating our adult learners. The new model must focus on the whole student, not just the amount of information that a student can ingest and then regurgitate for examinations. Schools must offer more physical, intellectual, and moral programs that work together to produce citizens who will be better able to cope with the needs of our 21st century society and beyond. The changes required are neither insignificant nor easy, and the transformation will be painful. Radical change cannot be realized by a simple reformation of our present schools; we must *deconstruct* the system and build anew.

Faculty and administrators of public schools will say that their present programs already meet many of the academic needs of their students, and when those are combined with sports, and even community service activities, they most often produce well-rounded citizens. For some, that is undoubtedly true. But, their programs remain mired in an ideology that was developed to maintain and serve the ruling class during the Roman Empire. The United States and other Western societies may not have a ruling class that resembles the monarchies or dictatorships of the past, but they do have governments that are filled with people of money and power, and of course, the United States has Wall Street and radical consumerism. The people who benefit the most, the now infamous 1% and their minions, are the products of an educational system that favors them, and encourages them to be *takers* above all else. The recent worldwide recession was, however, as much the fault of the education system as it was corporate greed. We need to take apart and scrap the archaic liberal arts curriculum, cut many programs, and dissolve self-serving school districts. There comes a point when just adding to or remodeling an old structure, especially one designed for Roman times, isn't what is needed – in fact it is detrimental to the welfare of the majority. Instead the current education system needs to be completely replaced. To state it plainly: public education in the United States must be *deconstructed* for several reasons; lack of funding and escalating costs, increased pressure on social services, and, most importantly, the dropout rate.

The funding for public schools is unfair and divisive. It needs to be equal and based upon a state established per student minimum, not necessarily abolishing property tax as a source, but rather equalizing any disparity among schools by state funding, which is the practice already in a number of states. Continuing to fund a significant portion of school needs through property taxes is important, because it helps to sustain a sense of community ownership in the educative process. The principal problem today is that state-controlled social services costs are increasing dramatically, at least partly because the public school systems are failing to graduate students, and those who do graduate are not adequately equipped to segue into the work force or to higher education without extensive training, or remedial non-credit course work. According to research completed by the Bill and Melinda Gates Foundation's Strong American Schools initiative, remedial education costs states and students as much as $2.3 billion a year because 43% of all community college students need some remedial education (math, reading and writing).[1] Independent School Districts (ISDs) have to compete for tax dollars with social services agencies that are seeing their abilities stretched and funding cut because of increasing competition from, and need by, school districts. This is a vicious cycle that will only get worse unless the source of the malady is changed. Some states have state income tax that *may* make up for the disparity in funding sources among districts.

But if funding were the only issue, we could expect to see fewer problems in the states that ensure equal funding for all students – unfortunately, that is just not the case.

During the 2009 State of the Union Address to the Joint Session of Congress, President Barack Obama read a letter from eighth-grade student, Ty'Sheoma Bethea, who said her school needed help; she was afraid it was going to be closed. Ty'Sheoma said that she and her classmates were trying to become lawyers and doctors and such, "We are not quitters," wrote Ty'Sheoma. The young girl and her classmates may not be quitters, but if public school formatting and funding remains as it is, *we* are the ones who have quit on these students. As the President intimated, dropouts quit on themselves and their country, but in reality our country and its public education system provide students with reasons to quit. We can and must do better.

At issue here is that Western-style global economics almost exclusively focus on the acquisition of wealth for a few massive corporations and their shareholders (a form of fundamentalism) with the idea that the wealth will trickle down to individuals and the community. Community schools and their development are, however, the antithesis of globalization, and are often hotbeds of activism that call for any change away from the historical system that has favored the few over the many. But hopefully there is some common ground and a framework can be found that facilitates success for global economics while, at the same time, fostering the economic health within and for communities which includes excellent education and schools.

Until that day comes, however, school districts must and will collapse upon themselves; a situation that is already happening in some parts of the country. In a 2008–2009 survey by the American Association of School Administrators, 11% of all public schools in the United States closed in 2009, up from 6% in 2008 and 3% in 2007.[2] The landslide of closings is surely in part associated with the nation's overall economic downturn, but it is important to consider that the economic downturn has been caused at least in part *by* poor schools.

Many schools have been marginal for years. Yet, instead of dealing with the root of the problem, administrators and school board members have let it lie and allowed the schools to continue because closing them would have a potentially disastrous effect on neighborhoods. Moreover, paradoxically, it serves an economic purpose by producing dropouts. For example, after years of systematically closing a large number of schools and abandoning thousands upon thousands of children due to a lack of funds, it was announced that the Detroit ISD was to be taken over in June 2011 by the state of Michigan.[3] In the previous year Kansas City ISD closed nearly half its buildings, and the district now has a director for its "repurposing" initiative which is seeking to reuse or dispense with aging or vacant school buildings.[4] And the Los Angeles Board of Education has voted to turn over to private charter providers one-third of its under-performing schools[5], but from previous experience many believe that only a fraction of the 250 charter schools proposed will actually open, and many of those will fail within the first year or so. This will cost the community from which all these children come much more than anyone can imagine, because these neighborhoods will become wastelands.

Charter schools are contributing to the demise of ISDs by pulling away students for which schools would normally receive state money. At first blush charter schools such as the rapidly growing nationwide Knowledge is Power Program (KIPP) seem to be working as they focus on minority and low income students, and have posted some impressive standardized test scores. One attribute of a KIPP school is a signed commitment by parents and students not only to succeed, but also to have ten-hour days, extra classes on Saturdays, and a longer school year. The increase in the school day and year will account for increased learner outcomes and is a step in the right direction, but clearly the high expectations the students encounter within these schools is also a critical factor. But unfortunately the real secret to their success is that they are self-selecting to start with, and when a student drops out they are replaced most often with a less "at risk" higher potential student who has been "skimmed" away from public schools. By skimming, charter schools will always do better because they replace a failing student with one not only from the top of their waiting list, but also often from the top percentage of the public school population. KIPP schools essentially are pullout programs (preparatory schools) for minority and low-income students. This is not necessarily a bad thing, but they should neither be confused with nor compared to public schools. Despite some positive attributes, charter schools should not be seen as the preferred model to replace public schools, partly because, despite the national hype and hope, they are failing at a greater rate than public schools. Stanford University researchers have found that, nationally, 37% of charter schools were "significantly worse" than their local public schools, and the data produced by the National Center for Research on Education Outcomes indicates that the majority of charter school students in the United States would be better off in the local public schools.[6] The research also found that charter schools, that have been effective in narrowing achievement gaps, often have their origins associated with celebrities or minority philanthropists, and restrict enrollment, which simply makes them de facto private schools. Charter schools, academies, and magnet schools are the forerunners of community schools, but they do not have a community-based philosophy. That is one reason, and a good one, that virtually all teachers' organizations oppose the spread of the charter movement.

Urban ISDs and states will surely absorb more and more cost from the inevitable legal challenges to school closures. When any district abandons any child, that organization is already dead; it just doesn't know it. For example, Detroit's dropout rate is 52%. On hearing this figure, the city's state appointed emergency financial manager, Robert Bobb, commented that the school system is "academically bankrupt." He went on to condemn the situation as "almost academic homicide."[7] The present and future children living in these school districts are not responsible for the situation, but in the end it will be *their* education that suffers and *their* futures, and those of their own children, that are put at risk. It does not go unnoticed that those affected are nearly all minority students, and that their system's failure will ensure the perpetuation of increasing social strife for generations to come. And the question must be asked; would these schools be closed if the students were white?

Clearly, the school dropout problem is not restricted to Detroit, Kansas City, and Los Angeles. In Texas, 70% of the state's population lives within what is referred to as the Texas Triangle—Houston, San Antonio, Dallas-Fort Worth, and Austin. For the academic year 2009–2010 those three cities' ISDs respectively had a dropout rate of 57%, 52% and 55% according to state data. Other agencies, such as the Intercultural Developmental Research Association (IDRA), claim that these numbers are not accurate and that the real attrition rate is significantly higher! Regardless, even using the state's data, there is no justifiable reason for the existence of any educational entity that has more dropouts than graduates. Administrators and board members of these cities will come up with creative solutions to keep these schools open and people employed, but citizens need to know that what they are paying for is not education. They are simply providing life-support to an already dead entity. The dropout rate in Texas is so bad that it even became a political issue in the recent election for governor. In the throes of the campaign, the state released new data which put the dropout rate at a mere 9%, but everyone knows that is far from the truth and just politics.[8] In fact, overall, Texas schools are losing over one-third of their students, and the racial ethnic gaps between whites and minorities have increased in all regions throughout the state.[9] It is not too often that a major newspaper editorial chides a state for keeping fake records with regard to school dropout rates, but in the San Antonio Express News, May 29, 2010, its editorial board did just that with a piece entitled "Deceptive Records Hide School Dropout Rates." There is little doubt that the state of Texas has grossly and purposefully underreported its dropout rates. The question is—why? Is it simply poor record keeping, or is there a darker, and sinister intentional reason?

Of even greater importance is the position of the rest of the country. Is this only a Texas issue, or is it possible that the whole nation is purposefully underreporting dropout rates? Apparently it is. In an Associated Press article, Heather Hollingsworth and Dorie Turner reported that because many states have had "flawed measurement formulas that often undercounted dropouts and produced inflated results," the United States Education Department has introduced a new standard formula for calculating graduation rates. Many states are expected to see large discrepancies between previous reports and the new figures.[10] So, apparently it is not just Texas! In response to inquiries about this article, United States Secretary of Education Arne Duncan said that "[t]hrough this uniform method, states are raising the bar on data standards, and simply being more honest."[11]

In the year 2006–2007, there were 28 of 254 counties in Texas that had at least a 65% dropout rate for black and Hispanic students. Twelve counties had a 100% dropout rate for black students in its public schools. Two counties had a 100% dropout rate for Hispanic students. Perhaps even more startling was that there were forty counties where the dropout rate for white students was 0%.[12] Statistics can be misleading and surely there are at least a few of those locations which only had one or two black students in the whole county and perhaps the family moved outside the county. However, it is less likely that so few Hispanic students exist in any county. But there is no denying that any school with a 100% graduation rate for white students and a high dropout rate for all minority students is guilty of institutional racism—plain and simple. It is probable, however, that those teachers, school officials, and the majority of the citizens of these counties would adamantly deny this claim; but they would be wrong. They are wrong because they are favoring and perpetuating an educational system which maintains a privileged society and worldview, and they are doing it either knowingly or through ignorance, and more specifically through *ignorantia affectata*; a term coined by Thomas Aquinas to describe cultivated ignorance resulting from a collective and willful lack of knowledge to protect privilege or self interest. And it is not just a state problem; it is a national problem because in 2010 a staggering 47% of all black males across the United States were high school dropouts. These men often turn to crime because they cannot get a decent job. African American men between 16 and 29 comprise 40% of all those incarcerated within the criminal justice system yet they only represent 14% of all men in this age group.[13] Moreover, *none* of them is considered a dropout since the National Center for Educational Statistics does not count incarcerated populations in their national dropout rate. So we have both the state *and* the federal governments inaccurately counting dropouts. In sum, dropouts become inmates, yet inmates do not equal dropouts – this is absurd. Nationally, 75% of all state prison inmates and 59% of federal inmates (and 69% of jail populations nationwide) are dropouts. The United States has only 5% of the world's population yet 25% of the world's inmates—and the vast majority are dropouts.[14] And, all told, the United States presently spends over $50 billion annually on inmates! Considering these numbers, it is obvious that someone is profiting, as it seems that dropouts and incarceration profoundly contribute to the United States economy. The raw material fueling this aspect of the economy is the dropout.

The problem is not just that dropout rates are increasing, and that it is difficult for those who do drop out of school to find meaningful work, it is that far too many are illiterate or functionally illiterate, which is the real reason they can neither succeed in school nor find meaningful employment. According to the National Adult Literacy Survey, as many as 40% of incarcerated individuals are at the lowest level of literacy. Thus, finding them jobs is not the solution; if we want to integrate incarcerated individuals back into society, they must be re-educated. If that is not possible, society will be forced to accept the reality that these people have little hope beyond a life of crime. Deep rooted sociological, political, and economic bias, perpetuated by an education system derived from and favoring a philosophical and epistemological ideology of a few over all others, will always preserve and sustain educational inequality and an under-society. The National Center for Educational Statistics reports that between 1970 (when they began keeping data) and 2006, never was the dropout rate of schools with low income students remotely as low as middle income schools, nor were middle income schools remotely as low in attrition as high income schools—clearly privilege begets privilege.

Even the most naïve among us must finally realize that this abandonment of education for these children is being done on purpose. Federal and state educational policies have adhered to the *human capital model*[15] of education over all other models. Students are the fuel pumped into economic engines (or the streets), which create a product (or prisoners) that is then sold (or provided) to make a profit. Not too long ago, early childhood through high schools for-profit schools were a rarity, but now early childhood programs, private learning centers, and charter schools proliferate and are big business. So too, are juvenile detention centers many of which are now run by large profit making corporations. It should be clear to most that a low dropout rate helps to make the country economically successful. However, it is also important to realize that there are long standing and powerful economic interests for some which benefit from a *high* dropout rate, such as the service industries. We cannot have illegal immigrants waiting on tables. Moreover, illegal and legal immigrants are needed in the fields, ranches, and other service industries, but there are nowhere near enough of them to fill all the low-wage, unattractive work positions—thus schools must produce dropouts. Powerful economic forces—owners, stockholders, CEOs, and the 1% who fund the campaigns of political leaders mostly prefer the human capital model.[16]

Many throughout the United States will say this is an inner city problem, a black and Latino problem, a lower socio-economic problem, or an immigrant problem; and if those communities cannot save their own schools, then too bad. And in the short term that is what many believe because they will not admit the extent of the problem. But unless we wish to become a de facto nation within a nation—the Un-united Oppressed Minorities and Poor of America and the United Whites and Invited Others of America, which some say it is now anyway—then education **must** change. Critical theorists are saying that this schism is not an accident of history or a sign of history repeating itself, but rather it was deliberately designed that way. Today, there are many wealthy Americans whose riches come from the sweat of immigrants (both legal and illegal) and the intentionally poorly educated. Seventy-five percent of United States farm workers were born in other countries (mostly in Mexico), and two-thirds are illegal, meaning they will work well below the minimum wage.[17] One can speculate that the ranching industry also benefits and contributes to keeping food costs down and profits up by employing illegal immigrants, and paying them much less than they would a legal citizen. The intentionally poorly educated provide workers for our service industries which, just like illegal workers, allow owners to keep costs down and profits up.[18]

These assertions suggest that there have been conspiracies within education to maintain a separation of social classes in our schools, and that educational outcomes perpetuate the chasm between rich and poor. Far-fetched? Not really. Consider the editorial recently in the Richmond-Times Dispatch which admitted to a long-standing "dreadful doctrine of massive resistance," toward desegregating the State of Virginia's public schools. The editors admitted to participating in hegemony with the state's white political leaders to ensure the state government cut funds to any school that tried to integrate.[19] This conspiracy goes well beyond institutional racism as it effectively maintains a form of slavery via economic and political policy.

The long-term cost of sustaining an increasingly uneducated segment of the population to the overall economic health of this country is billions upon billions of dollars in lost productivity and lost purchasing power, along with massive increases in crime and other social woes. As early as 2008, the IDRA predicted that, at the then current dropout rate, schools would lose not only the present generation, but also those of the future – that is, the trend and pace of dropping out would only get worse because of past practices. And sure enough, just two years later the dropout rate was worse – much worse.

Although they will not want to, the white and well-off people of color must help bail the boat as the water rises. They cannot cast themselves away from the major cities and its masses. A educational disaster is already here, and they cannot just pretend it is not happening. Class action law suits have already been filed across the United States based on the same argument as the 1954 *Brown vs. Board of Education*; that is, there cannot be a good and bad public education for whites and non-whites respectively. The civil rights struggle of the 21st century is not in the work place, it is in our schools.

Given the recent worldwide recession, it is reasonable to assume that most high schools, colleges, and universities are providing students knowledge and skills that are no longer relevant because many of the associated jobs no longer exist. Too many high schools in Western society still reflect the needs and dispositions of the factories of the long-past industrial revolution. The only product mass-produced in these "factory" schools these days is the dropout. If the long-suffering and wailing of public education critics cannot force the deconstruction of education, the new economic world order may. Most countries are going through an economic de-development. But this is not necessarily a bad thing, considering that many countries have become over-developed and over consume for the benefit of the global economy. Yet the curricula in high schools and degree programs in colleges and universities are preparing students for jobs and professions that are no longer always applicable to the real world. If high school does not prepare students to move smoothly into either employment or higher education, and the college or university degree does not translate into even better employment opportunities, what is the point of all those years in school? If education is no longer relevant to the "new normal" society, perhaps dropping out is a better option. Why should someone rack up a mountain of student loans if there is little or no chance of securing a job related to the degree? So it isn't just bad schools and dropouts that comprise the problems surrounding public education. The correlation between education and livelihood must be revisited and revised. The solution lies in abolishing the "factory focused" skills and dispositions, and the archaic and crippling hierarchy of public schools, as well as executing profound curricular change.

Without going into the history of curriculum (there are many accounts to satisfy the most curious reader), it is safe to say that the adherence to the human capital model and direct instruction after World War Two promoted economic globalization. Thus, the measure of education was and is reflected in economic growth and development – more is better. But there are three other major educational models of curriculum that have been, and are presently being used: the progressive model, the religious model, and the indigenous world model. A study of the four major models reflects different philosophical and cultural principles. Although advocates of each would say that their model is superior to the others, all are valued differently by different societies, or even by different segments within societies; and naturally, all have attributes and liabilities. As so many have embraced economic globalization, the human capital model has enjoyed such favor that integration of other educational models has not happened. They are viewed as an impediment to the worldwide economic engine. For example, the religious model inclines toward fundamentalism, the progressive model has a blind passion for constructivism, and the indigenous model leans toward tribalism. But at its extreme end, the human capital model has an obsession with money and consumerism, and the costs associated with these fixations are now becoming evident.

Clearly none of the four major models alone can provide the content and education needed for all societies in the new century. The extremism inherent in each model has to be avoided. But it is also clear that significant change is required, and a serious analysis is needed to assess, select, and amalgamate parts of the four historical curriculum models into a series of new systems that can meet the needs of the disparate communities which comprise the whole population. Education cannot be provided in a "one size fits all" scenario, and no organization must be allowed to create a single new model that is destined to serve just one segment of society. It is time to think about, and to address, the educational needs of all members of society. It is time for an educational paradigm shift that will change not just school life but all aspects of human existence.

Today, many people are caught up in the hamster wheel of never-ending progress, the obsessive accumulation of "stuff," and multitasking to the point of mental paralysis. People have moved so far from natural ways of living, and other ways of acquiring knowledge, that any shift toward harmony and equity will have to be revolutionary. The question is, can it be done, or are we beyond redemption? Significant change from the debilitating effects of the incessant drive to progress and past educational systems will be difficult, because these practices have become so inculcated into our lifestyles that it is difficult to imagine not having them. There is, however, little doubt that our modern lifestyle is more hectic than that of earlier generations. But it is difficult to envisage the 12-hour or more working days that earlier generations had to endure simply to put food on the table – food that had to be put up or bought daily and prepared from scratch. Nevertheless, we do feel busy, and a byproduct of that situation is a probable reduction in creativity, critical thinking, and play. The same could be said for our reliance on, and infatuation with, technology. The fear is not just that being busy and technology use dull our senses of the natural world, but that we already have habituated to both. Habituation creates change, and in this instance the change has normalized a reduction of time on task, and has corresponded with alarmingly high increases in the diagnosis of Attention Deficit Disorder (ADD) and Attention Deficit Hyperactivity Disorder (ADHD) in children. As young people flock to technology in their increasing quest not to be bored, ADD behaviors are becoming the norm, and the attention span of "Millennium Kids" is significantly less than that of the previous generation.[20]

The American Academy of Pediatrics (AAP) has recommended that children under two years of age not watch any television, because rapid visual images may alter their brain development. This rewiring of the brain had been linked to attention deficit problems as early as 2004.[21] It is disconcerting to realize that years earlier, many were warning about the effects of video monitors and television programming on children. It is not unrealistic to believe that the increase in incidences of ADD/ ADHD can be attributed to a lack of attention to, or belief in, those warnings. Nearly five years ago, the AAP strongly warned the public not only that two year olds should not be watching television, but also that other children including teenagers should not have television sets in their bedrooms. Further, research in 2007 found twenty percent of infants had television sets in their bedroom. Forty percent of all three to four year-olds and two-thirds of all teenagers had television sets in their rooms. Five years later undoubtedly those percentages have risen, along with a proliferation of video monitors. Profit should never trump the well-being of children.[22] It is the obligation of the government to protect its citizens – especially its children – including alleviating threats that prevent them from developing and reaching their fullest cognitive potential. As with cigarettes and alcohol, it has been suggested that the government should affix warning labels to all forms of video monitors, and run commercials between television programs to warn viewers of the link between ADD/ADHD and excessive time in front of screens. If the misuse of technology is contributing to a reduction in the attention span of our young, who are being diagnosed more and more frequently with ADD, one might muse that the makers of technology and the drug industry are in cahoots, if not knowingly perhaps unknowingly. It is important to point out that many believe that ADD and ADHD are heavily over diagnosed, thus increasing drug sales and drug company profits. It is easy to assume that doctors over diagnose and overprescribe to increase their own income, but parents who are looking to place blame for their children's bad behavior or lack of concentration often place undue pressure on physicians to affix a diagnostic label to a child and medicate accordingly. In 2010 testimony, the National Institute of Mental Health admitted that there had been "bias in prescribing practices" because of physicians' ties to the drug industry, and that a newly signed law would require doctors to make known their links to the drug industry and other unreported fees paid by the drug industry, to prominent researchers and doctors.[23]

European countries, notably France, are recognizing the danger of inappropriate practices often used in daycare settings and early childhood educational environments. The danger is television.[24] In a setting without a television, children are likely to be active and social; they play with other children and find activities to keep themselves amused. Children who watch television for long periods, even when the subject is educational, are disadvantaged because the time spent in front of the screen can isolate them, limit their ability to amuse themselves, and make them less physically fit. It is perhaps sacrilegious to many who were raised on Sesame Street that programs marketed for children are now raising serious concern about attention span and self-control associated with a child's ability to learn. Albeit a small study, recent research has found as little as nine minutes of watching a popular television program has been linked to long-term attention problems in children, including immediate impairment in four year olds.[25]

Health problems in children can manifest in many ways. A joint review of past research by scholars from the University of Southern Denmark and the Harvard School of Public Health has found that as few as two hours of television a day increases a viewer's chance of contracting Type 2 diabetes by twenty percent, and heart disease by fifteen percent. The study found that watching television isn't just hours not engaged in physical activity, but also snacking and being exposed to commercials promoting unhealthy foods.[26] And an increase in weight creates many health complications including diabetes. The people of China are generally not considered to have an overweight problem but, as the country rapidly embraces capitalism and consumerism, it finds itself with a diabetes rate nearly as high as that of the United States.[27] Schools in the United States have long been criticized for providing junk food and many are now under pressure to remove their vending machines, or to stock them with healthy alternatives. Unfortunately, however, many schools depend on revenue from the sale of snacks and drinks to supplement their income. Once again, the very institutions that should be bettering the lives of children are providing not only the wrong type of education, but also contributing to students becoming overweight and passing on long-term health costs to society.

Returning to technology, if France and other northern European countries have or are now considering passing laws banning the type of television broadcasts aimed at children, along with suggestions with regard to the amount of time a young person can watch, restrictions on computer use cannot be far behind, yet the United States continues to integrate more and more technology (including television monitors) into our schools. It is well known that watching too much television retards cognitive development[28], yet is it possible that using some other technological tools may be just as insidious?

Imagine not having televisions, computers, smartphones, iPods, and the like— what would we do? We would probably go outdoors, rediscover nature, be more reflective, be physically more active, be healthier, spend more time with our family and neighbors, read, and find novel ways to occupy our newfound time. Technological progress and tool use are necessary, and should provide us with a higher quality of life and a better means to preserve nature. But the misuse of technology is divorcing us from nature and if we ultimately value technology over nature, we will lose our humanity. Over-developed nations are consuming and then discarding gadgets for newer technology at a dizzying pace, and unbridled advances in the development of technology leads to ecological and social problems, not only widening the cyber gap between those who can afford it and those who cannot, but also creating ecologically ruined areas where those who cannot afford technology are destined to live, while those who can afford it live in environmentally preferred areas. We must seriously consider the possible effects of radiation from cell phones and other technological devices despite the industry saying that there is no cause for alarm (remember the tobacco industry); the city of San Francisco requires disclosure of cell phone radiation levels, lest the ecological spoiled area be between our ears. We must watch out for warning signs of environmental health problems. It is generally assumed that cancer, for instance, was quite rare among ancient people. Yet it is pandemic among modern societies for a variety of lifestyle and environmental reasons. It is always worth reminding ourselves that those who introduce new technology are doing so not to improve our quality of life but to make a profit, and students and schools are unfortunately easy targets.

As toddlers, children begin playing with toys or fake versions of technology (that is, toy cell phones and computers). However, children from about age nine are increasingly seen in possession of real portable media players (PMPs), cell phones, and even laptop computers, and these devices are increasingly brought to school. While education authorities and teachers extol the value of technology in the classroom, we have perhaps been naïve with regard to the deleterious effects of some types of technology. Consider that manufacturers are rushing to provide the PMP market with recordings that stimulate the same area of the brain as marijuana, cocaine, methamphetamines, peyote, and other illegal and highly addictive drugs. "Digital drugs" and "iDosing"[29] are said to create brain waves from two different sounds coming from separate headphones which in turn target and stimulate a specific area of the brain. There are numerous iDosing websites devoted to promoting and selling digital drugs.[30] To date, there are no laws against this. The reviews of the effectiveness of digital drugs doing nothing beyond the imagination are as many as those that tout their effectiveness. It is, however, clear that while technological tools can be useful in an educational setting, it is also necessary to be aware of possible dangers with regard to their use. PMP devices are not intended to be bad for students; and when television was introduced we didn't realize the correlation between watching and increased weight. With any new technology, we must be cautious and be prepared to educate ourselves about what children are exposed to in the name of education.

It would be easy to take a pessimistic stance and state that most Western societies, with lifestyles that pollute their surroundings, their blind acceptance of the notion that progress must be achieved at all cost, and governments and institutions that pander to the wealthy and neglect those who are most in need, are unwilling, or worse unable, to change. Yet in these times of uncertainty, people are questioning their way of life. Although there is much evidence of corporate greed and selfishness on the part of those who want for nothing, people are increasingly looking for a better way of living and a more meaningful reason for their existence. The former was clearly evident in the aftermath of Hurricanes Katrina, Rita, and Ike in 2005 and 2008. While government agencies and officials were busy blaming everyone but themselves for gross mismanagement and failure to provide basic aid for the neediest people in this country, fellow citizens opened their wallets, homes, and hearts to the refugees.

And so too with education; the best help comes from the people and their neighbors. Meaningful educational change must come from within communities. The framers of the United States Constitution knew this by rejecting a top down approach to education, yet today's school districts are the most top-down non-religious hierarchies in society. As John Dewey envisioned, schools are not the sole means to solve society's problems, but rather today's schools are the problem. And while society does not know how to fix the problem, the people do. Schools *must* serve their communities. Education cannot continue to favor consumerism, to operate for profit, and to perpetuate inequity. Schools need to reeducate both our young and old toward a better life that includes a *critical consciousness*, as espoused by Paulo Freire, and also leads to a self-sustaining world. Its natural by-product will be a world which is more equitable for all.

In chapter 11 we offer some recommendations that will begin the journey toward educating our children for tomorrow. Some may appear to be radical, but to change direction, radical change is necessary. Many of the ideas are not entirely new, but are modifications of existing workable systems; with so much work to do, there is no reason to reinvent the wheel. One thing for sure, however, is that there must be a new definition of education.

DAISY

As a teenager I spent much of my summers in the Boundary Waters Canoe Area Wilderness on the border between Minnesota and Ontario. I stayed at a remote cabin on Basswood Lake owned by Walt and Daisy Wiggens. Daisy had an Indian heritage and had been born and raised near the cabin. Both Walt and Daisy, had spent most of their lives on the site and were pretty much self sufficient, but they were getting up in age and always welcomed a young pair of legs.

I assisted Walt in his small sawmill operation, which was their primary means of income, but I have to admit I spent more time fishing than working, though they didn't seem to mind. Walt was a practical man, but Daisy was different. She seemed to be surrounded by an aura of serenity and had an uncanny ability to attract animals not only with her pancakes, but also by her singing.

In 1963 the federal government removed virtually all of the residents of that area by destroying their homes and cabins and making the area accessible only by canoe. Walt and Daisy moved to Seattle to be near family, and both passed away a few years thereafter.

In the 1990s, my wife and I canoed into the area and pitched a tent near Wiggens' Point. Late one afternoon as we relaxed at our camp, I heard singing. After a few minutes, I found the source of the sound – a lone woman paddling a canoe. It was Daisy.

Of course, my wife thought I had lost my mind as I hurried her into our canoe so that we could catch up with a woman who had died 20 years earlier. The woman was a strong paddler - like Daisy, and seemed nearly impossible to catch. Finally, right by the old cabin site we pulled a respectable distance alongside the mysterious woman. My eyes met hers, and I realized she was not Daisy. Nevertheless, although she was in her 30s, she bore a striking resemblance to Daisy. Not wanting to alarm the woman, we pulled away and returned to our campsite. I will not forget the unusual sight of this woman paddling alone on that large wild body of water. More importantly, I will never forget her song. I now know the woman really was Daisy, and I feel she came to me with a message to stay true to my path. To this day, I often think of her serene song reminding me that there is so much more to life than collecting stuff. The really important aspects of life are this planet, all of its occupants, and our relationships with them. Education must stress this connectivity and strive to teach and perpetuate this organic worldview. It is not enough for me to just believe this; I must share it with others.

CHAPTER 11

THE WAY FORWARD

Old quotes are not appropriate for a new beginning.

Risku and Harding

The previous chapters document the entrenched, archaic, and broken condition of traditional educational practices, and offer evidence to support our contention that it is too late for simple reform. We believe that most people realize that there must be change, but do not know where to start. Total reform is difficult; it is always easier simply to add or remove something in the hope that the effect will be sufficient to allow difficult changes to be postponed to another time and, importantly, passed to someone else. But while total deconstruction is painful, it is easier if the need for change and the direction are clear. In this case, while the *why* is easy and the *where* is murky, it is the *how* that will prove to be the most daunting and challenging, yet exciting. Understanding the need for change, however, does make the task of formulating a plan more palatable. Cutting new paths is, of course, never without problems, and progress is usually pedestrian at best, but any progress that is achieved will be satisfying. Even those who agree with the need for educational overhaul will find it hard to envision what a new pathway and a new delivery system might look like. But start we must.

In chapters 1 to 8, we outlined the vast differences that lie between the ways of knowing and living of indigenous people and white settlers, and the tragic consequences of forced assimilation when their paths crossed. When the Europeans sought not to enslave native people but, instead, attempted to assimilate them into white society, they most often used education as both a persuasive tool and an instrument of change. Thus, after listening to speeches about broken treaties and lost land as a result of ignorance of European law and language difficulties, indigenous parents often handed their children over to the Europeans in the hope that they would be educated in the white ways, and be able to negotiate indigenous rights on a more equal footing. Of course, we know that the result was, more often than not, a European-style education that was, for the indigenous children, inadequate to secure a place in white society, yet successful enough to ensure the loss of their native language and culture, and ultimately alienation. That alienation created a sea of lost young people who found themselves in a no mans land that lay between white and indigenous societies; they belonged in neither. In Chapter 9 we turned to the United States' present education system, and offered a philosophical foundation from which to build a novel educational delivery structure. Chapter 10 explained why the present system is beyond redemption, and introduced the psychological and physiological components that must be added to the new system to improve people's lives and the overall health of the natural world. Education can no longer be divorced from real life. In this final chapter we present the structural changes necessary to implement radical reform. The emphasis is on replacement programs and policies for some of the low hanging fruit (classes that are easy to discard since they are irrelevant to a balanced, fair, and meaningful education plan). Many, if not most, public educators will disagree with our assessment of the situation, because they are vested within the huge public education hierarchical complex, and many others will say it cannot be done. But the changes suggested here are necessary and doable, and quiet conversations among many educators have been encouraging.

It is clear that any education system comprises several components, all of which are interconnected and interdependent in some way, and are vital to its success. These components; the students, the community, the teachers, and the schools, have but one joint function, the success of the students. Thus, the new system we envisage is entirely student-centered, with schools located in and run by the community, teachers locally based when possible and appropriately selected, trained, and remunerated for their work, and the physical plant, administration, and programs operating in a support role. The students and their educational needs become the central focus of all programs and are supported by the community, teachers, and schools. While it is impossible to separate the individual components completely, we will discuss each in turn, beginning, naturally, with the students, and indicate areas of overlap as they become evident.

STUDENTS

As we stated earlier, the nurturing, safety, and education of students must be at the forefront of all educational programs. Thus, all schools, whether public, private, or charter, should assist in developing the complete physical, emotional, and intellectual wellness of their students. Accordingly, in keeping with Maslow's Hierarchy of Needs pyramid, they should ensure that students are well fed, feel physically and emotionally secure, and are educationally challenged.

Individual schools need to work with their communities to guarantee that students have access to nourishing food. School supervisors must assure that the quality and variety of food served in school cafeterias meet not just the basic wants of the students and financial needs of the schools, but also be nutritious and balanced. Economics must not trump the nutritional needs of students, and schools must ban non-nutritious food and drinks. Physical well-being is crucial to mental well-being, and many students living in Western societies are profoundly sedentary and overweight. Movement is essential to brain development, and the obesity epidemic stems primarily from a lack of physical activity, an intake of too many high-calorie, high-fat foods and sugar-based drinks, and not enough protein based nutritious options. And because protein is needed for human brains to operate at their cognitive best, schools must provide protein rich, high quality food. It is a simple ratio of calories in versus calories out, and schools must take the lead in promoting a healthy lifestyle for everyone. Although teachers have borne the brunt of the blame for poor student performance over the last few decades, it may really lie in the hands of the school board members, businesses, parents, and society in general. The real problem is two-fold, and stems from a lack of proper nutrition and the general reduction in the amount of physical activity undertaken by children today. Schools must reemphasize physical education and mandate that not only all students but also all school personnel participate in either a physical education class or daily exercise program. There also needs to be much more emphasis given to intramural athletics and activities which are meaningful to more than just a small percentage of the student population. This will trim not only waistlines but also budgets. When possible, physical education should take place daily and outside, so that students can see and feel nature, and benefit from fresh air and sunshine. Unfortunately, it is not just weather that restricts physical education outdoors, because for physical education to be outside, the air must be safe to breath, but more than half of all American students live in areas where they are forced to breath dirty air.[1] Some students have plenty of exercise; those who are involved in interscholastic sports, but these activities do nothing for the vast majority of the student population. And interscholastic sports can deny other, less elite organizations, much needed school funding.

Socialization and assimilation of students are important by-products of the educative process, and while interscholastic activities are a minor part of this process, they are a significant drain on most district budgets. Interscholastic sports serve but a few select athletes, and so foster entitlement and discrimination. The overall level of priority, costs, and short and long-term injuries associated with interscholastic competition is self-serving, obscene, counter-educational, and socially unproductive. All too many high school students are allowed and, indeed, even encouraged to focus on athletic versus academic performance with the dream of attaining an athletic scholarship to a university where they can focus even more on sport and less on academics. Like gladiators of old, too many high school and university athletes are left under-educated and with lifetime injuries, all for the sake of entertainment. This is so much of a problem that United States Education Secretary, Arne Duncan, proposed that college teams be barred from postseason play if they fail to graduate at least 40% of their players. It is particularly odious that some university teams participating in the Men's National Collegiate Athletic Association (NCAA) basketball tournament have a 0% graduating rate for African American students. Numerous other schools also have a dismal graduation rate for their players. Of the NCAA 2010 postseason teams, twelve of the "Sweet Sixteen" schools had lower than a 40% graduation rate for the participating athletes.[2] The University of Maryland and University of California from 1999–2002 had no African American starters graduate.[3] And an ESPN study found thirty-six Division I programs failed to graduate any of their basketball players between 1990 and 1994, and there is little reason to believe that the graduation rate is any better now than it was then.[4] The vast majority of college athletes do not enter the professional ranks, and too many often become the detritus of society.

Too many universities are better known for their sports programs than for their academics. But there is so much money to be made that a recent interscholastic commission report states that the imbalance between sports and academics has been caused by a business model which has impinged upon the quality of academic programs.[5] And this all starts in our middle and junior high schools across the United States where sport is taking away financial resources from academics. A prime example of that can be found in Allen, Texas where a $60 million high school football stadium has recently opened. It isn't that the community can't afford the stadium, it is the inappropriate priorities and the message they send to its students. Admittedly, the stadium will be used by other teams and for other community purposes, but the reality is that this stadium was built primarily so that a few of the school's male students can play a game once a week for 12 or so weeks a year. Physical fitness and school and community spirit are, of course, critical to the well-being of the students and need to be enhanced, but that can be better achieved through low cost intramural programs that are available to all students at all skill levels. When questioned about the cost of interscholastic sport, ardent supporters point to privately raised discretionary funds that help to defray costs, but that support is erratically sustained and cannot be counted upon always to be there. Usually parents only give extra if *their* children are in school and in the programs, and community donations ebb and flow depending upon the success of teams. Schools should have intramural activities, events, and programs for the benefit of not only all students in the school, but also for the community; taxpayers would then feel better, especially those without children in school, when they see what their tax dollars were buying and could partake in the activities.

While it is important on a day-to-day basis to address appropriate nutritional and physical fitness needs for students, they will still be reluctant to attend school and, when there, will find it impossible to concentrate on learning if they do not feel safe. Working closely with community service personnel, school officials must make students' safety a priority. All staff need be attentive to students in distress and report safety concerns to supervisors and the appropriate outside agencies. Mandated reporting laws have to be strictly enforced, and criminal history background checks on all school staff should be reviewed annually. While still in their professional development programs, preservice teachers ought to have access to advice and practical training on subjects such as, but not restricted to, homelessness, gangs, bullying, sexual abuse, drug and alcohol addiction, and personal psychological problems. Only once the lower level needs of Maslow's Hierarchy have been fulfilled, can educators then turn their full attention to the learning needs of students. This is but one area of the education system where students and teachers interact in a realm that is not strictly based on the curriculum.

For students to learn successfully, they need to create a rapport with their teachers, and to feel that they can rely on them to be there for them. Unfortunately, however, one full year of the average United States' student's public school experience is taught by substitute teachers.[6] Teachers' unions have negotiated contracts that have abbreviated the already short school year with double digit paid sick days and personal leave days, all or most of which are taken on Fridays and Mondays. Many districts even have a sick day policy, wherein those not used can be allocated to another teacher. Hence, even though not all teachers use all of their paid days off, the days and required substitutes are still being used and paid for not just once but twice—the sick teacher is paid and the substitute is paid. There needs to either be incentives not to use sick or personal leave days, or at least rules to limit their use both by the teachers themselves and by others to whom they did not originally belong. Substitute teaching is a hard task, and there are some who take it seriously and actually teach or at least try to. Most school administrators will, however, confess to their peers that they have few or no expectations of substitutes, and it is a good day if they just keep order in the classroom.

Students' well-being is not only a concern during school hours; their out-of-school schedules and activities can also affect greatly their ability to perform, and their success in class. Many students today are chronically sleep deprived, because they go to bed late and schools generally start early. Studies have shown that school starting times, especially for adolescents, influence cognitive development; sleepy children are not sharp. Schools with a starting time later than the traditional 7:30 or 8:00 a.m. have a significant increase in learner outcomes, and provide more options and a safer environment for students to get to school. Thus, the structure of the school day should also be changed. Students have reported that they feel better and teachers know that students are more alert with a later start. This does mean that students will be in school later in the day, but time can also be shaved off between classes, study halls, and lunch. Extending the school day also means fewer latchkey children. Peer pressure being what it is, unsupervised children get into far more trouble than those who are in the care of responsible adults, but they are less likely to get into trouble *before* school than after. A later start could significantly reduce some societal issues. Advocates of interscholastic programs and business owners will argue that a later dismissal time reduces extracurricular opportunities and takes away student income from after school jobs, and that may be true; but let us not forget why students are in school.

Students are in school to learn; but what about those who do not want to learn or feel that they have learned as much as they need to make a living in their adult lives. Compulsory schooling, a state law that requires a student to stay in school until a particular age, should be revisited with the idea of lowering the leaving age. One-to-three year community-based apprenticeship or vocational programs could transition students who do not want an extended high school education, and would rather enter into a meaningful employment-based program instead and earlier. The belief among many is that raising the compulsory education age would lower the dropout rate. That seemingly makes sense, but in reality there is little research supporting this policy.[7] Why do we have compulsory education laws? If it is to ensure an educated population, test scores suggest that the plan is not working. Many will say that we have compulsory education laws to keep students from becoming dropouts along with all the associated costs to society; but that is not working either. In reality, one of the main reasons for compulsory education is to keep juveniles off the streets. But 7,200 United States public school students drop out every day[8] so that isn't working either. So how would raising the compulsory education age affect the drop-out rate? A national study found no credible empirical evidence that raising the age to eighteen years will reduce dropouts.[9] The real reason that school districts lobby to raise the age of compulsory education is, of course, money. The longer a student remains in school the more money the district acquires from the state. School districts are big business.

It goes without saying that schools are most effective for students who desire to be educated, so forcing students to attend school because of truancy law requirements does nothing, either for them or for those around them. Enforcement of truancy laws results in criminalizing absent students, and in creating parental resentment since absent students are not criminals; they merely want to do things other than attend school. Moreover, if students do not want to be in the classroom, their attitude will impinge upon their own learning, and their negative behaviors will impact the classroom climate affecting, more often than not, the learning outcomes of their fellow students. When this happens, students' right to learn is violated. It is the teacher's responsibility to ensure an appropriate classroom climate, and there are few, if any, who are not frustrated with the disruptions caused by students who wish to be anywhere other than in school. Financial reasons should not trump meaningful learning and academic freedom. Compulsory education is an admirable societal goal, but not compulsory schooling.

If being a dropout has dire consequences, being labeled a dropout may be even worse. Students who leave school before they graduate from the twelfth grade are considered dropouts in most people's minds. The stigma of such a tag forces many into a life of crime or welfare, because they don't feel that they can achieve meaningful employment. And they are usually right. But what if they didn't dropout but rather were given options early on to leave or to stay in school? In Europe, once students have reached the minimum leaving age, usually 16, many simply do just that; they leave school. They do not carry with them the title of "dropout"; they move on to other endeavors that suit their needs such as vocational schools, apprenticeships, marriage, employment, or the military. There isn't a graduation. No one graduates from high school. Instantly, there are few, if any, dropouts and the stigma surrounding the label is eliminated! With the dropout problem either solved or rendered manageable, teachers, community leaders, and school administrators can turn their attention to the real reason for schools' existence, education.

To ensure that an educational program is appropriate for the student body, it is important to understand learning theory. Content knowledge is important, but it must be taught when it is developmentally appropriate to do so, or it can do more harm than good. Educationally, the most popular theorist of cognitive development is Jean Piaget. Piaget posits that the four stages of cognitive development are sensorimotor, pre-operational, concrete operational, and formal operational. The stages are hierarchal, in that each provides a foundation upon which the next, more complex level is developed. Learning activities should, therefore, be set at a level that is high enough to challenge the student's abilities, but not so high as to cause anxiety.[10] In light of Piaget's theories, there are also negative connotations surrounding formal learning in early childhood. Consequently, by sending very young children to a structured learning environment, we are shackling them by not allowing them to develop and learn through play, especially outside. More structured education is not better, and exposing young children to the expectations that they must learn to read and do mathematics when they should be outside playing is putting them at risk of developing emotional stress. There is no doubt that early childhood education is big business, but the benefits are over stated. Certainly, not all children are the same, and some benefit from early childhood programs, but that is true only if they are provided in appropriate environments and conducted properly; the primary benefit is, however, socialization.

Bruce Fuller, author of *Standardized Childhood: The Political and Cultural Struggle over Early Education* published in 2007, claims that a group of "born-again preschool advocates" are self-serving and seek to create a standards-driven, school-based preschool program that will maintain and privilege those who attend. Fuller fears that "leave no toddler behind" will standardize childhood to the point where parents and communities no longer have any influence over the early development and education of their children.[11] Undoubtedly, the primary concern of preschool programs should be to nurture the individual stages of early child development, so accelerating academic expectations before a child is developmentally ready is not only unnecessary, but counterproductive. Fuller argues that early childhood education must remain in the communities, and rooted in their cultural context. Furthermore, he says, a nurturing environment is best provided by parents and elders, and not by state certified college graduates from outside the area who will impose not only state standards, but cultural disinterest. The popular Waldorf Schools, founded by Rudolf Steiner, actually delay academics, including learning to read, until age seven. Steiner, agrees with many other educators, including child psychologist David Elkind, that over-emphasis on academics within early childhood education does not account for the wide range of individual differences in the development of children. Teaching reading and mathematics to children who are not cognitively ready to learn such concepts puts them at risk of emotional problems. Further, premature exposure to formal schooling puts children inside buildings and hence removes them from freer environments, including the outside world, where they could foster creativity and explore the wonders of nature.

Rudolph Steiner's early educational philosophy is aligned with Johann Pestalozzi's belief that any type of teaching is supposed to be for the betterment of students – not for the promotion and financial benefit of educational programs, including those of early childhood. A child's early education needs to come from the family first, and then from added socialization in informal settings with other children within small community settings. The standardization, professionalization, and commercialization of early childhood education, as we know it today, border on the abuse of children in the name of profit; this is sinful. So should most of the early childhood education programs that exist today be scrapped? Yes. After decades of a proliferation of programs and hype, there is scant research that shows they are achieving their claimed and advertised goals. Not only that; they have existed primarily throughout the time when learner outcomes have diminished. So a legitimate question must be, have early childhood programs, despite all the good intentions and expense, actually hurt children? That very well may be so. This is not, however, to say that programs should not exist. We understand that many parents enroll their young children into such programs because both parents are working, and they need to provide a safe environment for their children. For these children, parents must search for programs that focus on their cognitive development through play. For parents who are more able to spend time with their young children, a rapidly growing alternative to early childhood educational programs is Home Instruction for Parents of Preschool Youngsters (HIPPY). The federally approved HIPPY program has research support from the Harvard Family Research Project and the United States Department of Education among others. The organization's website provides extensive explanation and instructions on how parents, families, and communities can provide age appropriate home instruction for their three, four, and five year old children.[12] The beauty of the HIPPY program is not just that it has a well-established model, albeit not as well-known as the factory-based for-profit versions, but that its philosophical foundation is well established, simple, and usually free for participating parents and their children. There are some costs involved in setting up and running the program but, because the parents, with training and support, are the teachers, and the activities are generally conducted in the children's homes, these are far lower than those imposed by traditional early childhood programs.

Once educators and others who are engaged in supportive roles embrace the idea of a student-focused system from early childhood onward, reformers can turn their attention to creating the physical space needed to house and deliver programs.

COMMUNITY

Communities must be reflected in their schools. So it makes consummate sense for them to be operated by the community. This can be achieved through a site-based system comprised of parents, teachers, business owners, elders, and anyone else within the local area with an interest in the education of its children. Smaller schools cost less to operate than the behemoths to which we have become accustomed, because fewer personnel are needed to run them. The day-to-day administration of the schools would not be an oligarchy; but more likely a teacher-coordinator led consortium of educators supported by community-based staff. Community schools would solve many of the problems currently associated with the education system by offering mentors and role models to parents as well as to students, reducing student commuting time and expense, reducing the instances and effects of cultural alienation, and addressing environmental issues.

The physical locations of schools, especially high schools, would serve students best if they were inside the communities where their students live. Smaller high schools help to instill a sense of community (unlike the massive, open, prison-like structures many have become today). Federal Bureau of Investigation statistics since 1950 show serious crimes committed by children has increased 11,000%, and most crimes committed by males in the nation are perpetrated between the ages of 13–24. Schools and school schedules have contributed to this frightening trend.[13] There is no easy solution, but a good place to start is to ensure that all students have a mentor or role model in the school and community, especially if they live with only one parent or caregiver. For students who are missing either a male or female role model, school personnel can fill that void and help the young person grow under the influence of both sexes. Robert Bly states, "Women can change the embryo to a boy, but only men can change the boy to a man."[14]

A significant portion of our present day expense for public education is going to transportation because districts are now so large. Nationally in early 2010, over 120 mostly rural school districts had moved to a four-day school week because it reduced not only transportation costs, but also utilities costs, and part-time jobs.[15] Fewer bus drivers, fewer substitute teachers, fewer cafeteria workers, fewer custodial staff, and fewer general office support personnel do not mean fewer people to do more work, but instead full-time positions are created by combining the work load of two part-time employees which gives a now part-time worker a full-time position. Although research needs to be done on the academic and financial impact of four days a week schools, districts are reporting higher attendance and less need for substitute teachers. This is in part offset by longer school days. Unsurprisingly, Monday or Friday are the most popular days to cut, and a strong case can be made that given a choice, the more academically focused schools would opt for a Monday-Thursday school week. Regardless of the additional day cut, it is very important that it should not be considered a day off. On that day, partnering institutions, community education, community involvement, and local organizations and businesses should be a source for volunteering, mentorships, and apprenticeships, along with organized tutoring at on-campus locations. One of the advantages here is that outside agencies can be charged for using the location, thus helping to defray operational costs. The four-day school movement is economically driven and will reduce direct costs, but it will also increase daycare costs for working parents, and potentially have other unforeseen family and social consequences. It may, however, prove to be the only reasonable option for some rural schools.

All across the country and in every type of community, yellow school busses add to the morning and afternoon commutes as they transport millions of students to and from schools that are miles from their homes. Not only are these vehicles prohibitively expensive to run, they also pollute the atmosphere and risk students' health. Standing alongside a passing school bus, it is evident that its emissions are toxic, and it is only reasonable to imagine that because of the repetitive opening and closing of the school bus door, those emissions must find their way into the interior of the bus. Research should be done on the health of long-term bus riders versus students who do not ride buses. The time has come for the yellow dinosaur to become extinct. In urban areas, long school bus rides and forced integration need to become a thing of the past. Community schools will greatly reduce the need for gas-guzzling, air-polluting school transportation which is often a source of embarrassment to many students who are required to ride long distances and waste instruction or sleep time on the "Loser Cruisers," as school buses are often called by local non-riding students. When bus transportation is needed, it must keep the students safe. Thus, in the interest of student safety, all school busses must be fitted with restraint systems. As soon as possible, schools need to purchase hybrid vehicles which, in the long run, will reduce transportation costs and pollution. Indeed, the cost savings from cutting administration, bus transportation, and interscholastic sports will more than offset the costs of more neighborhood community schools.

The creation of neighborhood schools will result in a natural re-segregation of students who will learn by means of a curriculum and methodology that reflect their culture and community, and offer instruction by teachers and members from that same community. Forced integration across Independent School District (ISD) boundaries and busing (exceeded only perhaps by sex education) is the greatest educational reform failure. Modern society needs to be released from the burdensome and naïve belief that our schools should be integrated. Beverly Tatum's, *Can We Talk About Race? And Other Conversations in an Era of Resegregation*[16], and writings by other critical race theorists provide interesting and sound arguments that, despite good intentions, integration has many shortcomings. Large elementary schools and monolithic secondary schools built outside of the community force the integration of students and impose culture. These schools should be replaced with smaller neighborhood schools which will provide students with an increased sense of identity and place. Culturally distinct communities need be part of the educational equation—but schools can't save a community by themselves. The community must take responsibility for its schools and the education provided therein; it is not enough to talk and complain and wail about the injustices of the past. Communities must provide support for their schools and their students which extends well beyond rhetoric. As the saying goes, it may take a village to raise a child, but it takes a community to truly educate a child. Forced integration will always be counterproductive. It has been assumed that because the United States comprises an immigrant and diverse society, schools need to be a major assimilative agent. Historically there was a time when that may have been true, but with multimedia and the ease of travel, forced assimilation is no more necessary today than summer vacations to work on the family farm. Schools are not only too large but are designed to impede divergent and higher order thinking, and to exclude the community. Schools should have a *community commons* component where the educative process is shared with the neighborhood citizens. Everyone needs a geographic place where he or she can physically and also mentally go, and a community commons area serves that need. When possible this area should be outside, and when that is not feasible, schools should provide adequate natural lighting and living greenery. A recent study by the Nature Conservancy found that only two out of five American youths partake in outdoor activities.[17]

The environment in which a child is truly educated should not reflect the "factory schools" of the past; it should reflect all that is important to the values and future aspirations of the community. Yet even to question the cannon of school desegregation brings accusations of racism and elitism. Critical theorists in education have, however, spawned just such a critique of our present and failing system of schools with a growing number of researchers, academics, and civic leaders called *racialists*. Racialists recognize that there are differences among ethnic groups and in many instances these groups are best served within their own culture. The principles supporting racialism can be found in many of the best examples of ethnocentric charter schools across the nation, such as Chicago's Urban Prep Academy. A number of successful Afro-centric and tribal schools are serving their students and communities very well, and they could serve as exemplary models for community schools. One key purpose of any education is to transmit the cultural values of a society to its young. So education should be in harmony with the norms and desires of elders, teachers, and the community at large. Small homogeneous community cultures are not static, and change comes from both within and without their borders. Many educators have wondered about the past great success of the "one room school houses" all across America. Their success is attributed to a culturally-centered, community-based educational focus that used teachers, parents, older students and community elders to aid the learning process.

Many residential neighborhoods today, especially those in suburban areas, have little or no community spirit of cooperation, and those that do often lose their young adults to educational institutions and employment far from home. To reestablish proud communities and to encourage their young to stay, it will be necessary to help the next generation feel a connection to, and a responsibility for, their immediate surroundings. The most effective way of doing so is to integrate community elders into the educative process. There is no good reason why every classroom does not have community "elder teachers" to assist the professional teacher. We have an exceptionally highly educated generation retiring, yet most in retirement will be unable to use their skills and education. Relegating this very productive generation to the role of onlooker is a waste for the community, and a tragedy for the young.

A lack of community-based education has caused, and will continue to cause, cultural unrest and conflict. Among immigrant nations there is a long history of cultural imposition, forced assimilation, and the denial of a culturally based education for their young. Culturally distinct communities will naturally evolve and will remain healthy if they have good schools with good educators and role models.

To continue to have cultural wastelands, and dismal education available therein, is a danger to the whole country, and a waste of both human and financial resources.

It is not only cultural wastelands about which we need to worry. Increasing populations, a general apathy toward conservation, and global climate change are all contributing to an increasingly unnatural and unhealthy environment. Future schools must be constructed to foster community involvement and remodeling, and meet, or be striving to meet, the goal of certification of the United States Green Building Council Leadership in Energy and Environmental Design. This would demonstrate to students the importance of community in their lives, and the importance of conservation and ecology to their community. There should be a "Green Steward" in every school as too many of us, and virtually all of the younger generations, suffer from NDD (*nature-deficit disorder*), a term coined by Richard Louv, author of *Last Child in the Woods.* In this work, that has launched the international movement "Leave No Child Inside," Louv bemoans the increasing separation of children from the natural world. He writes:

> The postmodern notion that reality is only a construct—that we are what we program—suggests limitless human possibilities; but as the young spend less and less of their lives in natural surroundings, their senses narrow, physiologically and psychologically, and this reduces the richness of human experience.[18]

An educational focus on global and national economic interests must be balanced by environmental and social responsibility in the neighborhood "e-community." Environmental sciences courses should be related to the local environs and, besides energy conservation and recycling, should include organic gardening, and food and nutrition sciences. Indigenous science and an understanding of women's intuition also need to be part of the new curriculum. Community environmental awareness, along with intuition, will be particularly beneficial for healing local surroundings from ecological damage. All teachers need to be role models of sustainability and eco-stewards. But before that can happen we need to retrain our teachers, and change our teacher preparation programs, toward educating an environmentally literate citizenry as described by the North American Association for Environmental Education (NAAEE) thus:

- Fostering clear awareness of and concern about, economic, social, political and ecological interdependence in urban and rural areas.
- Providing every person with opportunities to acquire the knowledge, values, attitudes, commitment and skills needed to protect and improve the environment.
- Creating new patterns of behavior of individuals, groups and society as a whole towards the environment.[19]

Despite bitter rhetoric on both sides of the debate, most scientists now agree that human activity has greatly influenced global climate change. Yet in spite of warnings that the present rise in average global temperatures will cause undue stress to natural resources and disrupt the lives of many species including humans, it is not uncommon to hear people dismissing the phenomenon as a myth. Because much of the doubt is fueled by ignorance, it is imperative that the principles of conservation and ecology be integrated in all courses at all grade levels so that children learn to be stewards of the earth from the earliest age.

If we are to expect young people to care about the world, they must know about it. Thus, we must teach geography, not only to ensure that students recognize borders and understand concepts such as gross national product, but also to help them understand the earth and its living populations more fully, and to know the relationships between places, people, and natural resources. Geographic knowledge will also help students to know where they are and how to find their way in the world. Having a sense of place is a critical ingredient toward having a sense of community, both local and global; too many people in the United States, young and old, are comfortably wrapped in a cloak of isolationism. That may have been acceptable in the past, but now we must instill in our students a worldview that really does consider the needs and actions of *all* people. Few people today carry maps or, indeed, even know how to use them. The reason is most probably the modern reliance upon global positioning systems (GPS) to provide location then direction. All animals have an inherent sense of where they are, but that may not be true for contemporary humans. A map provides a visual picture of place and direction, but to read it intelligently a person must use his or her brain. On the other hand, by following the verbal or visual directions of a GPS machine, a person can travel from point A to point B without having to think or to understand map literacy. This unilateral reliance on technology for direction is certainly convenient in urban environments, but it can prove deadly in remote areas. Over the last fifteen years at least a dozen people have died in California's Death Valley following incorrect directions on their GPS.[20]

It is clear from our suggestions so far that changing the structure, control, and financing of schools is but a small part of the reform necessary to adequately prepare students for the rest of the 21st century; the current situation must be replaced by new disciplines and a new curriculum, such as the one defined by the NAAEE and outlined above. Programs for all students in K-12 education (and in universities for that matter) should have goal requirements that include both knowledge and skills in the area of environmental literacy. Education specialists Courtney Crim, Christine Moseley, and Blanche Desjean-Perrotta suggest that the key principles of environmental education should include "an understanding of systems, interdependence, the importance of where one lives, the integration and infusion of concepts across the curriculum, the use of real-world experiences for understanding, and the need for lifelong learning skills such as critical thinking and decision-making."[21] Learning gardens could play a substantial role in establishing a love of nature in young children. These areas should be actual gardens where children learn to plan, plant, and grow food cooperatively, which can then be shared with families and the community. Once students are competent in maintaining school gardens, they can be encouraged to take their skills to family and community gardens. These learning areas are not just gardens, but laboratories in which a variety of subjects are integrated to provide life-long lessons in sustainability and ecology.

TEACHERS

Teacher certification and licensing programs, and the accreditation agencies which have advocated "one size fits all" state and federal content standards, cannot meet the needs of community-based education. The establishment of community education will, therefore, necessitate profound change in teacher certification and licensing, which will give rise to resistance and rile those in higher education who run preservice teacher programs. Historically, these programs have been "cash cows," and few institutions will be willing to see them diminished without some type of battle. Despite state and federal regulations and increased standards, there are virtually no restrictions on the number of teachers a university can produce. Some state legislatures have come to realize that resident students, financially subsidized by virtue of being enrolled in state universities, are migrating to other places to find teaching positions. This is neither cost effective, nor a good use of state finances. These states have countered by increasing the requirements to become a teacher. Too many, however, still over-produce teachers who have little chance of finding relevant work. It is also a sad reality that a significant number of students go into interdisciplinary teaching programs because they are "undecided" and insecure about other majors, or are underprepared to specialize; can that ever be a good reason to teach?

There are also reasons why states and school districts not only allow, but actually want an over-production of teachers. The practice ensures a surplus of teachers, which in turn keeps teachers' salaries low. Teacher education programs must reduce intake to only the most qualified and dedicated students by increasing entry requirements and graduation standards. Education cannot improve unless those running the classrooms are of the highest quality, well remunerated, and excited to be there. Teachers' salaries should be set by the state, and adjusted for experience, performance, and cost of living. Many prefer their teachers to come from within the communities and, with state-determined compensation, teachers would be less likely to move away. This would reduce teacher retention problems in urban communities, and increase the quality of teachers in schools within low socio-economic communities. Numerous nationwide studies have concluded, not surprisingly, that teacher quality is critical to student learning. The Hoover Institute at Stanford University, for example, recently found that an "above average teacher" with 30 students will increase his or her students' collective earning by $430,000 a *year* above an "average teacher."[22] Despite the results of the Hoover Institute research, however, a recent two-year study of 90,000 teachers found that virtually no efforts were being made, especially by urban districts, to retain the top 20% of their teachers because they felt that they would just lose them anyway. This top

20% of teachers, which account for the best student outcomes on state examinations, were called "The Irreplaceables" by the study's researchers.[23] Many variables make a teacher "Irreplaceable," but experience and motivation are certainly two of the most important.

Student achievement needs to be *the* critical part of a teacher's performance evaluation. Many have criticized this as being too difficult and likely to foster bias, but these fears are not valid if proper diagnostic assessment is performed before instruction. Simply put, poor teachers need be dismissed, and above average and excellent teachers need to be paid significantly more to keep them in the profession. But money alone cannot solve education's woes. A federal grant was recently awarded that provides urban districts with funds to pay $10,000 "combat pay" to excellent veteran teachers to move to struggling minority schools. Excellent pedagogy will make a difference, but only if there are students. Similar programs have been tried with little result because, as any veteran teacher will attest, he or she can get results, but not if absenteeism is high. The problem goes back to families and communities who feel isolated from large urban schools, and to students who do not feel safe, and who believe that the educational experience is not relevant to their lives. Importing excellent teachers will treat the symptoms, but it will not cure the educational ills. Smaller neighborhood schools with highly qualified teachers from the community will be far more effective. These schools must also offer teachers enough support and respect that they would want to stay in the profession.

High levels of stress, low remuneration, difficult working conditions, and lack of respect are just some of the reasons that teachers give when they decide to leave the profession. Most teachers enter the field full of high hopes and excitement, but soon these emotions are replaced by frustration and weariness. It is understandable that difficult working conditions can cause health issues, but it is important to ensure that new teachers are physically and emotionally able to teach our young. Another area of concern that needs attention and research is the emotional intelligence and affect of all teachers. Effective teachers have healthy and positive dispositions. Personality inventories are required in virtually all social service professions except teaching, yet the strong lobby and influence of teacher organizations have stopped any meaningful assessment of a person's disposition to teach children. There are now criminal history background checks, but children are still entrusted to adults who may have significant mental health issues and personality disorders. Although there has been some research into the correlation between the existence of the dropout rate, and the low emotional intelligence of students, little has been done to investigate a possible correlation between the emotional intelligence level of students, and that of their teachers.[24] The emotional intelligence of *all* our teachers must be assessed and, with the large surplus that now exists, this might be the perfect time to undertake this task.

Teachers are often asked to cope with a far greater workload than is possible while still maintaining classroom standards. The same is true for areas of school discipline and program implementation. Thus, schools need also to be supplemented with, and supported by, the presence of community teachers; mentors or role models who are committed to the betterment of the community. Community teachers are a rich untapped human resource, from retirees to business people who will not only add a wealth of knowledge about the economic and social needs of the community, but also will be able to assist the certified classroom teacher. In every community there are many very successful older people who are wasting away from a poverty of purpose.

The teachers in a school can only be as successful as the administration allows. Schools that are poorly run, inadequately supplied, and that are not able to enforce attendance and disciplinary policy cannot expect high teacher performance. Unfortunately, many schools today have such unwieldy bureaucracies that the needs and the maintenance of the administration has become the primary focus (the all-too-familiar inverted pyramid). In cases like these, the schools decline, the teachers become disillusioned, and the students suffer. This is often the situation when schools are administered by large ISDs. For teachers to be allowed to do their job unencumbered, schools must offer a supportive administration, a curriculum that is relevant to the students and their future, and a student body in each classroom that well represents the overall level of talent in the community.

SCHOOLS

School districts need to be dismantled; they are hierarchical, laden with bureaucracy, beset with politics, too often vulnerable to mismanagement and less than honest operations and procedures. It used to be that school board members were frequently representatives from the business community dedicated to monitoring district costs. Too often today, however, school board members are there to ensure that lucrative contracts are awarded to family or friends; while district administrators, in concert with the school boards who have hired them, have created partnerships to ensure high administrative salaries and perks. Schools are being bled to death by parasitic businesses, programs, and systems whose owners are only involved to make money for themselves and their shareholders; these people have no real interest in the school or its students. Of course, there are many honest hard-working well-intended superintendents and school board members, but it is doubtful that there is a school district or tax payer in the United States that has not been victimized by some hegemonic relationships. The curriculum of a school should reflect the whole culture of the community, past, present, and future. Economic realities and businesses must also be part of the educative process, but corporate advertising and infringements upon curriculum as pay back need to be stopped. If a school does run out of money, the local community will be expected to find more. Moreover, if a school underperforms, it will hurt its own community. In that case, the state will have the option to stop funding, call for change and, if necessary, close the school. Schools are unlikely to fail, however, if they put their students first and create a curriculum that is relevant to them, their needs, and their aspirations.

More engaging community-centered and student-centered lessons will make for more student interest, more motivation to learn, and hopefully less disruption and absenteeism. There is a significant disconnect between student-centeredness, motivation, and relevance and present day content-driven public school instruction, and the greatest disconnect is within mathematics departments. There are some who believe that God can be discovered and the mysteries of the universe unraveled through mathematics. Very few people question the importance of mathematics education, and the mathematics pendulum has swung from Old Mathematics to New Mathematics and back again, but the real mystery is that after trying every mathematical method imaginable, pouring more money into mathematics curricula than any other discipline, and replacing more principals and teachers than most other programs, mathematics scores continue to fall. And when blame must be apportioned, whether justified or not, it more often than not is laid at the feet of the teachers.

In many regions of the nation high schools are historically grades 9–12, and dropout rates unfortunately can be linked more often to ineffective mathematics teaching than to any other subject. Data over several years in Texas clearly identify that most students who drop out do so in or around the 9th grade. Recent national figures identifying 8th grade mathematics scores as failing to improve correlates with, and helps to explain, this dropout statistic. Recent mathematics scores nationwide for 4th and 8th graders have not significantly changed even after the emphasis and threat of No Child Left Behind (NCLB). NCLB's goal of *all children* being proficient at grade level in mathematics by 2014 is laughable, and in no subject area is there greater disparity between whites and minority students. As of 2009, only four states showed improvements in mathematics scores.

The major factor impinging upon students learning any subject, and especially mathematics, is their ability to access prior knowledge. Mathematics is not necessarily complex, but what students are asked to learn is most often building on earlier content knowledge. Mathematics is hierarchical, and the combination of that together with the critical importance of prior knowledge means that just one poor teacher can set a student behind forever. A student can survive a bad teacher in a variety of subjects, but the results of a bad mathematics teacher are harder to overcome, because students then lack the prior knowledge necessary to move forward. If the vital foundation for the next year's mathematics instruction is missing, the students struggle. They come to fear and thus hate mathematics and, understandably, they begin to lose their confidence in other subjects knowing that success in school and graduation is dependent upon a mathematics standard. Secondary and middle school teachers tend to be blamed, but it is more accurate to say that far too many elementary teachers are products of a flawed certification or licensure system.

Many elementary teachers have simply scraped by in mathematics because they only have a procedural understanding and not a conceptual knowledge understanding of the subject. They then, because of their own lack of knowledge and confidence, hold their students back by not teaching methods that lead to a conceptual understanding, or by simply avoiding mathematics as much as possible. The use of calculators and computer games is not meaningful instruction and, consequently, too many students are mathematically challenged by the time they reach secondary level. It is also accurate to say that far too many high school minority students are taught by unqualified teachers without a degree in mathematics. Most states have allowed teachers who are already certified in one area to teach other courses with an emergency certification, which is often gained simply by the school principal calling the state and making the request. Initial certification comes with the clearance to teach only in that discipline, but after their probationary period many teachers are allowed to take the certification examination in other disciplines despite not having a degree in those areas. In the areas of mathematics and the sciences where there have been historical shortages of teachers, it is not unusual, especially in urban areas with very high minority populations, to learn that students are being taught mathematics and science by teachers who have no corresponding degrees.[25] In NCLB, a "highly qualified" status requires a degree in the content area, and grade level state certification. For a variety of reasons, many states have allowed teachers with other degrees such as English or history to teach in shortage areas (such as mathematics and science). Although an educator may be an excellent teacher of his or her own area of interest, teaching another subject, like mathematics, without a degree is far from ideal because a lack of content knowledge necessary to ensure student understanding much beyond a lower cognitive level is not probable. If we really want mathematics and science scores to increase nationwide, beyond the fourth grade, these subjects must be taught by teachers with appropriate qualifications.

Failure in mathematics is not only the greatest factor in the so-called 9th grade hump[26], but has also been identified as the biggest "logjam" in higher education, and a major reason why many students give up on their dream of a college degree. A staggering 27% of all college graduates nationwide have had to take non-credit remedial mathematics courses in college.[27] But before we throw all mathematics teachers under the bus, maybe we need to question the need for, and relevance of, mathematics in today's curriculum. Do we really need it? Radical as this may seem, people, such as Andrew Hacker who wrote a July 29, 2012 New York Times article entitled, *Is Algebra Necessary?* are now openly asking the same question. The article identifies mathematics curricula problems, and provides alternative solutions which fundamentally change how we think about mathematics. We are told that the subject is important not for the product but the process.[28] Doing mathematics certainly makes people smarter, but only if they learn to understand the process, and then use that process to solve mathematical problems. Using technology developed several thousand years ago: the abacus, Plato's students studied mathematics so that they could visualize and conceptually understand the problem-solving process. Texas, the home of Texas Instruments, apparently has had enough of low mathematics scores such that, stunningly, it has taken an important step by restricting calculators through much of elementary school.[29] Restricting calculators is an important start to looking at the problem surrounding the teaching of mathematics, but something is drastically wrong; so instead of another curriculum innovation, research is needed to determine when students first start to struggle and why.

There may, however, be a simpler solution to this dilemma. It is now known that the acquisition of a second language, and learning music develop the same part of the brain that is used in solving mathematical problems. Consequently, every student competent in language or music should also be competent in mathematics or any variation thereof. When this is not the case, the probable variable making it otherwise is the instruction. If the object of learning mathematics is primarily to make people smarter, and not necessarily the acquisition of mathematical proficiency itself, why not teach more language or music? There are calculators to cope with everyday arithmetic, and mathematically-trained professionals and software to solve more difficult questions, so why are all students required to demonstrate proficiency in mathematics? Music isn't compulsory beyond early elementary school, and second language requirements are usually only introduced in secondary school. As technological progress allows, and indeed often forces, people from all over the world to communicate across boundaries and cultures, surely a second language should be more widely promoted and expected. We propose that a second language be a required goal, and that mathematics be subject to the same scheduling as music; make them both required only in the early years of schooling. These innovations would go a long way toward taking the fear, one of the main obstacles to learning, out of mathematics for many students, and thus solve many associated problems. Furthermore, when mathematics and science are taught in the elementary schools, the instruction should again come from qualified teachers. Schools certainly need excellent elementary teachers who are good generalists for grades K-four, but students in grades five and six should be taught only by qualified teachers with degrees in the subjects being taught. All programs, including mathematics and science, would also gain from having students of all abilities included in main classroom teaching sessions.

Compensatory education and pullout programs are often associated with special education and Talented and Gifted (TAG) programs. In pullout programs, students in as early as the first grade are taken out of the regular classroom for either remediation or enriched activities. Despite the purpose and the great expense, research does not overly embrace this educational practice. It does, however, offer significant benefit for the inclusive student, despite growing concerns about inclusion practices. The point of the practice of inclusion, initially known as mainstreaming, is to provide a normal classroom experience mostly to cognitively and physically disabled students. But what is a normal classroom? Because it is not unusual to have more than one inclusive student in the classroom, the regular classroom teacher and the special education teacher or aid often sit the inclusive students close together for convenience. By doing this, they create de-facto segregation within the regular classroom, which is not in the spirit of the least restrictive environment which is to be provided to the inclusive student. Moreover, when inclusive students are added to the classroom and the talented and gifted are pulled out, it no longer is a normal classroom. Students of all abilities should be able to benefit from dialogue and cooperative grouping activities. The increased population of students with disabilities, and the legal requirement of inclusion programs, have resulted in nearly seventy-five percent of students with disabilities now being within the regular classroom. It is easy to see the benefit of a normal classroom for such students but, given this profound increase over the last few decades, one must question the educational cost to other students.[30] The addition of inclusive students can often cause confusion and disruption in the classroom and may force the teacher to focus primarily on basic content knowledge for lower achieving students, thus denying all students the opportunity to learn more conceptual and abstract thinking skills. Responding to the above concern, Title I programs funded by the United States Department of Education, which focus on improving the academic achievement of all disadvantaged children, now favor eliminating pullout programs in schools. Increased learner outcomes, including cognitive diversity, are best facilitated in a heterogeneous classroom. The reality is, however, that TAG programs are basically providing white students with an educational haven away from low achieving, inclusive, low socio-economic status, minority students. TAG programs often employ the best and most qualified teachers to bring critical and higher order thinking skills to the most talented students earlier and more frequently than regular classroom students; in essence, they are thinly veiled forms of segregation, and that is precisely why they were developed in the first place.

To be more effective, inclusive classrooms need to be small – smaller than the average regular education classroom, yet more often the reverse is true. In addition, educators need more training to develop the special skill set needed to serve special needs children. Schools and their communities need to demonstrate the same dedication and commitment to serving special education students as do their classroom teachers. It is more often the case, however, that regular classroom teachers are left to fend for themselves, and to cope with increasing inclusion class populations without sufficient training and good support. Recent research by the Texas Education Agency found that of the students who receive in-school or out-of-school suspension, special education students represent the highest or close to the highest of every disciplinary action.[31] These statistics lead to a questioning of the types of students who are being labeled "special education."

Inclusion practices and TAG programs are, of course, politically charged issues, with many legal and parent groups fighting to sustain, and even to enhance, them throughout public schools. But the big loser in all of this may be the so-called average student, as the law as it now stands requires accommodation only for the special needs and the privileged cadres. What we should be asking and researching is how much attention and resources are being diverted from average students who want only to behave and learn, but too often find themselves ignored by overstretched teachers and distracted by disruptive students. Moreover, what is the collateral damage of removing better students from the classroom? Isn't it reasonable to suggest that it lowers the overall cognitive level of the classroom? If an inclusive student benefits from a regular classroom of average students, how can culling the brightest students fail to harm the average student? If we have inclusive students in the classroom, we should not allow other students to be pulled out because, when we do, it causes a general cognitive imbalance and a slowing down of instruction. To be fair, more research is needed on the ways that inclusive students in the classroom affect the speed of instruction and the learning outcomes of all students. There can be little doubt about the socialization benefits for all students in inclusive settings, but few researchers dare address the nagging suspicion that special education students in regular classrooms limit progress for other students. It is only right and fair that schools should adhere to the legal requirement to provide a least restrictive environment (LRE) for students with disability, but this type of accommodation should not be at the educational expense of other students.

It is important to point out that, while education authorities boast about inclusive practices, the gifted and talented are deliberately excluded and placed in their own *special* environment. Clearly, both practices place the "normal' classroom and school ratios in disequilibrium. Political correctness should never be allowed to trump the educational needs of students. At one time it was thought that forced busing was good, and laws were created to enforce it. The practice did not work. Serious studies need to be conducted by non-vested researchers to determine if inclusive students are negatively impacting the learning outcomes of other students within the regular classroom. If that is determined to be the case, then this practice must stop. Similarly, TAG students need to be accommodated within the regular classroom, and the programs and practices that take them out should be abolished. While educational researchers often disagree about ways to combat the decline of the public school system, most do agree that for inclusion to be more successful, schools must be restructured.[32]

Alternative education programs (not so much pullout, but rather pushout programs) are popular among school districts because they cost little to maintain, and bring in additional funding per student from federal and state sources. These additional sources of money pad the district's general funds, so they are unlikely to be voluntarily closed down. Of course, they also allow districts to remove disruptive students from regular classrooms. But Disciplinary Alternative Education Programs (DAEPs) are a reform nightmare. Alternative programs are not effective and have evolved from the old GED curriculum into little more than tracking that segregates mostly minority, troublesome students from the general population.[33] In too many cities they have, in essence, become induction centers for gangs. Smaller community schools, and a strong community presence, will be more successful in putting these students back into the regular classroom where they belong. Teachers need to be made more responsible for the learning climate within their classrooms, but that will require better classroom management skills, effective discipline, promulgated consequences for student misbehavior, and real and reliable support. Community leadership teams need to support effective teachers by removing disruptive students from the privilege of attending school. If these students, after a reasonable period, wish to be readmitted, they should be allowed to do so, but only once. If they reoffend and disrupt the learning of other students, they should be expelled permanently. If they wish to continue their education, they may do so by other means; distance education might be a possibility in this instance. Keeping continually disruptive students in school, placing them all together in one program, and then calling it education is a waste of money and resources. DEAPs need be eliminated and replaced with more effective methods of either rehabilitating disruptive students who wish to reform their behavior, or providing other programs that allow students to continue their studies isolated both from the students they have harmed and other offenders.

It is not, however, only disruptive students who might make use of distance education. As gated communities expand and increase in number, neighborhood community-based education could, via virtual delivery systems, become a viable alternative and eventually the norm. Virtual colleges and universities are well established; less known, however, is the proliferation of virtual K-12 education. Virtual high schools are providing the same conveniences that distance higher education has, such as attending classes at the student's own pace in his or her own home, reducing formal vacation time, and often accelerating the accumulation of credits leading to early leaving (graduation), and duel credit. In addition, the virtual student would not face transportation costs and would not be physically fearful of the public school environment. Florida Virtual School is such a program, which provides fully accredited K-12 courses via computer, telephone, and video delivery systems that can be transferred into a student's regular school program. The spread of virtual courses has expanded over the last several years to the point that 70% of all public school districts in the United States are providing some form of distance learning; such virtual schools and courses have grown by 40% in the last three years.[34]

Online education does not require bricks and mortar or buses. What it does require, however, is an exceptionally reliable and efficient delivery system. It is difficult right now to envision how elementary schooling could be delivered online, but research in every aspect of distance learning is underway, and if it can be done successfully, someone will produce the evidence, the curriculum, and the expected results. Private preparatory online high schools have sprung up in recent years, but they are perhaps too new to assess their effectiveness. Clearly, however, they will not provide one of the original articulated purposes of public schools; that is assimilation through compulsory socialization. Distance education has been around for a long while, and has been successful, using the technology of the time, including telephones, live television and radio broadcasts, and, in times past, the postal service, for submitting assignments and receiving feedback. Modern technology is continually improving both student and teacher experience of distance education, and there is a wealth of ongoing research into incorporating learning styles, creating communities of online learners, increasing levels of student satisfaction, and retention.[35] Perhaps the physical school will no longer be the norm; instead students will attend a virtual school and learn via avatars. This may seem futuristic and not plausible, but online environments are already offering real alternatives to the traditional bricks and mortar schools. Online options for an increasingly technology competent population, spiraling costs of public education, transportation costs and availability, and environmental factors, together with chronic dissatisfaction with the present system all combine to suggest that this will become a reality sooner rather than later.

Regardless, however, of where a student attends school, the when must be longer than it is right now. The school year must be lengthened radically to a year-round format favored by many other countries. Up to a third of the start of any school year is spent re-teaching. Further, schools can start by actually teaching on Fridays. Friday should be like Tuesday and Wednesday, it should not be a pep rally, a travel day, a resource day, a T-shirt day, or a jeans day for teachers. The last week of the school year and the day or so before every holiday are beset with disruptions and a festive atmosphere, and somehow this attitude and the resulting behavior has extended beyond Fridays to often include Thursday. Mondays are often considered sleepy with low expectations, so that leaves Tuesdays and Wednesdays for teaching and learning. Perhaps the above is an exaggeration but there are many high schools on this schedule.

Some schools, especially those with overcrowding issues, have gone to a 45/15 school year which comprises nine weeks of classwork followed by three weeks off with a break during all four seasons, and no single long break during the summer. The 45/15 is the most popular of the proffered alternative schedules, and although the school year is not actually longer, it provides students with the option of attending school all year round, and the authorities the ability to accommodate more students within a year. To actually lengthen the school year, a 45/10 would surely increase learners' outcomes and diminish summer decay. This could be achieved by having more than just the traditional single tract where all students and teachers are either in school or on vacation at the same time. Having three to five tracks allows an equal number of students in each track. For example, in a four-track model, three tracks are always in school while another track is always on break. A year-round calendar is used. A high school that only has room for 1,000 students can now accommodate 1,333 so increasing its yearly enrollment by 33%. Students have an option to accelerate their credit acquisition, and teachers have the option to teach and earn more over the year by not taking so many holidays. Although there are variations of these plans, the disadvantage is problematic scheduling, possible increased transportation costs, and higher utility bills. But solutions to these difficulties must be sought, and the tail should not wag the dog. The best way to lengthen the school year is to go to a variation of a trimester system, which is popular in higher education. Other options are Saturday school, half day Saturday school, and online or hybrid courses. If as a nation we are serious about increasing learner outcomes, the school year must be lengthened and technology must be employed to make the curriculum as flexible as possible.

Technology, information, and content knowledge will never replace wisdom. Today's curriculum standards place significant emphasis not just on increased literacy, but also on the development of Information Technology (IT) as a means to economic growth. Educators are pressured into integrating technology into all areas of the curriculum, with upgrades touted with evangelical fervor. The Governor of Texas, Rick Perry, recently called for abandoning textbooks in public schools, and replacing them with computer technology. Recognizing the digital divide as a problem, Perry suggested that parents who do not have computer access at home need to purchase it.[36] His proposal was announced during a computer conference in Austin, the silicon valley of Texas. Presently teachers (and university and college professors) who do not attend the latest district or institutional IT workshops on the recent upgrade of some new software, are often condemned as "not part of the team" or considered Luddites. (Luddites were members of a 19th century movement where English workers destroyed technology as a resistance statement to new machinery that improved work efficiency but often adversely affected working conditions.) Yet districts and universities rarely supply the support necessary to either sustain technology for daily use, or respond in a timely manner when the technology breaks down or help is needed. The solution too often has been to purchase the next supposedly more user-friendly upgrade. Lost within the technology race and furor is the reality that there is little research showing that technology used in schools is actually helping students, especially female and minority students.[37] Computer technology is characterized by the Command-Control-Communication-Intelligence (C3I) Model developed at the height of the Cold War for military application. It was developed by males to be used by males for a specific application. The IT world today is still dominated by males in both hardware and software development, so how confident can we be that the curriculum, delivery, and content will not be any less male-centric than when it was first developed? The students and teacher should be the focus. IT and cyberspace are means of support and nothing more.

SUMMARY AND CONCLUSION

The student-focused approach to education that we have outlined above will not be easy to introduce, but it will, we believe, be worth the effort despite the pain. Naturally, some of the changes will be more easily implemented than others, so a thoroughly-planned process with a realistic timeline will be vital to a successful transformation. One of the first and easiest changes should be the selection, training, and placement of teachers. Today's schools by their very nature and structure, perpetuate inherent disadvantages faced by low social economic status children. Nationwide, the teaching profession comprises predominately white, English-speaking, middle class, suburban females, while the student population increasingly is minority, of low social economic status, and with formal and informal language issues. There is no inherent problem with teachers being significantly different from the students they teach, nor should there be, but it is understandable and reasonable to expect that students will learn better when they can relate to their teacher, thus creating a sense of ancestral connectivity that increases learning potential. Additionally, if teachers live within the same community as their students, so much the better. Hence, we need programs that recruit and retain minority teachers, and especially males, to all school programs and at all levels. Yet while teaching continues to be considered by many to be a vocation and not a profession, and as such, poorly compensated, it will be virtually impossible to compete with higher paying employment opportunities in industry and business. The standard argument is that teachers have long holidays, so it is right that they earn less money that those who work for 48–50 weeks a year does not fly; time off does not put food on the table. Many teachers are forced into minimum wage, menial work during the summer just to make ends meet. This does nothing to attract good students into the profession, and so the downward spiral of low salary/ low expectations/low standards is perpetuated. Once salaries are corrected, it will be time to turn toward expectations. These are two-fold; teachers' expectations of the job, and the people's expectations of the teachers. Some of the former are clear and have been discussed earlier; fair remuneration, high levels of support, and good work conditions, but we would add to that, classrooms with a good balance of students (TAG students are not separated), superior training, and respect. The best students will think about teaching if they feel that they will be part of a respected profession, be fairly compensated, and be supported by an administration that is student-oriented instead of self-absorbed.

It is clear that physical schools cannot be torn down and rebuilt overnight, but with good planning and forethought, new schools can be built to accommodate the new system while older schools transform their student body, teacher cadre, and administration through planned attrition. As student classes graduate or move on to the next stage of their lives, they should be replaced by students who are connected to the community in which the school is located. Retiring teachers should be replaced by local teachers who have been qualified under new teacher education guidelines, and administration responsibilities could be gradually handed over to community leaders and community-based professional educators. Curriculum reform should also be introduced as new classes of students enter the system.

People will ask if it is even possible to create this type of conceptual learning framework for our young people, which will allow them to gain the skills needed for success in society while at the same time nurturing their relationship with their families, culture, and community. The "At-Promise" model, which was first introduced by the Intercultural Development Research Association (IDRA) in 2000, already offers such a framework, but while the concept is sound, the support it has received has rendered it impotent. It is time for educators to help with the process of implementing At-Promise, but this time, communities and their leaders must add their voices, their money, their commitment, and their physical effort to ensure its success. If the will is there to make the necessary changes, the new schools and their new teachers, community members, and elders, can provide both excellent human resources and local education that reflect community values and local knowledge.

Howard Gardner's book, *Five Minds for the Future*[38], states that in today's super-connected world, education should be disciplined, synthesized, creative, respectful, and ethical. Further, he claims that in order for the planet to survive, these mental dispositions need to be actively taught in schools in order to be inculcated into society. These dispositions align closely with the concept of community-based education, and with the IDRA's published commitment to educational reform for the benefit of the students, their communities, and society at large. One IDRA article, *Development Through Engagement: Valuing the "At-Promise" Community*, includes international leader and educational visionary Peter Benson's description of an multi-point framework that would gather the necessary community assets to create an effective educational model. The points are:

- Support
- Empowerment
- Boundaries
- Expectations
- Constructive use of time
- Commitment to learning
- Positive values
- Social competence
- Positive identity

This type of framework can only work, however, if the people in the community have control over their own lives, value their community, have high expectations for everyone, including their young people, and do all that they can to promote student success, by working together with integrity and dignity.[39]

Of critical importance to the success of this, or any other educational concept, is an understanding and promulgation of student expectation. Low expectations beget poor results. It is time to expect the best effort from all students regardless of cultural or socio-economic background. For too long expectations of performance have been biased by culture and economic status, and that practice must stop. Of course, not every student can excel, but imposing high expectations for effort and diligence on all students will ensure that everyone has the potential to make the most of their diverse talents.

Many of the ideas that we have proffered in this book will probably be dismissed as interesting but impractical to implement. But we suggest that there is no time to waste. The education system in its present state is not only ineffectual; it is harmful, and the planet is in peril because of human-induced forces, and apathy. Students must be taught to care about themselves, their society, and the global implications of their actions. They must be given, through education, the knowledge to demonstrate care in practical terms, and they must also see their role in their community and beyond as meaningful and necessary. Students can and will do all that their community members expect of them, but that will only be the cure if those expectations are targeted in a way that will encourage them to aim high. The young people of today have the potential to do great things, but we must look at them as individuals with differing learning styles, aspirations, and talents. Each and every one of them must also know that he or she matters. Let us move away from concentrating our educational efforts on one tiny part of the brain of one tiny part of the population. Let us look back to the educational models of indigenous people who educated their young to be fully functional members of their community. No-one was deemed useless or less worthy of training; everyone had his or her place and his or her role. Now it is time for us to show our young people that we believe in the same for them; the contributions of all people from all cultures must be integrated into an educational process that places a high value, not only on personal success, but also on the health of the environment, and the wellbeing of all living things.

NOTES

PREFACE

[1] The No Child Left Behind Act was an initiative of the Clinton administration and became a key issue of the George W. Bush administration's education policy.

CHAPTER 1: INTRODUCTION

[1] James Redfield's *The Celestine Prophecy* is a 1993 novel that discusses psychological and spiritual ideas that are rooted in far eastern religion. The main character of the novel undertakes a journey throughout Peru to find and understand a series of nine spiritual insights, and that synchronicity is much more meaningful than we understand. The book is a first-person narrative that results in a spiritual awakening.

[2] Carlos Castaneda's work detailing the lifestyle and philosophy of shamanism earned him a bachelor's degree and a PhD from the University of California at Los Angeles. Later, however, his work was discredited by conventional anthropologists who considered him to be more of a talented literary writer who had created a fictional, magical world with an indigenous flavor, than a research anthropologist. Castaneda wrote many books dealing with the paranormal including the psychic effects of the drugs peyote and datura. His books have sold many millions of copies and have been translated into several languages.

[3] Colin Wilson is a prolific British writer best known for his book, *The Outsider* (1956). Wilson claims that "Outsiders" are people who possess knowledge beyond the mainstream, but society and universities shun them, and "Outsiders" in turn fail to contribute their potential to the evolution of society. Wilson also contends that one's *peak experiences* offer a short glimpse of the wonder of the real world and its potential for all humans and society. Wilson believes that humans are defeatists because the human mind tricks people into under performance by *blinkering*, shrouding reality because it is too intense and wondrous.

[4] Redfield, J. (1993). *The celestine prophecy*. New York: Warner Books.

[5] Redfield, J. "Celestine vision: James Redfield and the celestine prophecy movie," Retrieved from http://www.celestinevision.com

[6] Castaneda, C. (1968). *The teachings of Don Juan: A Yaqui way of knowledge*. New York: Pocket Books.

[7] Wilson, C. (1969). *The philosopher's stone*. New York: Warner Books.

[8] Toor, R. (2007, September 14)). The care and feeding of the reader. *The Chronicle of Higher Education* 54(3), C2.

[9] Toor, R. (2007, September 14)). The care and feeding of the reader. *The Chronicle of Higher Education* 54(3), C2.

[10] Toor, R. (2007, September 14)). The care and feeding of the reader. *The Chronicle of Higher Education* 54(3), C2.

[11] The term *highly qualified* is part of the NCLB and basically requires that all K-12 classroom teachers have a degree and certification and are teaching in that subject only. Many U.S. teachers are teaching subjects that they neither have a degree nor original certification in. It is estimated that over half of all inner city math and science teachers do not have a degree in math or science.

[12] "Crabs in the bucket" syndrome describes the process in which peer pressure prevents talented, highly motivated students from reaching their potential. When crabs are placed in a bucket there is no need for a lid – the crabs will continually pull each other down so that none can climb out of the bucket.

CHAPTER 2: INDIGENOUS WAYS OF KNOWING

1. The Mashco-Piro is one of the few remaining non-contact tribes of nomadic indigenous hunter-gatherers who inhabit remote regions of the Amazon rainforest.

2. The Sng'oi are members of the Orang Ali (original people) of Malaysia.

3. Bushmen, or San (because they do not have a collective name for themselves, both terms have been imposed by outsiders) were traditionally hunters and gatherers ranging across the Kalahari Desert. Because they are believed to be the oldest extant cultural group, they are of considerable interest to anthropologists.

4. Lama, A. (2005, April 16). "'Transitory' reserves for Mashco-Piro Indians," Tierrámerica, under "Accents." Retrieved from http://www.tierramerica.org/2005/0416/iacentos.shtml. The Mashco-Piro live in voluntary isolation from Western-style civilization in the Amazon jungle. Their very existence is threatened by loggers who encroach upon their territory, and who bring them into contact with diseases against which they have no defense.

5. Established in 2004, Alto Purús is the largest national park in Peru.

6. Linda Lema Tucker is a sociologist who has worked as a consultant with the Peruvian National Commission of Aboriginal People. The statement is quoted from Abraham Lama's article (see note 4 above).

7. Cevallos, D. (2003, June 30). Isolated indigenous groups face extinction. Tierrámerica. Retrieved from http://www.tierramerica.net/english/2003/0630/iarticulo.shtml

8. Cevallos, D. (2003, June 30). Isolated indigenous groups face extinction. Tierrámerica. Retrieved from http://www.tierramerica.net/english/2003/0630/iarticulo.shtml

9. Hill, D. (2012, January 19). Amazon 'uncontacted' tribes at risk from new highway plan. *The Ecologist* Retrieved from http://www.theecologist.org/News/news_analysis/1202915/amazon uncontacted_tribes_at_risk_from_new_highway_plan.html

10. Malone, A., & McConnell, A. (Writers), & Maybury-Lewis, D. (host). (1992). *The shock of the other/ strange relations, pt. 1 of Millennium: Tribal Wisdom and the Modern World*, VHS, Los Angeles, CA: PBS Home Video.

11. Malone, A., & McConnell, A. (Writers), & Maybury-Lewis, D. (host). (1992). *The shock of the other/ strange relations, pt. 1 of Millennium: Tribal Wisdom and the Modern World*, VHS, Los Angeles, CA: PBS Home Video.

12. Malone, A., & McConnell, A. (Writers), & Maybury-Lewis, D. (host). (1992). *The shock of the other/ strange relations, pt. 1 of Millennium: Tribal Wisdom and the Modern World*, VHS, Los Angeles, CA: PBS Home Video.

13. Malone, A., & McConnell, A. (Writers), & Maybury-Lewis, D. (host). (1992). *The shock of the other/ strange relations, pt. 1 of Millennium: Tribal Wisdom and the Modern World*, VHS, Los Angeles, CA: PBS Home Video.

14. Wolff, R. (2001). Original wisdom: Stories of an ancient way of knowing. Rochester, VT: Inner Traditions, p. 119.

15. Wolff, R. (2001). Original wisdom: Stories of an ancient way of knowing. Rochester, VT: Inner Traditions, p. 88.

16. Redfield, J. (1997). The celestine vision: Living the new spiritual awareness. New York: Warner Books, p. 130.

17. Wolff, R. (2001). *Original wisdom: Stories of an ancient way of knowing*. Rochester, VT: Inner Traditions, p. 197.

18. Membrane or m theory is an extension of string theory. M theory mathematically predicts that multiple parallel dimensions exist, but science at this time lacks the technology to demonstrate the unique duality of the theory.

19. Hawking, S. W. Glossary, Stephen W. Hawking. Retrieved from http://ww w.hawking.org.uk/ index.php/glossary

20. Wolff, R. (2001). Original wisdom: Stories of an ancient way of knowing. Rochester, VT: Inner Traditions, p. 176.

21. Laurens van der Post was a widely respected writer, broadcaster, and conservationist who introduced many readers to the Bushmen of the Kalahari.

22. Van der Post, L. (1986). *The lost world of the Kalahari*. San Diego: Harcourt Brace. (Original work published 1958), p. 225.

23. Van der Post, L. (1986). *The lost world of the Kalahari*. San Diego: Harcourt Brace. (Original work published 1958), p. 6.

24. Van der Post, L. (1986). *The lost world of the Kalahari*. San Diego: Harcourt Brace. (Original work published 1958), p. 10.

25. Van der Post, L. (1986). *The lost world of the Kalahari*. San Diego: Harcourt Brace. (Original work published 1958), pp. 14–15.

26. Van der Post, L. (1986). *The lost world of the Kalahari*. San Diego: Harcourt Brace. (Original work published 1958), p. 15.

27. Van der Post, L. (1986). *The lost world of the Kalahari*. San Diego: Harcourt Brace. (Original work published 1958), p. 26.

28. Van der Post, L. (1986). *The lost world of the Kalahari*. San Diego: Harcourt Brace. (Original work published 1958), pp. 29–30.

29. Van der Post, L. (1986). *The lost world of the Kalahari*. San Diego: Harcourt Brace. (Original work published 1958), p. 19.

30. Isaacson, R. (2001). *The healing land*. New York: Grove Press. p. 38.

31. Isaacson, R. (2001). *The healing land*. New York: Grove Press. p. 274.

32. Van der Post, L. (1986). *The lost world of the Kalahari*. San Diego: Harcourt Brace. (Original work published 1958), p. 269.

33. To be Eurocentric is to focus consciously or unconsciously one's worldview toward Europe and European people and to favor this interpretation over all other countries, cultures, and people.

34. To fully understand cosmology requires running down rabbit holes full of metaphysical cobwebs. For the purposes of this text, however, think of cosmology as the study of individual's beliefs about nature and the order of the universe. People's upbringing provides a conceptual framework of the universe and their place within it, which is determined by exposure to culture, religion and education.

35. Van der Post, L. (1986). *The lost world of the Kalahari*. San Diego: Harcourt Brace. (Original work published 1958), p. 65.

36. Van der Post, L. (1986). *The lost world of the Kalahari*. San Diego: Harcourt Brace. (Original work published 1958), p. 23.

37. Yanko, D. (2010, November 4). Visions on rock. *Virtual Saskatchewan*, Retrieved from http://www.virtualsk.com/current_issue/visions_on_rock.html. For more information about Tim Jones and his work, see his 1981 book Aboriginal rock paintings of Churchill River. Saskatchewan Department of Culture and Youth.

38. See Preamble to Chapter 1.

39. Kafka, F. (1933). Investigations of a dog. *In The Great Wall of China and Other Pieces*. London: Morrison & Gibb. p. 22.

40. Jewish Publication Society. (1985). Genesis, Tanakh: The Holy Scriptures. Quoted in Abram, D. (1996). *The spell of the sensuous: Perception and language in a more-than-human world*. New York: Vintage Books, p. 94. Abram states that this quote is from the traditional Hebrew text, the Tanakh: The Holy Scriptures.

41. Jewish Publication Society. (1985). Genesis, Tanakh: The Holy Scriptures. Quoted in Abram, D. (1996). *The spell of the sensuous: Perception and language in a more-than-human world*. New York: Vintage Books, pp. 94–95.

42. Hegemony exists when a dominant group or groups exert excessive power, most often political and economic, within a society. Historically, it was and still is common that these powerful groups join forces to achieve even greater influence and privilege. In Western civilization, religion and royalty have frequently forged such a partnership. A religious and political alliance is often referred to as a priest-king hegemony.

43. Rasmussen, K. (1975). Magic words. In E. Field (Trans. and Ed.), *Eskimo songs and stories*. Cambridge: Delcorte Press/Seymour Lawrence, pp.7–8.

CHAPTER 3: THE ROLE OF INTUITION

1. Misra, N. (2005, January 4). Stone Age Cultures Survive Tsunami Waves: Indian Islanders Apparently Heeded Ancient Lore, *Associated Press*. Retrieved from http://www.msnbc.msn.com/id/6786476/ns/world_news-tsunami_a_year_later/

2. Misra, N. (2005, January 4). Stone Age Cultures Survive Tsunami Waves: Indian Islanders Apparently Heeded Ancient Lore, *Associated Press*. Retrieved from http://www.msnbc.msn.com/id/6786476/ns/world_news-tsunami_a_year_later/

3. Belkora, L. (2005). Steering by the Stars. *StarDate* 33(4) p.16.

4. Belkora, L. (2005). Steering by the Stars. *StarDate* 33(4) p.16.

5. Belkora, L. (2005). Steering by the Stars. *StarDate* 33(4) p.18.

6. Belkora, L. (2005). Steering by the Stars. *StarDate* 33(4) p.18.

7. Belkora, L. (2005). Steering by the Stars. *StarDate* 33(4) p.19.

8. Radio New Zealand International. (2010 July 14). Legendary FSM Master Navigator Dies. Retrieved from http://www.rnzi.com/pages/news.php?op=read&id=54698

9. Polynesian Voyaging Society promulgates information on its website http://hokulea.org/. It also has a presence on Facebook and Twitter.

10. Sabine, C. (2005 January 6). Senses Helped Animals Survive the Tsunami: Few Carcasses Turning Up in Affected Region, *NBC Nightly News*. Retrieved from http://www.msnbc.msn.com /id/6795562/#.UDJ1A7_CKes

11. Mott, M. (2005 January 4). Did Animals Sense Tsunami Was Coming? *National Geographic News*. Retrieved from http://news.nationalgeographic.com/news/ 2005/01/0104_050104_tsunami_animals.html

12. Mott, M. (2005 January 4). Did Animals Sense Tsunami Was Coming? *National Geographic News*. Retrieved from http://news.nationalgeographic.com/news/ 2005/01/0104_050104_tsunami_animals.html

13. 1 Ecc. 7:26 (King James Bible)

14. Menahoth 43b-44a. Other translations of this prayer vary and have changed over time. This version is as true to the original as can be found.

15. 1 Tim. 2:11–14 (New Testament) (King James Bible).

16. Prov. 8:22–31 (King James Bible).

17. www. malleusmaleficarum.org

18. www. malleusmaleficarum.org

19. Ahmed, L. (1992). *Women and gender in Islam: Historical roots of a modern debate*. New Haven: Yale University Press, p. 29.

20. Ahmed, L. (1992). *Women and gender in Islam: Historical roots of a modern debate*. New Haven: Yale University Press, p. 33.

21. Brown, E. (2003). An intimate spectator: Jewish women reflect on adult study. *Religious Education* 98(1), p. 66.

22. Heller, R. T. Men & women: A Jewish view on gender differences. *Judaism Online*. Retrieved from http://www.simpletoremember.com/articles/a/jewish-view-on-gender-differences

23. McGivern, R.F., Mutter, K. L., Anderson, J., Wideman, G., Bodnar, M., Huston, P. J. (1998, August). Gender differences in incidental learning and visual recognition memory: Support for sex difference in unconscious environmental awareness. *Personality and Individual Differences* 25(2), p. 231.

24. McGivern, R.F., Mutter, K. L., Anderson, J., Wideman, G., Bodnar, M., Huston, P. J. (1998, August). Gender differences in incidental learning and visual recognition memory: Support for sex difference in unconscious environmental awareness. *Personality and Individual Differences* 25(2), p. 224.

25. Pomeroy, S. B. (1975). *Goddesses, whores, wives, and slaves: Women in classical antiquity*. New York: Schocken Books, p. 2.

26. Aristotle. (1946). *The politics of Aristotle*. E. Barker (trans. and ed.). Oxford: Oxford University Press, p. 130.

27. Aristotle. (1984). *Generations of animals*. J. Barnes (Ed.). Princeton: Princeton University Press, p. 1199.

28. Gilligan, C., & Attanucci, J. (1988, July). Two moral orientations: Gender differences and similarities, *Merrill-Palmer Quarterly* 34(3), p. 233.

29. Lawrence Summers made this remark on January 14, 2005 during a National Board of Economic Research (NBER) Conference.

30. Perry, W. (1998). *Forms of intellectual and ethical development in the college years: A scheme.* San Francisco, CA: Jossey-Bass.

31. Belenky, M. F., Clinchy, B. M., Goldberger, N. R., Tarule, J. M. (1986). *Women's ways of knowing: The development of self, voice, and mind.* New York: Basic Books, p. 229.

32. Ransom, W., & Moulton, M. M. (2001, December). Why girls' schools? The difference in girl-centered education. *Fordham Urban Law Journal* 29(2), p. 592. Retrieved from http:www.thefreelibrary.com/why+girls'+schools%3f+the+ difference+in+girl-centered+education-a083701146

33. Ransom, W., & Moulton, M. M. (2001, December). Why girls' schools? The difference in girl-centered education. *Fordham Urban Law Journal* 29(2). Retrieved from http:www.thefreelibrary.com/why+girls'+schools%3f+the+ difference+in+girl-centered+education-a083701146

34. Lee, V. E., & Lockheed, M. E. (1990 May). The effects of single-sex school on achievement and attitudes in Nigeria. *Comparative Education Review* 34(2), p. 228.

35. Lee, V. E., & Lockheed, M. E. (1990 May). The effects of single-sex school on achievement and attitudes in Nigeria. *Comparative Education Review* 34(2), p. 228.

36. Ransom, W., & Moulton, M. M. (2001, December). Why girls' schools? The difference in girl-centered education. *Fordham Urban Law Journal* 29(2), pp. 593–594. Retrieved from http:www.thefreelibrary.com/why+girls'+schools%3f+the+ difference+in+girl-centered+education-a083701146

37. Society for Neuroscience. (2004, October, 24). Mothers have brains primed for care and certain techniques may reverse problems in offspring related to poor parenting. *News release.* Retrieved from http://www.sfn.org/index.aspx?pagename=news_102404c

38. Tedlock, B. (2005). *The woman in the shaman's body.* New York: Bantam, pp. 3–4.

39. Agamben, G. (1999). *The man without content.* Stanford: Stanford University Press, p. 70.

40. Adler, M. J. (1985). *Ten philosophical mistakes.* New York: Collier Books, p. 34.

41. Adler, M. J. (1985). *Ten philosophical mistakes.* New York: Collier Books, p. 89.

42. Gould, S. J. (1997, January). The basis of creativity in evolution. (Lecture presented at the University of Rochester, Rochester, NY). Quoted in Broomfield, J. (1997). *Other ways of knowing: Recharting our future with ageless wisdom.* Rochester, VT: Inner Traditions, p. 85.

43. Jablonka, E., & Lamb, M. (2005). *Evolution in four dimensions: Genetic, epigenetic, behavioral, and symbolic variation in the history of life.* Cambridge: MIT Press, p. 1.

44. Jablonka, E., & Lamb, M. (2005). *Evolution in four dimensions: Genetic, epigenetic, behavioral, and symbolic variation in the history of life.* Cambridge: MIT Press, p. 344.

45. Vitousek, P. M., D'Antonio, C. M., Loope, L.L., Rejmanek, M., Westbrooks, R. (1997). Introduced species: A Significant component of human-caused global change. *New Zealand Journal of Ecology* 21(1), p. 2.

46. Vitousek, P. M., D'Antonio, C. M., Loope, L.L., Rejmanek, M., Westbrooks, R. (1997). Introduced species: A Significant component of human-caused global change. *New Zealand Journal of Ecology* 21(1), p. 2.

47. Vitousek, P. M., D'Antonio, C. M., Loope, L.L., Rejmanek, M., Westbrooks, R. (1997). Introduced species: A Significant component of human-caused global change. *New Zealand Journal of Ecology* 21(1), p. 9.

48. Vitousek, P. M., D'Antonio, C. M., Loope, L.L., Rejmanek, M., Westbrooks, R. (1997). Introduced species: A Significant component of human-caused global change. *New Zealand Journal of Ecology* 21(1), p. 10.

49. Vitousek, P. M., Mooney, H. A., Lubchenco, J., Melillo, J. M. (1997, July 25). Human domination of earth's ecosystems. *Science* 277(5325), no. 5325, p. 495.

50. Vitousek, P. M., Mooney, H. A., Lubchenco, J., Melillo, J. M. (1997, July 25). Human domination of earth's ecosystems. *Science* 277(5325), no. 5325, p. 495.

51. Vitousek, P. M., Mooney, H. A., Lubchenco, J., Melillo, J. M. (1997, July 25). Human domination of earth's ecosystems. *Science* 277(5325), no. 5325, p. 498.

52. Vitousek, P. M., D'Antonio, C. M., Loope, L.L., Rejmanek, M., Westbrooks, R. (1997). Introduced species: A Significant component of human-caused global change. *New Zealand Journal of Ecology* 21(1), p. 7.

53. Mann, C. C. (2006). *1491: New revelations of the Americas before Columbus*. New York: Vantage, p. 351.

54. Mann, C. C. (2006). *1491: New revelations of the Americas before Columbus*. New York: Vantage, p. 107.

55. Mann, C. C. (2006). *1491: New revelations of the Americas before Columbus*. New York: Vantage, p. 109.

56. Hallowell, E. M. (2005, January). Overloaded circuits: Why smart people underperform. *Harvard Business Review*, p. 1.

57. Foerde, K., Knowlton, B. J., & Poldrack, R. A. (2006). Modulation of Competing Memory Systems by Distraction. *Proceedings of the National Academy of Sciences* 103(31). Retrieved from http://www.pnas.org/content/103/31/11778.full

58. Hallowell, E. M. (2005, January). Overloaded circuits: Why smart people underperform. *Harvard Business Review*, p. 4.

59. Hallowell, E. M. (2005, January). Overloaded circuits: Why smart people underperform. *Harvard Business Review*, p. 4.

CHAPTER 4: TRADITIONAL INDIGENOUS EDUCATION

1. National Geographic Expeditions. (2012). *National Geographic adventures: Tanzania: Walking safari with the Maasi.* Retrieved from http://www.nationalgeographicexpeditions.com/expeditions/maasai-walking-safari/detail

2. Callañaupa. N. (2009). Newsletter 3(2). The American & Canadian Association of Peru. Retrieved from http://www.acap-peru.org/newsletter/2009-02/nilda-callanaupa-alvarez.html

3. Isaacson, R. (2001). *The healing land.* New York: Grove Press. p. 50.

4. Hughes, P. & More, A. J. (1997, December 4). *Aboriginal ways of learning and learning styles.* Speech presented at the Annual Conference of the Australian Association form Research in Education. Brisbane, Australia.

5. Hughes, P. & More, A. J. (1997, December 4). *Aboriginal ways of learning and learning styles.* Speech presented at the Annual Conference of the Australian Association form Research in Education. Brisbane, Australia. Section 5.1.

6. Blanchard, A. (1985). *Aboriginal Education (Blanchard Report)*, House of Representatives Select Committee on Aboriginal Education, Parliament of the Commonwealth of Australia, Canberra.

7. Kirkness, V. J. (1998). Our people' education: Cut the shackles; cut the crap; cut the mustard. *Canadian Journal of Native Education*, 22(1), p. 10.

8. Kirkness, V. J. (1998). Our people' education: Cut the shackles; cut the crap; cut the mustard. *Canadian Journal of Native Education*, 22(1), p. 10.

9. Kirkness, V. J. (1998). Our people' education: Cut the shackles; cut the crap; cut the mustard. *Canadian Journal of Native Education*, 22(1), p. 10.

10. Standing Bear, L. (1978). *Land of the Spotted Eagle.* Lincoln: University of Nebraska Press. (Original work published 1933), p. 2.

11. Standing Bear, L. (1978). *Land of the Spotted Eagle.* Lincoln: University of Nebraska Press. (Original work published 1933), p. 2.

12. Standing Bear, L. (1978). *Land of the Spotted Eagle.* Lincoln: University of Nebraska Press. (Original work published 1933), p. 2.

13. Standing Bear, L. (1978). *Land of the Spotted Eagle.* Lincoln: University of Nebraska Press. (Original work published 1933), p. 10.

14. Standing Bear, L. (1988). *My Indian boyhood.* Lincoln: University of Nebraska Press. (Original work published 1931), p.16.

15. Standing Bear, L. (1988). *My Indian boyhood.* Lincoln: University of Nebraska Press. (Original work published 1931), p.24.
16. Standing Bear, L. (1988). *My Indian boyhood.* Lincoln: University of Nebraska Press. (Original work published 1931), p. 16.
17. Standing Bear, L. (1988). *My Indian boyhood.* Lincoln: University of Nebraska Press. (Original work published 1931), p. 31.
18. Standing Bear, L. (1988). *My Indian boyhood.* Lincoln: University of Nebraska Press. (Original work published 1931), p. 31.
19. Standing Bear, L. (1978). *Land of the Spotted Eagle.* Lincoln: University of Nebraska Press. (Original work published 1933), p. 14.
20. Standing Bear, L. (1978). *Land of the Spotted Eagle.* Lincoln: University of Nebraska Press. (Original work published 1933), p. 15.
21. Standing Bear, L. (1975). *My People the Sioux.* Lincoln: University of Nebraska Press. (Original work published 1928), p. 48.
22. Cajete, G. (2000). *Native science: Natural laws of interdependence.* Santa Fe, NM: Clear Light Publishers, p. 87.
23. Cajete, G. (2000). *Native science: Natural laws of interdependence.* Santa Fe, NM: Clear Light Publishers, p.87.
24. Cajete, G. (2000). *Native science: Natural laws of interdependence.* Santa Fe, NM: Clear Light Publishers, p. 88.
25. Cajete, G. (2000). *Native science: Natural laws of interdependence.* Santa Fe, NM: Clear Light Publishers, p 89.
26. Hirschfelder, A. (Ed.). (1995). Native heritage: Personal accounts by American Indians 1790 to the present. New York: Macmillan, p 91.
27. Aupaummut, H. (1995). Teaching the children. In *Native heritage: Personal accounts by American Indians 1790 to the present.* A. Hirschfelder (Ed.). New York: Macmillan, pp.92–93.
28. Shield, P. (1995). I tried to be like my mother. In *Native heritage: Personal accounts by American Indians 1790 to the present.* A. Hirschfelder (Ed.). New York: Macmillan, p. 97.
29. Price, A. (1995). Playing wickiup. In *Native heritage: Personal accounts by American Indians 1790 to the present.* A. Hirschfelder (Ed.). New York: Macmillan, p. 100.
30. Nowell, C. J. (1995). Play potlaches. In *Native heritage: Personal accounts by American Indians 1790 to the present.* A. Hirschfelder (Ed.). New York: Macmillan, pp. 103–104
31. Tafoya, T. (1995). The old ways teach us. In *Native heritage: Personal accounts by American Indians 1790 to the present.* A. Hirschfelder (Ed.). New York: Macmillan, p. 113.
32. Emory, K. (1999). *Ancient Hawaiian civilization.* Honolulu, HI: Mutual Publishing, p. v.
33. Emory, K. (1999). *Ancient Hawaiian civilization.* Honolulu, HI: Mutual Publishing, p. 50.
34. Emory, K. (1999). *Ancient Hawaiian civilization.* Honolulu, HI: Mutual Publishing, p.55.
35. Federation of Saskatchewan Indian Nations. (1990). An act respecting Indian nations' jurisdiction and control over the establishment and delivery of child welfare and family support services to treaty Indian children and family

PREAMBLE TO CHAPTER 5: THE RIGHT OF MAN – SEEK AND DESTROY?

1. Joseph Campbell was perhaps the world's foremost researcher on mythology and its significance to cultural identities and social norms. His immensely popular, *The Power of the Myth*, was made into a public television series. His analysis of myths has proven to be a source of knowledge that includes human selfhood and actuality.
2. Robert Bly, a National Book Award winning poet and author, wrote the national bestselling, *Iron John*. Bly uses ancient stories, legend, and myth regarding what it is to be a man, and the importance of mentorship to the stages of male growth.

CHAPTER 5: INDIGENOUS AND WESTERN WAYS OF KNOWING: A CONFLICT OF INTERESTS

1. Teleology – a philosophical term for the study of purpose, particularly its effect on humans.
2. Ontology – a philosophical term for the nature of being including reality and existence. Humans have a sense of being which distinguishes us from other animals.
3. Axiology – a philosophical term for the study of values and ethics.
4. Richard Rodriguez is a Mexican American author who wrote the critically acclaimed *Hunger of Memory: The Education of Richard Rodriguez*. He is an outspoken critic of bilingual education and affirmative action.
5. Rodriguez, R. (1982). *Hunger of memory: The education of Richard Rodriguez*. New York: Dial Press, p.70.
6. Anzaldúa, G. (2001). Borderlands/La Frontera. In P Bizzell & B Herzberg (Eds.), *The rhetorical tradition: Readings from classical times to the present*. Boston: Bedford/St. Martin's, p. 1601.
7. Chinua Achebe is a Nigerian novelist critical of both pre-colonial tribal life and British colonialism.
8. Tikly, L. (2004). Education and the new imperialism. *Comparative education 40*(2), p. 173.
9. Tikly, L. (2004). Education and the new imperialism. *Comparative education 40*(2), p. 189.
10. Ectopia – One of the nine culturally distinct nations in North America. It is a narrow strip of land starting from Northern California to Alaska where the environment is worshipped and is the homeland of radical environmentalism.
11. Earth First!ers are members of the Earth First! environmental movements, and can be found in high concentrations in Ectopia and other places where environmentalism has taken on a religious connotation.
12. Earth First! "About Earth First!" Earth First! Worldwide Retrieved from http://www.earthfirst.org/about.htm
13. Earth First! "About Earth First!" Earth First! Worldwide Retrieved from http://www.earthfirst.org/about.htm
14. Earth First! "About Earth First!" Earth First! Worldwide Retrieved from http://www.earthfirst.org/about.htm
15. David Abram is the founder of the Alliance for Wild Ethics and the author of *The spell of the sensuous: Perception and language in a more-than-human world*. Abram has been named by the Utne Reader as one of a hundred visionaries currently transforming the world relative to science, ethics, and environmentalism. Besides research in sensory perception, he has a passionate interest in interspecies communication and in the rejuvenation of oral culture.
16. Abram, D. (1996). *The spell of the sensuous: Perception and language in a more-than-human world*. New York: Vintage Books, p. 271.
17. Michael W. Apple is a leading critical theorist in education.
18. Apple, M. W. (2000). *Official knowledge: Democratic education in a conservative age*, 2nd ed. New York: Routledge, p. 43.
19. Foucalt, M. (1995). *Discipline & punish: The birth of the prison*. New York: Vintage Books, p. 201.
20. Foucault, M. (2001). The order of discourse. In P. Bizzell & B. Herzberg (Eds.), *The rhetorical tradition: Readings from classical times to the present*. Boston: Bedford/St.Martin's, p. 1469.
21. Apple, M. W. (1996). *Cultural politics and education*. New York: Teachers College Press, p. 22.
22. Apple, M. W. (2006), *Educating the "right" way: Markets, standards, God, and inequality*, 2nd ed. New York: Routledge, p. 23.
23. Apple, M. W. (2006), *Educating the "right" way: Markets, standards, God, and inequality*, 2nd ed. New York: Routledge, pp. 147–148.
24. Apple, M. W. (2006), *Educating the "right" way: Markets, standards, God, and inequality*, 2nd ed. New York: Routledge, p. 262.
25. The Brazilian Paulo Freire is arguably the most important educational philosopher for the new century. Freire's *Pedagogy of the Oppressed*, published in 1970, is considered by many to be the bible of critical theorists worldwide.
26. Freire, P. (2000). *Pedagogy of the oppressed*. M Bergman Ramos (trans). New York: Continuum. (Original work published 1970), p. 72.

[27.] Glass, R. D. (2001). On Paulo Freire's philosophy of praxis and the foundation of liberation education. *Educational Researcher* 30(2), p. 15.

[28.] Herndl, C. G. (1993). Teaching discourse and reproducing culture: A critique of research and pedagogy in professional and non-academic writing. *College composition and communication 44*(3), p. 359.

[29.] Selfe, C. L. & Selfe, R. J. Jr. (1994). The politics of the interface: Power and its exercise in electronic contact zones. *College composition and communication 45*(4), pp. 481–482.

[30.] Selfe, C. L. & Selfe, R. J. Jr. (1994). The politics of the interface: Power and its exercise in electronic contact zones. *College composition and communication 45*(4), p. 495.

[31.] Selfe, C. L. & Selfe, R. J. Jr. (1994). The politics of the interface: Power and its exercise in electronic contact zones. *College composition and communication 45*(4), p. 482.

[32.] Feenberg, A. (2003). Democratic rationalization: Technology, power, and freedom. In Scharff, R. C., & Dusek, V. (Eds.), *Philosophy of technology: The technological condition: An anthology* (pp. 652–665). Malden, MA: Blackwell Publishing, p. 658.

[33.] One Step Toward Bridging the Racial Computer Gap. (Winter 1999–2000). *The Journal of Blacks in Higher Education*, 26, p. 62.

[34.] One Step Toward Bridging the Racial Computer Gap. (Winter 1999–2000). *The Journal of Blacks in Higher Education*, 26, p. 62.

[35.] Sheingold, K., Martin, L. M. W., & Endreweit, M. E. (1987, July 20–24). Preparing urban teachers for the technological future. Paper presented at the World Assembly of the International Council on Education for Teaching, Eindhoven, NL, p. 9.

CHAPTER 6: THE WESTERN EDUCATION SYSTEM

[1.] Tamaoka, K. (1986). *Congruence between learning styles of Cree, Dene and Métis students, and instructional styles of Native and Non-Native teachers.* (Paper presented at the Mokakit Conference of the Indian Education Research Association, Winnipeg, Manitoba, Canada, October 17–19, 1986) Retrieved from ERIC Document Reproduction Service #289667.

[2.] For additional studies supporting Tamaoka's research see Jablonka, E. & Lamb,M. (2005). *Evolution in four dimensions: Genetic, epigenetic, behavioral, and symbolic variation in the history of life.* Cambridge: MIT Press; Chrystal , S. C. (1991). *Assessing prior knowledge across culture (Native American and caucasian).* PhD diss., Marquette University; Risku, M. (1996). American Indian learning style: The illusion. In S. M. Schacher (ed), *Celebration of Indigenous Thought and Expression* (pp. 267–272). Sault Ste. Marie, MI: Lake Superior State University Press.

[3.] Heaney, T. W. Issues in Freirean Pedagogy. *National-Louis University*. Retrieved from http://www.nl.edu/academics/cas/ace/facultypapers/ ThomasHeaney_Freirean.cfm

[4.] Smith, M. K. (2008). Howard Gardner, multiple intelligences and education. In *The encyclopedia of informal education*. Retrieved from http://www.infed.org/thinkers/gardner.htm

[5.] Smith, M. K. (2008). Howard Gardner, multiple intelligences and education. In *The encyclopedia of informal education*. Retrieved from http://www.infed.org/thinkers/gardner.htm

[6.] Smith, M. K. (2008). Howard Gardner, multiple intelligences and education. In *The encyclopedia of informal education*. Retrieved from http://www.infed.org/thinkers/gardner.htm

[7.] An external locus of control is a person's belief in or realization that there are both positive and negative outside forces that will influence his or her life. Acknowledging that these forces are not necessarily a person's fault allows him or her to more easily overcome them.

[8.] Noriega, J. (1992). American Indian education in the United States: Indoctrination for subordination to colonialism. In M. A. Jaimes (ed.), *The state of Native America: Genocide, colonization, and resistance*. Boston: South End Press, pp. 371–372.

[9.] Noriega, J. (1992). American Indian education in the United States: Indoctrination for subordination to colonialism. In M. A. Jaimes (ed.), *The state of Native America: Genocide, colonization, and resistance*. Boston: South End Press, p. 374.

[10.] Mann, C. C. (2006). *1491: New Revelations of the Americas Before Columbus.* New York: Vintage Books (Original work published 2005), p.321.

NOTES

11. Many in the academic community did more than ignore Meggers, not only discrediting her research and scholarship, but also calling her a socialist during the McCarthy Era. Meggers outlived her critics and others have since substantiated her *Amazonian farmland theory*. She was appointed director of the Latin American Archeology Program at the National Museum of Natural History at the Smithsonian Institute.

12. Noriega, J. (1992). American Indian education in the United States: Indoctrination for subordination to colonialism. In M. A. Jaimes (ed.), *The state of Native America: Genocide, colonization, and resistance.* Boston: South End Press, p. 375.

13. Atkins, J. D. C. 1886 annual report U.S. commisionary of Indian affairs. Quoted in Noriega J, (1992). American Indian education in the United States: Indoctrination for subordination to colonialism. In M. A. Jaimes (ed.), *The state of Native America: Genocide, colonization, and resistance.* Boston: South End Press, p. 379.

14. Noriega, J. (1992). American Indian education in the United States: Indoctrination for subordination to colonialism. In M. A. Jaimes (ed.), *The state of Native America: Genocide, colonization, and resistance.* Boston: South End Press, p. 380.

15. Pratt, R. H. (1964). *Battlefield and Classroom: Four Decades with the American Indian, 1867–1904.* R. M. Utley (Ed.). New Haven, CT: Yale University Press, p. 119.

16. Pratt, R. H. (1964). *Battlefield and Classroom: Four Decades with the American Indian, 1867–1904.* R. M. Utley (Ed.). New Haven, CT: Yale University Press, pp. 118–121.

17. Adams, D. W. (1995). *Education for extinction: American Indians and the boarding school experience, 1875 – 1928.* Lawrence, KS: University Press of Kansas, p. 43.

18. Pratt, R. H. (1964). *Battlefield and Classroom: Four Decades with the American Indian, 1867–1904.* R. M. Utley (Ed.). New Haven, CT: Yale University Press, p. 283.

19. Pratt, R. H. (1964). *Battlefield and Classroom: Four Decades with the American Indian, 1867–1904.* R. M. Utley (Ed.). New Haven, CT: Yale University Press, p. 100.

20. Dejong, D. H. (1993). *Promises of the Past: A History of Indian Education in the United States* Golden, CO: North American Press, pp. 4–5.

21. Adams, D. W. (1995). *Education for extinction: American Indians and the boarding school experience, 1875 – 1928.* Lawrence, KS: University Press of Kansas, p. 211.

22. Pratt, R. H. (1964). *Battlefield and Classroom: Four Decades with the American Indian, 1867–1904.* R. M. Utley (Ed.). New Haven, CT: Yale University Press, p. 223.

23. Adams, D. W. (1995). *Education for extinction: American Indians and the boarding school experience, 1875 – 1928.* Lawrence, KS: University Press of Kansas, p. 211.

24. Standing Bear, L. (1978). *Land of the Spotted Eagle.* Lincoln: University of Nebraska Press. (Original work published 1933), pp. 68–69.

25. Standing Bear, L. (1975). *My People the Sioux.* Lincoln: University of Nebraska Press. (Original work published 1928), p.128.

26. Standing Bear, L. (1975). *My People the Sioux.* Lincoln: University of Nebraska Press. (Original work published 1928), p.130.

27. Adams, D. W. (1995). *Education for extinction: American Indians and the boarding school experience, 1875 – 1928.* Lawrence, KS: University Press of Kansas, p. 109.

28. Standing Bear, L. (1975). *My People the Sioux.* Lincoln: University of Nebraska Press. (Original work published 1928), p.137.

29. Adams, D. W. (1995). *Education for extinction: American Indians and the boarding school experience, 1875 – 1928.* Lawrence, KS: University Press of Kansas, p. 140.

30. Sweezy, C. We Counted Time by Sleeps. Quoted in A.Hirschfelder (ed.) (1995). *Native Heritage* New York: Mcmillan, pp. 174–175.

31. Beliveau, A. (1929, October 29). [Letter to Duncan Campbell Scott, Deputy Superintendent General]. National Archives of Canada (CN 65-4, Vol. 1, File 494/25-1-015), Ottawa, CA.

32. Perrault, F. (1930, May 2). [Letter to Frank Edwards, DIAND, May 2, 1930, CN 65-4, Vol. 1, File 494/25-1-015. This letter was requested from the National Archives in Ottawa, Canada.

33. Swartman, G. (1945, December 31). [Letter to Department of Indian Affairs]. National Archives of Canada (CN 65-4, Vol. 1, File 494/25-1-015).

34. Pratt, R. H. (1964). *Battlefield and Classroom: Four Decades with the American Indian, 1867–1904.* R. M. Utley (Ed.). New Haven, CT: Yale University Press, p. 318.
35. Giago, T. A. (1978). *The Aboriginal Sin.* San Francisco: Indian Historian Press, p. 81–82.
36. The first author has also witnessed the return of former students to the site.
37. Tileston, D. W. (2004). *What Every Teacher Should Know About: Instructional Planning.* Thousand Oaks, CA: Corwin Press, p. 10.
38. Kastner, L. (2008, October 22). 2,500 Dropouts a Week. *San Antonio Express-News*, 12B.
39. Kastner, L. (2008, October 22). 2,500 Dropouts a Week. *San Antonio Express-News*, 12B.
40. The knowledge and writing skills of government job applicants were tested using standardized tests.

CHAPTER 7: LANGUAGE AND POWER

1. Adams, D. W. (1995). *Education for extinction: American Indians and the boarding school experience, 1875 – 1928.* Lawrence, KS: University Press of Kansas, p. 139.
2. Standing Bear, L. (1975). *My People the Sioux.* Lincoln: University of Nebraska Press. (Original work published 1928), pp.155–156.
3. Momaday, N. S. (1998). *The man made of words: Essays, stories, passages.* New York: St. Martin's Griffin, p. 28.
4. Momaday, N. S. (1998). *The man made of words: Essays, stories, passages.* New York: St. Martin's Griffin, p. 16.
5. Western education models have, on paper, embraced the critical thinking taxonomy of educational psychologist Benjamin Bloom that highlights the distinction between lower order cognitive skills (knowledge, comprehension, and application) and higher order thinking skills (analysis, synthesis, and evaluation). In practice, however, many teachers fail to offer opportunities for students to master the higher order thinking skills. They adopt Paulo Freire's "banking system" of education that requires little more than internalization and regurgitation without employing or nurturing critical thinking skills.
6. Winchester, S. (2003). *Krakatoa.* New York: HarperCollins, pp. 100–101.
7. Momaday, N. S. (1998). *The man made of words: Essays, stories, passages.* New York: St. Martin's Griffin, p.103.
8. Momaday, N. S. (1998). *The man made of words: Essays, stories, passages.* New York: St. Martin's Griffin, p.25.
9. Momaday, N. S. (1998). *The man made of words: Essays, stories, passages.* New York: St. Martin's Griffin, p. 104.
10. Momaday, N. S. (1998). *The man made of words: Essays, stories, passages.* New York: St. Martin's Griffin, p. 15.
11. Nabokov, P. (Ed.). (1991). *Native American testimony: A chronicle of Indian-White relations from prophecy to present, 1492–1992.* New York: Penguin, p. 221.
12. Nabokov, P. (Ed.). (1991). *Native American testimony: A chronicle of Indian-White relations from prophecy to present, 1492–1992.* New York: Penguin, p. 221.
13. Nabokov, P. (Ed.). (1991). *Native American testimony: A chronicle of Indian-White relations from prophecy to present, 1492–1992.* New York: Penguin, p. 221.
14. Nabokov, P. (Ed.). (1991). *Native American testimony: A chronicle of Indian-White relations from prophecy to present, 1492–1992.* New York: Penguin, p. 222.
15. Nabokov, P. (Ed.). (1991). *Native American testimony: A chronicle of Indian-White relations from prophecy to present, 1492–1992.* New York: Penguin, p..221
16. Nabokov, P. (Ed.). (1991). *Native American testimony: A chronicle of Indian-White relations from prophecy to present, 1492–1992.* New York: Penguin, pp. 223–224.
17. Nabokov, P. (Ed.). (1991). *Native American testimony: A chronicle of Indian-White relations from prophecy to present, 1492–1992.* New York: Penguin, p. 224.
18. Nabokov, P. (Ed.). (1991). *Native American testimony: A chronicle of Indian-White relations from prophecy to present, 1492–1992.* New York: Penguin, p. 224.

19. Nabokov, P. (Ed.). (1991). *Native American testimony: A chronicle of Indian-White relations from prophecy to present, 1492–1992*. New York: Penguin, p. 224.

20. Baker, C. (2006). *Foundations of bilingual education and bilingualism*, 4th ed. Clevedon, UK: Multilingual Matters, p. 74.

21. Frankfurt International School. Second language acquisition—essential information. Retrieved from http://esl.fis.edu/teachers/support/cummin.htm

22. Social semioticians study the social processes and implications that surround the production, dissemination, and analysis of communication.

23. Kress, G. R., & Van Leeuwen, T. (2006). *Reading images: The grammar of visual design*. Abingdon, UK: Routledge, p. 9.

24. Kress, G. R., & Van Leeuwen, T. (2006). *Reading images: The grammar of visual design*. Abingdon, UK: Routledge, p. 9.

25. M.A.K. Halliday is a British linguist who pioneered the social and meaning-making aspects of language. While describing himself as a generalist, he was especially interested in the ways in which language distinguished human society from that of other life forms.

26. Halliday, M.A.K. (2005). *The language of science*. J.J. Webster (ed). New York: Continuum, p. 16.

27. Halliday, M.A.K. (2005). *The language of science*. J.J. Webster (ed). New York: Continuum, p. 17.

28. Halliday, M.A.K. (2005). *The language of science*. J.J. Webster (ed). New York: Continuum, p. 17.

29. Kress, G. R., & Van Leeuwen, T. (2006). *Reading images: The grammar of visual design*. Abingdon, UK: Routledge, p. 20.

30. Kress, G. R., & Van Leeuwen, T. (2006). *Reading images: The grammar of visual design*. Abingdon, UK: Routledge, p. 23.

31. Halliday, M.A.K. (2005). *The language of science*. J.J. Webster (ed). New York: Continuum, p. 25.

32. San rock art depicts not only the way of life experienced by the San people thousands of years ago but is also believed to offer insight to their all aspects of their existence.

33. Lewis-Williams, D. (2004). *The mind in the cave: Consciousness and the origins of art*. London: Thames & Hudson. (Original work published 2002), p. 144.

34. Lewis-Williams, D. (2004). *The mind in the cave: Consciousness and the origins of art*. London: Thames & Hudson. (Original work published 2002), p. 144.

35. Momaday, N. S. (1998). *The man made of words: Essays, stories, passages*. New York: St. Martin's Griffin, p. 15.

36. Momaday, N. S. (1998). *The man made of words: Essays, stories, passages*. New York: St. Martin's Griffin, p. 15.

37. Christie, M. (2003, September 24). Databases which support rather than inhibit Australian Aboriginal ways of knowing and making knowledge. (Seminar, Charles Darwin University), p. 1.

38. Christie, M. (2003, September 24). Databases which support rather than inhibit Australian Aboriginal ways of knowing and making knowledge. (Seminar, Charles Darwin University), p. 4.

39. Mann, C. C. (2006). *1491: New revelations of the Americas before Columbus*. New York: Vintage Books (Original work published 2005), p. 290.

40. Abram, D. (1996). *The spell of the sensuous: Perception and language in a more-than-human world*. New York: Vintage Books, pp. 71–72.

41. Abram, D. (1996). *The spell of the sensuous: Perception and language in a more-than-human world*. New York: Vintage Books, p. 240.

42. Abram, D. (1996). *The spell of the sensuous: Perception and language in a more-than-human world*. New York: Vintage Books, p. 194.

CHAPTER 8: NEITHER WOLF NOR DOG

1. Wagamese, R. (1994). *Keeper 'n Me*. Toronto, Canada: Doubleday, p. 51.

2. Ethnogenesis describes the creation or emergence of a cultural group that is distinct from their social surroundings.

3. Overholt, T. W., & Callicott, J. B. (1982). *Clothed-in-fur and other tales: An Introduction to an Ojibwa World View*. Washington, DC: University Press of America, p. 1.

4. Erik Erikson was a developmental psychologist whose pioneering research described the stages of development of human beings and contributed greatly to an understanding of personality development. See the Erikson Institute webpage at http://www.erikson.edu

5. Colin Powell is a retired four-star general who served from 2001 to 2005 as Secretary of State in President George W Bush's administration.

6. Although a Southern social construction, the One-Drop Rule originates from the days of slavery where it helped sustain a slave population as the importation of slaves was illegal. The rule was simply that no matter what people looked like or how much white ancestry they had, if they had any Black-African ancestry, they could not be considered white. If no longer legal, many in the United States still recognize this designation although not necessarily for other races.

7. Tucker, N. C., Kojetin, B. A., & Harrison, R. (1996). A statistical analysis of the CPS supplement on race and ethnic origin. *Proceedings of the Bureau of the Census' 1996 annual research conference.* p. 5. Retrieved from http://www.census.gov/prod/2/gen/96arc/arc96.html

8. Means, R. (1980, July). *On what to call indigenous people of North America.* Speech presented at the Black Hills International Survival Gathering, South Dakota.

9. McMurtry, L. (2005). *Crazy Horse: A life* (Penguin Lives biographies). New York: Penguin Books, pp.7–8.

10. Sandoz, M. (1997). *Crazy Horse.* New York: Fine Communications, pp. xxiv.

11. Paul Gauguin was a French Post-Impressionist artist whose work was appreciated more after his death than during his life. His adult life was dogged with bouts of depression, mixed business success, and failed relationships, but his most constant aim was to escape European society. His travels took him to, among other places, Tahiti where he found an exotic people who were far more grounded and free than any he had known before.

12. Nerburn, K. (1994). *Neither wolf nor dog: On forgotten roads with an Indian elder.* Novato, CA: New World Library, p. 229.

13. Gilbert, S. (2000). *The tattoo history source book.* New York: Juno Books, p. 101.

14. The Dawes Rolls, more formally known as *The Final Rolls of the Citizens and Freedmen of the Five Civilized Tribes in Indian Territory*, lists the names of members of the Cherokee, Creek, Choctaw, Chickasaw, and Seminole tribes who were deemed eligible to receive land allotments in return for recognizing Federal laws. The Rolls are used today to establish eligibility for tribal membership.

15. Morris, F. (2007, February 21). *Cherokee tribe faces decision on freedmen*, National Public Radio.

16. History has had many instances of ethnic cleansing, but perhaps the most notorious was during the Second World War when Hitler attempted to establish a Judenfrei (free of Jews) society.

17. The melting pot is a term that has been in use since the formation of the United States to suggest the harmonious blending of separate immigrant cultures into one homogenous population. The rise of multiculturalism in the 1970s, which promotes the celebration of cultural differences, has challenged the melting pot metaphor suggesting instead the notion of a salad bowl of mixed, but separate, cultures.

18. The tuition waver policy is articulated in a letter from the University of Minnesota, Office of the University Attorney, June 13, 1990 to the Director of Admissions at the University of Minnesota, Morris. The policy allowed the tuition waver to anyone able to provide documentation or certification of American Indian ancestry. The primary author was a member of the faculty during this time and also worked within the minority student program. He consulted with the aforementioned committee on a number of these decisions.

19. According to the Bureau of Indian Affairs, a federal Indian reservation is "an area of land reserved for a tribe or tribes under treaty or other agreement with the United States, executive order, or federal statute or administrative action as permanent tribal homelands, and where the federal government holds title to the land in trust on behalf of the tribe." In addition the relationship between the U.S. government and an Indian tribe is one of equals or government to government. Retrieved from http://www.bia.gov.

20. Prior to 1985 Indian women and any resulting children lost their tribal membership (status) if they married a man outside their band, and they were not automatically accorded status in their husband's band even if he had status. Illegitimate children were also denied tribal status if the father was not a member of the women's band. After 1985, women were allowed to regain their status after "marrying out," as were their children. But if the children of a woman who married out also married out, they lost their status forever. This practice is presently in place and is commonly referred to as the "two generation cut-off clause."

21. The Métis are indigenous Canadians whose ancestry is a mix of Indians and Europeans.
22. The red road is a spiritual life path that is guided by native teachings and beliefs.
23. Kurt Vonnegut's *Harrison Bergeron* is a satirical and cautionary tale of enforcing equality via technology to a level that individuality and freedom no longer exist. The short story was first published in October 1961 in The Magazine of Fantasy and Science Fiction.

CHAPTER 9: A UNIFIED THEORY

1. Kuhn, T. (1996). *The structure of scientific revolution. (3rd Ed.).* Chicago, IL: University of Chicago Press, p. 2.
2. Kuhn, T. (1996). *The structure of scientific revolution. (3rd Ed.).* Chicago, IL: University of Chicago Press, p. 6.
3. Kuhn, T. (1996). *The structure of scientific revolution. (3rd Ed.).* Chicago, IL: University of Chicago Press, p. 6.
4. Dualism is the idea most commonly credited to Plato who said that the world has fundamental opposites. Plato's dualism of the mind and body gave birth to Idealism, which favors the world of ideas over the imperfect body. Examples in religion are good versus evil, and God over the Devil. Dualism is a central ingredient of Western thought and historically a way of making sense of the world. Dualism also lent itself to the development of linearity—the belief that there is a past, present, and future.
5. The terms "takers" and "leavers" is defined in the 1992 novel *Ishmael* by David Quinn. Quinn suggests that "takers" were the cause of, and the reasons for, the continuation of androcentrism. "Takers" have the belief that progress is the only option, and value humans over everything else. And they have created a worldview that perpetuates their ideology thus maintaining power. "Leavers," on the other hand, are the "primitives." Ultimately believing in a biocentric worldview, they do not take for profit and, conversely, try to sustain earth's resources.
6. Georges Sioui is a Canadian scholar, advocate, and activist for Amerindians. His, *For an Amerindian Autohistory, An Essay on the Foundations of a Social Ethic*, published in 1992 is an important study toward understanding American aboriginal history and philosophy.
7. Sioui, G. E. (1992). *For an Amerindian autohistory, An essay on the foundations of a social ethic.* S. Fischman (trans.). Montreal: McGill-Queen's University Press, p. 64.
8. Sioui, G. E. (1992). *For an Amerindian autohistory, An essay on the foundations of a social ethic.* S. Fischman (trans.). Montreal: McGill-Queen's University Press, p. 66.
9. Sioui, G. E. (1992). *For an Amerindian autohistory, An essay on the foundations of a social ethic.* S. Fischman (trans.). Montreal: McGill-Queen's University Press, p. 68.
10. Sioui, G. E. (1992). *For an Amerindian autohistory, An essay on the foundations of a social ethic.* S. Fischman (trans.). Montreal: McGill-Queen's University Press, p. 105.
11. John Dewey made these points in the forward that he wrote for Radin's book. See Radin, P. (1927). *Primitive man as philosopher.* New York: D. Appleton, pp. xv – xviii.
12. Sioui, G. E. (1992). *For an Amerindian autohistory, An essay on the foundations of a social ethic.* S. Fischman (trans.). Montreal: McGill-Queen's University Press, p. 81.
13. Freire, P. (2000). *Pedagogy of the oppressed.* M. Bergman Ramos (trans.). New York: Continuum. (Original work published 1970), p. 174.
14. Pierre Furter is a Swiss professor of pedagogy and adult education, and was a contemporary and influence on Paulo Freire's writings. Furter has focused on worldwide education and region disparities and its devastating results. His book, *Educação e Vida*, provides an alternative education model that is more humanistic and environmentally friendly than the economic education model.
15. Furter, P. (1966). *Educação e vida.* Rio de Janiero: Vozes, pp. 26–27. Quoted in Freire, P. (2000). *Pedagogy of the oppressed.* M. Bergman Ramos (trans). New York: Continuum. (Original work published 1970), p. 92.
16. Freire, P. (2000). *Pedagogy of the oppressed.* M. Bergman Ramos (trans). New York: Continuum. (Original work published 1970), p. 92.

[17.] Van der Post, L. (1986). *The lost world of the Kalahari.* San Diego: Harcourt Brace. (Original work published 1958), pp. 60–61.

[18.] Van der Post, L. (1986). *The lost world of the Kalahari.* San Diego: Harcourt Brace. (Original work published 1958), pp. 279.

[19.] Freire, P. (2000). *Pedagogy of the oppressed.* M. Bergman Ramos (trans). New York: Continuum. (Original work published 1970), p. 101.

[20.] Rideout, V. J., Foehr, U. G., & Roberts, D. E. (2010). *Generation M2: Media in the lives of 8 to 18-year-olds.* Menlo Park, CA: Kaiser Family Foundation. Retrieved from http://www.kff.org/entmedia/upload/8010.pdf

[21.] Mortimer Adler felt that intensive specialization is one of the worst movements that has happened in education over the last century, and is destructive to society.

[22.] Forest time is a form of biological time that reflects the growth and seasonal cycles of flora and fauna. Different plants and animals grow at different rates, yet for humans there is no particular value associated to this natural rhythm of life. But there is a pulse to the forest and to feel it is serene.

[23.] This quote is a frequently used variation of what Albert Schweitzer wrote in his 1949 *Philosophy of Civilisation.* Schweitzer, who was a German theologian, musician, and medical doctor, spent much of his life as a medical missionary in Africa. He was deeply concerned about the decay of Western civilization and man's abuse of the earth's natural resources. He was awarded the Nobel Peace Prize in 1952 for his *Reverence of Life,* which is considered by many as an important contribution to the modern day environmental movement.

[24.] Sigrud Olson was one of the most significant conservationists of the 20th century. His book, *The Singing Wilderness,* stands with Aldo Leopold's *Sand County Almanac* and Rachel Carson's *Silent Spring.* Olson worked tirelessly for the preservation of America's natural plants and animals. He argued "the wilderness" and "the wild" are critical to human development.

[25.] Freire, P. (2000). *Pedagogy of the oppressed.* M. Bergman Ramos (trans). New York: Continuum. (Original work published 1970), p. 59.

[26.] Blessed Earth, *Mission and beliefs.* Retrieved from http://www.blessedearth.org/about/mission-and-beliefs/

[27.] The little known Eckhart is recognized as having had a profound influence upon Nicholas of Cusa, who provided foundational thinking on relativity, and had a similar influence on Einstein.

[28.] Pierre Teilhard de Chardin, besides being a renowned paleontologist, was a Jesuit priest and philosopher. His *Phenomenon of Man,* published in 1941, posits that humans need to form a psychological unification with "Omega Point," his name for God. Teilhad felt that religions were archaic and not serving human needs and that they needed to evolve and foster unification. He was frequently in disfavor with the Catholic Church and his writings were often censored but eventually published.

[29.] Abram, D. (1996). *The spell of the sensuous: Perception and language in a more-than-human world.* New York: Vintage Books, p. 10.

[30.] Olson, S. (1964, May 23). *Testimony before the Selke Committee on the fate of the Boundary Waters Canoe Area.* Saint Paul, MN.

[31.] Dewey, J. (1938). Quoted in United States Department of the Interior, National Park Service, *Yearbook: Park and Recreation Progress.* Washington, D. C.: U.S. G.P.O., p. 38.

[32.] Freire, P. (2000). *Pedagogy of the oppressed.* M. Bergman Ramos (trans). New York: Continuum. (Original work published 1970), p. 43.

[33.] PestalozziWorld. (2012). *Educating children for a better world.* Retrieved from http://www.pestalozziworld.com/pestalozzi/methods/html

[34.] American Montessori Society. (2011). *Public schools.* Retrieved from http://www.amshq.org/School%20Resources/Public.aspx

[35.] Moore, T. (1992). *Care of the soul: A guide for cultivating depth and sacredness in everyday life.* New York: HarperColins, p. xiii.

[36.] Moore, T. (1992). *Care of the soul: A guide for cultivating depth and sacredness in everyday life.* New York: HarperColins, p. xvi.

[37.] Moore, T. (1992). *Care of the soul: A guide for cultivating depth and sacredness in everyday life.* New York: HarperColins, p. xvi.

38. Moore, T. (1992). *Care of the soul: A guide for cultivating depth and sacredness in everyday life.* New York: HarperColins, p. xx.

39. Bly, R. (1996). *The sibling society.* Reading, MA: Addison Wesley, pp. viii-ix.

40. Bly, R. (1996). *The sibling society.* Reading, MA: Addison Wesley, p. 58.

CHAPTER 10: WHY A NEW PATHWAY

1. Vandal, B. (2010, May). Rebuilding the remedial education bridge to college success. Retrieved from http://www.gettingpastgo.org/docs/GPGpaper.pdf, p. 4.

2. American Association of School Administrators. (2009). *Report of findings one year later: How the economic downturn continues to impact schools districts.* Retrieved from http://www.aasa.org/uploadedFiles/Resources/files/OneYearLater%20FINAL.pdf.

3. Detroit schools closing: Michigan officials order Robert Bobb to shut half the city's schools. (2011, February 21). *Huffington Post.* Retrieved from http://www.huffingtonpost.com/2011/02/21/detroit-schools-closing_n_826007.html

4. Klaus, K. (2011, March 11). Kansas City Missouri school district looks for broker to 'repurpose' closed schools. *Kansas City Business Journal.* Retrieved from http://www.bizjournals.com/kansascity/print-edition/2011/03/11/kansas-city-missouri-school-district.html?page=all

5. Saxon, R. (2009, August 26). L.A. school board OKs school choice plan with private operators. *USA Today.* Retrieved from http://www.usatoday.com/news/ education/2009-08-26-los-angeles-schools_N.htm

6. Center for Research on Education Outcomes. (2009). *Multiple choice: Charter school performance in 16 states.* Retrieved from http://credo.stanford.edu/reports/MULTIPLE_CHOICE_CREDO.pdf

7. Gray, S. (2010, January 25). Can Robert Bobb fix Detroit's public schools? *Time Magazine.* Retrieved from http://www.time.com/time/magazine/article/0,9171,1953694,00.html

8. Scharrer, G. (2010, April 8). White flunks Perry's handling of dropouts. *San Antonio Express News,* p. 5B.

9. Intercultural Development Research Association. (2011, April). Five Texas regions have persistently high student attrition rates. Retrieved from http://www.idra.org/IDRA_Newsletter/ April_2011_Curriculum_Quality/Five_Texas_Regions/

10. Hollingsworth, H, & Turner, D. (2011, July 28). States Brace for Grad Rate Dips as Formula changes. *San Antonio Express News,* p. 5A.

11. Kissell, M. R. (2011, July 28). High school graduation rates expected to drop. Dayton Daily News. Retrieved from http://www.daytondailynews.com/blogs/content/shared-gen/blogs/dayton/ education/entries/2011/07/28/

12. Intercultural Development Research Association. (2008, October 9). Attrition rates in Texas public schools by race – ethnicity, 2007–2008. *Newsletter,* 35(9).

13. Swaminathan, N. (2010, August 17). Is public education failing black male students? Good Education. Retrieved from http://www.good.is/post/is-public-education-failing-black-male-students/

14. Liptak A. (2008, April 23). Inmate count in U.S. dwarfs other nations. *New York Times.* Retrieved from http://www.nytimes.com/2008/04/23/us/23prison.html?pagewanted=all

15. Global Models of Education historically comprise the Human Capital Model, the Progressive Model, the Religious Model, and Indigenous Model. Given America's colonial history and the influence of the industrial revolution on its economic policies, the American educational system was destined to favor the Human Capital Model over all others. The effectiveness of education has therefore been measured by economic growth and development. Standardization of curriculum and content through mandatory textual materials lend themselves to standardized exams and sorting (tracking) to guarantee that workers are ensured for all levels of need within the economy.

16. Spring, J. (2010). *American education.* Boston, MA: McGraw Hill, p. 242.

17. Finz, S. (2012, June 6). *Study tackles low wages in food industry.* San Antonio Express News, p. C4.

18. Martin, P. (2011, June 21). Migration's economic tradeoffs: Farm worker wages and food costs. *Population Reference Bureau*. Retrieved from http://www.prb.org/Articles/ 2010/ usfarmworkersfoodprices.aspx

19. Times-Dispatch. (2009, July 16). Times-Dispatch Editorial Expresses Regret for Massive Resistance. Richmond Times-Dispatch. Retrieved from http://www2.timesdispatch.com/news/2009/jul/16/ed-mass16_20090715-183204-ar-37136/

20. Pomerantz, J. (2005, September 6). ADHD: More prevalent or better recognized. *MedScape News Today*. Retrieved from http://www.medscape.com/viewarticle/511173_print

21. Tanner, L. (2004, April 5). Watching TV linked to attention deficit problems. *San Antonio Express News*, p. 5A

22. Strasberber, V. C. (2007, October). First do no harm: Why have parents and pediatricians missed the boat on children and media. *Journal of Pediatrics,* 151(4), pp. 334–336. Retrieved from http://www.jpeds.com/article/S0022-3476(07)00491-X/fulltext

23. Johnson, C. K. (2010, March 24). Psychiatrist called too close to drug makers: New rules enable consumers to look up doctors' ties. *San Antonio Express News*, p. 6A.

24. Ollivier, C. (2008, August 20). France bans broadcasting of TV programs for babies. *San Antonio Express News*.

25. Lillard, A. S., & Peterson, J. (2011, September 12). The immediate impact of different types of television on young children's executive function. *Pediatrics*. Retrieved from http://pediatrics. aappublications.org/content/early/011/09/08/peds.2010-1919.full.pdf

26. Salamon, M. (2011, June 14). Too much TV raises risk of diabetes, heart disease and death. *Health*. Retrieved from http://news.health.com/2011/06/14/too-much-tv-raises-risk-of-diabetes-heart-disease-and-death/

27. CBS News. (2010, March 24). China faces diabetes epidemic. Retrieved from http://www.cbsnews.com/2100-202_162-6330788.html

28. Tanner, L. (2004, April 5). Watching TV linked to attention deficit problems. *San Antonio Express News*. p. 5A.

29. Fauber, J. (2004, November 29). Brain shrinks as body swells. *San Antonio Express News*.

30. The following is one of the less offensive internet sites from which to purchase "digital drugs." http:// itunes.apple.com/us/artist/i-doser/id367837407 However, just another click away lurks the seedier side of illegal drugs.

CHAPTER 11: THE WAY AHEAD

1. American Lung Association. (2011). *State of the air 2011*. Washington, DC: p.6. Retrieved from http:// www.stateoftheair.org/2011/assets/SOTA2011.pdf.

2. Gorski, E. (2010, March 18). Ed Secretary: Ban NCAA teams with low grad rates. *Associated press*. Retrieved from http://www.thegrio.com/news/ed-secretary-ban-ncaa-teams-with-low-grad-rates.php

3. Gorski, E. (2010, March 18). Ed Secretary: Ban NCAA teams with low grad rates. *Associated press*. Retrieved from http://www.thegrio.com/news/ed-secretary-ban-ncaa-teams-with-low-grad-rates.php

4. Griffin, T. (2003, March 26). Sour news from NCAA. *San Antonio Express News*, p. 1C.

5. Pack, W. (2010, June 18). Panel envisions more frugal college athletics. *San Antonio Express News*.

6. Glatfelter, A.G. (2006). *Substitute teachers as effective classroom instructors.* (Doctoral dissertation). p. 7. Retrieved from Eric ED494940.

7. Rennie Center for Education Research and Policy. (2009). *Raise the age, Lower the dropout rate?*: *Considerations for policymakers*. Retrieved from http://www.aypf.org/ documents/renniecenter_ 25.pdf

8. CPB. *Public relations agency partner to develop dropout awareness*. Retrieved from http://www.cpb. org/grants/grant.php?id=332

9. Rennie Center for Education Research and Policy. (2009). *Raise the age, Lower the dropout rate?*: *Considerations for policymakers*. Retrieved from http://www.aypf.org/ documents/renniecenter_25. pdf

10. Webb, P. K. (1980). Piaget: Implications for teaching. *Theory into Practice*, 19(2), pp. 93–97.

NOTES

11. Fuller, B. (2007, April). Standardize childhood: The political and cultural struggle over early education. *Stanford, Press Release*. Retrieved from http://www.sup.org/html/book_pages/0804755795/Press%20 Release.pdf

12. Home Instruction for Parents of Preschool Youngsters. Retrieved from http://www.hippy.org

13. Postman, N. (1983). The disappearing child: Americans are confused about how they should be educating children because American culture is the enemy of childhood. *Educational Leadership, 40*(6), p.14. Retrieved from http://www.ascd.org/ASCD/pdf/journals/ed_lead/ el_198303_postman.pdf

14. Bly, R. (1992). *Iron John*. New York: Vintage Books, p. 16.

15. Associated Press. (2010, June 04). *4-day school weeks gain popularity across U.S.* Retrieved from http://www.cbsnews.com/stories/2010/06/04/national/main6548010.shtm

16. Tatum, B. (2008). Can we talk about race? And other conversations in an era of school resegregation. Boston, MA: Beacon Press, pp. ix-xvi.

17. Nature Conservancy. *Connecting America's youth to nature*. Retrieved from http://www. nature.org/ newsfeatures/kids-in-nature/youth-and-nature-poll-results.pdf

18. Louv, R. (2008). *Last child in the woods*. Chapel Hill: Algonquin Books, p.3.

19. North American Association for Environmental Education *(NAAEE) Guidelines for K-12 Learning*. Retrieved from http://eelinked.naaee.net/n/guidelines/topics/Excellence-in-EE-Guidelines-for-Learning-K-12

20. Experts warn of 'death by GPS' as more people visit remote wildernesses. (2011, February 4). *Fox News*. Retrieved from http://www.foxnews.com/tech/2011/02/04/death-gps-rise/

21. Crim, C., Moseley, C., & Desjean-Perrotta, B. (2008). Partnerships gone wild: Preparing teachers of young children to teach about the natural world. *Childhood Education,* 85(1), pp. 6–12.

22. Scharrer, G. (2010, July 20). Students need great teachers. *San Antonio Express News*. Retrieved from http://www.mysanantonio.com/news/education/article/Students-need-great-teachers-781469.php

23. Matthews, J. (2012, July 30). Large study says great teachers get little respect. *Washington Post*. Retrieved from http://www.washingtonpost.com/blogs/class-struggle/post/large-study-says-great-teachers-get-little-respect/2012/07/30/gJQAy6NqKX_blog.html

24. Kvapil, L. (2007). *The impact of emotional intelligence on the academic performance of at-risk high school students* (Unpublished doctoral dissertation). University of the Incarnate Word, San Antonio, TX, p. 95.

25. Russell, J. (2005, May 22). Teachers figure into the school gap. *San Antonio Express News*, p.1A.

26. In Texas schools it is estimated that 50% of all high school minority students are in the 9th grade. This is commonly referred to by educators as the 9th grade hump.

27. Spak, K. (2011, May 27). Report: Over a third of students entering college need remedial help. *Chicago Sun-Times*. Retrieved from 9336-418/college-can-be-a-rude-remedial-awakening.html

28. Hacker, A. (2012, July 29). Is algebra necessary? *The New York Times Sunday Review*. Retrieved from http://www.nytimes.com/2012/07/29/opinion/sunday/is-algebra-necessary.html?pagewanted=all&_moc.semityn.www

29. State board wants calculators out of grade schoolers' hands, (2012, April 19). *Houston Chronicle*, Retrieved from http://www.chron.com/news/houston-texas/article/Early-math-lesson-Put-calculators-aside-3496172.php

30. National Center for Education Statistics. (2012). Fast facts: Students with disabilities, inclusion of. *Institute of Education Sciences*. Retrieved from http://nces.ed.gov/fastfacts/ display.asp?id=59

31. Scharrer G., & Lloyd, J. R. (2011, July 19). Texas education report on discipline: 60% of kids in trouble, (San Antonio Express News, July 19, 2011), p. 1A.

32. Gartner, A., & Lipsky, D. K. (1987). Beyond special education: Toward a quality system for all students. *Harvard Educational Review*, 66(4), pp. 367–395.

33. Cortez, A. & Cortez, J. D. (2008). Disciplinary Alternative Education Programs in Texas, *Intercultural Development Research Association Newsletter*. Retrieved from http://www.idra.org/IDRA_Newsletter/May_2008_Enlightened_Public_Policy/ Disciplinary_Alternative_Education_Programs_in_Texas/

34. Glass, G. (2009). *The realities of k-12 virtual education*. Great Lakes Center for Education Research and Practice. Retrieved from http://greatlakescenter.org/docs/Policy_Briefs/Glass_Virtual.pdf

[35] Davis, J., Harding, L., & Mascle, D. (2010). Digital connections and learning styles. In W. Ritke-Jones (Ed.). *Virtual environments for corporate education: Employee learning and solutions* (pp. 302–320). Hershey, NY: Business Science Reference.

[36] Shannon, K. (2010, April 8). Governor makes a pitch for electronic schoolbooks. *San Antonio Express News.*

[37] Braundy, M., O'Riley, P., Dalley, S., Petrina, S., & Paxton, A. (2000). Missing XX Chromosomes or Gender In/Equity in Design and Technology Education? The case of British Columbia. *Journal of Industrial Teacher Education, 37(3)*, p. 21

[38] Gardner, H. (2007). *Five minds for the future.* Boston, MA: Harvard Business School Press

[39] Rodriguez, R., & Villarreal, A. (2000, April). Development through engagement: Valuing the "at-promise community. *Intercultural Development Research Association Newsletter,* Retrieved from *http://www.idra.org/IDRA_Newsletters/August_2000%3A_Educational_Pipeline/Development_Through_Engagement/*

BIBLIOGRAPHY

Abram, D. (1996). *The spell of the sensuous: Perception and language in a more-than-human world.* New York: Vintage Books.

Adams. D. W. (1995). *Education for extinction: American Indians and the boarding school experience,* 1875–1928. Lawrence, KS: University Press of Kansas.

Adler, M. J. (1985). *Ten philosophical mistakes.* New York: Collier Books.

Agamben, G. (1999). *The man without content.* Stanford: Stanford University Press.

Ahmed, L. (1992). *Women and gender in Islam: Historical roots of a modern debate.* New Haven: Yale University Press.

American Association of School Administrators. (2009). *Report of findings one year later: How the economic downturn continues to impact schools districts.* Retrieved from http://www.aasa.org/ uploadedFiles/Resources/files/OneYearLater%20FINAL.pdf

American Lung Association (2011), State of the air 2011. Retrieved from http://www.stateoftheair.org/2011/assets/SOTA2011.pdf

American Montessori Society. (2011). *Public schools.* Retrieved from http://www.amshq.org/ School%20 Resources/Public.aspx

Anzaldúa, G. (2001). Borderlands/La Frontera. In P. Bizzell & B. Herzberg (Eds.), The rhetorical tradition: Readings from classical times to the present. (pp. 1585–1604). Boston: Bedford/St. Martin's.

Apple, M. W. (1996). *Cultural politics and education.* New York: Teachers College Press.

Apple, M. W. (2000). *Official knowledge: Democratic education in a conservative age.* New York: Routledge.

Apple, M. W. (2006). *Educating the "right" way: Markets, standards, God, and inequality.* New York: Routledge.

Aristotle (1946). *The politics of Aristotle.* E. Barker (Trans. and Ed.). Oxford: Oxford University Press.

Aristotle. (1984). *Generations of animals.* J. Barnes (Ed.). Princeton: Princeton University Press.

Associated Press. (2011, June). 4-day school weeks gain popularity across U.S. Retrieved from http:// www.cbsnews.com/stories/2010/06/04/national/main6548010.shtm

Atkins, J. D. C. (1886). Annual report U.S. commisionary of Indian affairs. In M. A. Jaimes (Ed.), The state of Native America: Genocide, colonization, and resistance (p.379). Boston: South End Press.

Aupaummut, H. (1995). *Teaching the children.* In A. Hirschfelder (Ed.) Native heritage: Personal accounts by American Indians 1790 to the present. (pp. 92–93). New York: Macmillan.

Baker, C. (2006). *Foundations of bilingual education and bilingualism,* 4th ed. Clevedon, UK: Multilingual Matters

Beliveau, A. (1929, October 29). [Letter to Duncan Campbell Scott, Deputy Superintendent General]. National Archives of Canada (CN 65-4, Vol. 1, File 494/25-1-015), Ottawa, CA.

Belkora, L. (2005). Steering by the stars. *StarDate, 33*(4), 16–19.

Belenky, M. F., Clinchy, B.M., Goldberger, N.R. & Tarule, J.M. (1986). *Women's ways of knowing: The development of self, voice, and mind.* New York: Basic Books.

Blanchard, A. (1985). *Aboriginal education* (Blanchard Report). House of Representatives Select Committee on Aboriginal Education, Parliament of the Commonwealth of Australia. Canberra, AU.

Blessed Earth, Mission and beliefs. Retrieved from http://www.blessedearth.org/about/mission-and-beliefs/

Bly, R. (1992). *Iron John.* New York: Vintage Books.

Bly, R. (1996). *The sibling society.* Reading, MA: Addison Wesley.

Braundy,M., O'Riley, P., Dalley, S., Petrina, S., & Paxton, A. (2000). Missing xx chromosomes or gender in/equity in design and technology education? The case of British Columbia. *Journal of Industrial Teaching, 37*(3), 21. Retrieved from http://scholar.lib.vt.edu/ejournals/JITE/v37n3/braundy.html

Broomfield, J. (1997). *Other ways of knowing: Recharting our future with ageless wisdom.* Rochester, VT: Inner Traditions.

Brown, E. (2003). An intimate spectator: Jewish women reflect on adult study. *Religious Education, 98*(1), 66.

BIBLIOGRAPHY

Callañaupa, N. (2009). The American & Canadian Association of Peru Newsletter 3(2). Retrieved from http://www.acap-peru.org/newsletter/2009-02/nilda-callanaupa-alvarez.html
Castaneda, C. (1968). *The teachings of Don Juan: A Yaqui way of knowledge*. New York: Pocket Books.
Cajete, G. (2000). *Native science: Natural laws of interdependence*. Santa Fe, NM: Clear Light Publishers.
CBSNews. (2010, March 24). China faces diabetes epidemic. Retrieved from http://www.cbsnews.com/2100-202_162-6330788.html
CBS News, (2011, May 16). *Death by GPS: Warning about the devices*. CBS News, Retrieved from http://www.cbsnews.com/2102-502303
Center for Research on Education Outcomes. (2009). *Multiple choice: Charter school performance in 16 states*. Retrieved from http://credo.stanford.edu/reports/MULTIPLE_CHOICE_CREDO.pdf
Cevallos, D. (2003, July). *Isolated indigenous groups face extinction. Tierrámerica*. Retrieved from http://www.tierramerica.net/english/2003/0630/iarticulo.shtml
Christie, M. (2003, September 24). *Databases which support rather than inhibit Australian Aboriginal ways of knowing and making knowledge*. Seminar conducted at Faculty of Indigenous Research and Education Seminar Room, Charles Darwin University, Casuarina, AU.
Chrystal, S.C. (1991). *Assessing prior knowledge across culture: Native American and Caucasian (Unpublished doctoral dissertation)*. Marquette University, Milwaukee, WI.
Cortez, A., & Cortez, J.D. (2008). *Disciplinary alternative education programs in Texas*. Intercultural Development Research Association Newsletter, 3.
Corporation of Public Broadcasting. (2011). Public relations agency partner to develop dropout awareness. Retrieved from http://www.cpb.org/grants/grant.php?id=332
Crim, C., Moseley, C., & Desjean-Perrotta, B. (2009, October). *One wild partnership: Working together to infuse environmental education into a teacher preparation program*. Consortium of State Organizations for Texas Teacher Education, San Antonio, TX.
Davis, J., Harding, L., & Mascle, D. (2010). *Digital connections and learning styles*. In W. Ritke-Jones (Ed.). *Virtual environments for corporate education: Employee learning and solutions* (pp. 302–320). Hershey, NY: Business Science Reference.
Dejong, D. H. (1993). *Promises of the past: A history of Indian education in the United States*. Golden, CO: North American Press.
Detroit schools closing: Michigan officials order Robert Bobb to shut half the city's schools. (2011, February 21). Huffington Post. Retrieved from http://www.huffingtonpost.com/2011/02/21/detroit-schools-closing_n_826007.html
Emory, K. (1999). *Ancient Hawaiian civilization*. Honolulu, HI: Mutual Publishing.
Fauber, J. (2004, November 29). Brain shrinks as body swells. San Antonio Express News.
Feenberg, A. (2003). *Democratic rationalization: Technology, power, and freedom*. In Scharff, R. C., & Dusek, V. (Eds.), *Philosophy of technology: The technological condition: An anthology* (pp. 652–65). Malden, MA: Blackwell Publishing.
Finz, S. (2012, June 6). *Study tackles low wages in food industry*. San Antonio Express News.
Foerde, K., Knowlton, B. J., & Poldrack, R. A. (2006, April). *Modulation of competing memory systems by distraction*. Proceedings of the National Academy of Sciences, 103(31). Retrieved from http://www.pnas.org/content/103/31/11778.full
Foucault, M. (1995). *Discipline & punish: The birth of the prison*. New York: Vintage Books.
Foucault, M. (2001). *The order of discourse*. In P. Bizzell & B. Herzberg (Eds.), The rhetorical tradition: Readings from classical times to the present (pp.1460–1470). Boston: Bedford/St.Martin's.
Freire, P. (2000). *Pedagogy of the oppressed*. New York: Continuum.
Fuller, B. (2007, April). *Standardize childhood: The political and cultural struggle over early education*. Stanford, Press Release. Retrieved from http://www.sup.org/html/book_pages/0804755795/Press%20Release.pdf
Gardner, H. (2006). *Five minds for the future*. Boston: Harvard Business School Press.
Gartner, A., & Lipsky, D.K. (1987). *Beyond special education: Toward a quality system for all students*. Harvard Educational Review, 66(4). pp. 367–395.
Giago, T. A. (1978). *The Aboriginal sin*. San Francisco: Indian Historian Press.
Gilbert, S. (2000). *The tattoo history source book*. New York: Juno Books.

Gilligan, C., & Attanucci, J. (1988). *Two moral orientations: Gender differences and similarities*, Merrill-Palmer Quarterly, 34(3), 233.

Glass, G. (2009). *The realities of k-12 virtual education.* Great Lakes Center for Education Research and Practice. Retrieved from http://greatlakescenter.org/docs/Policy_Briefs/Glass_Virtual.pdf

Glass, R.D. (2001). On Paulo Freire's philosophy of praxis and the foundation of liberation education. *Educational Researcher*, 30(2), 15.

Glatfelter, A.G. (2006). *Substitute teachers as effective classroom instructors.* (Doctoral dissertation). Retrieved from Eric ED494940.

Gould, S.J. (1994). The evolution of life on earth. *Scientific American, 271*(4), 85–91

Gorski, E. (2010, March 18). Ed Secretary: Ban NCAA teams with low grad rates. Associated Press. Retrieved from http://www.thegrio.com/news/ed-secretary-ban-ncaa-teams-with-low-grad-rates.php

Gray, S. (2010, January 25). Can Robert Bobb fix Detroit's public schools? Time Magazine. Retrieved from http://www.time.com/time/magazine/article/0,9171,1953694,00.html

Griffin, T. (2003, March 26). *Sour news from NCAA.* San Antonio Express News, p.1C.

Hacker, A. (2012, July 29). Is algebra necessary? The New York Times Sunday Review. Retrieved from http://www.nytimes.com/2012/07/29/opinion/sunday/is-algebra-necessary.html?pagewanted=all&_moc.semityn.www

Halliday, M.A.K. (2005). *The language of science.* J.J. Webster (ed). New York: Continuum.

Hallowell, E.M. (2005). Overloaded circuits: Why smart people underperform. *Harvard Business Review, 83*(1), 54–62.

Hayden, T. (2009, February). What Darwin didn't know. Smithsonian Magazine, 39(11), 40–48. Retrieved from http://www.smithsonianmag.com/science-nature/What-Darwin-Didnt-Know.html?c=y&page=2

Heaney, T.W. (1995, June). *Issues in Freirean Pedagogy.* National-Louis University. Retrieved from http://www.nl.edu/academics/cas/ace/facultypapers/ ThomasHeaney_Freirean.cfm

Heller, R.T. *Men & women: A Jewish view on gender differences.* Judaism Online. Retrieved from http://www.simpletoremember.com/articles/a/jewish-view-on-gender-differences

Herndl, C.G. (1993). *Teaching discourse and reproducing culture: A critique of research and pedagogy in professional and non-academic writing.* College Composition and Communication, 44(3), 359.

High school graduation in Texas. (2006). *Editorial Projects in Education Research Center.* Retrieved from http://www.edweek.org/rc.

Hill, D. (2012, January 19). *Amazon uncontacted tribes at risk from new highway plan.* The Ecologist. Retrieved from http://www.theecologist.org/News/news_analysis/1202915/amazon uncontacted_ tribes_at_risk_from_new_highway_plan.html

Hirschfelder, A. (Ed.). (1995). *Native heritage: Personal accounts by American Indians 1790 to the present.* New York: Macmillan.

Hollingsworth, H, & Turner, D. (2011, July 28). *States Brace for Grad Rate Dips as Formula changes".* San Antonio Express News.

Home Instruction for Parents of Preschool Youngsters. Retrieved from http://www.hippy.org

Hughes, P., & More, A. J. (1997, December). *Aboriginal ways of learning and learning styles.* Australian Association of Research in Education, Brisbane, AU.

IDRA principles: Uncompromising expectations for graduating all students. (2007, November/December) Intercultural Development Research Association Newsletter.

Intercultural Development Research Association. (2008, October 9). *Attrition rates in Texas public schools by race – ethnicity*, 2007–2008. Newsletter. 35(9).

Intercultural Development Research Association. (2011, April). Five Texas regions have persistently high student attrition rates. Retrieved from http://www.idra.org/IDRA_Newsletter/ April_2011_ Curriculum_Quality/Five_Texas_Regions/

Intercultural Development Research Association, (2000). Valuing the "at-promise community.

Intercultural Development Research Association. Retrieved from www.idra.org/...2000%3A.../ Development_Through_Engagement/

Isaacson, R. (2001). *The healing land.* New York: Grove Press.

Jablonka, E., & Lamb, M. (2005). *Evolution in four dimensions: Genetic, epigenetic, behavioral, and symbolic variation in the history of life.* Cambridge: MIT Press.

Jewish Publication Society. (1985). *Genesis, Tanakh: The holy scriptures.* Philadelphia: Jewish Publication Society.

Johnson, C. K. (2010, March 24). *Psychiatrist called too close to drug makers: New rules enable consumers to look up doctors' ties.* San Antonio Express News.

Kafka, F. (1933). *Investigations of a dog. In the Great Wall of China and other pieces.* London: Morrison & Gibb.

Kastner, L. (2008, October 22). 2,500 dropouts a week. San Antonio Express-News.

Kirkness, V.J (1998). Our people's education: Cut the shackles; cut the crap; cut the mustard. *Canadian Journal of Native Education,* 22(1), 10.

Kissell, M.R. (2011, July 28). *High school graduation rates expected to drop.* Dayton Daily News. Retrieved from http://www.daytondailynews.com/blogs/content/shared-gen/blogs/dayton/ education/ entries/2011/07/28/

Klaus, K. (2011, March 11). *Kansas City Missouri school district looks for broker to 'repurpose' closed schools.* Kansas City Business Journal. Retrieved from http://www.bizjournals.com/ kansascity /print-edition/2011/03/11/kansas-city-missouri-school-district.html?page=all

Kress, G.R., & Van Leeuwen, T. (2006). *Reading images: The grammar of visual design.* Abingdon, UK: Routledge.

Kuhn, T. (1996). *The structure of scientific revolution.* (3rd Ed.). Chicago, IL: University of Chicago Press.

Kvapil, L. (2007). *The impact of emotional intelligence on the academic performance of at-risk high school students (Unpublished doctoral dissertation).* University of the Incarnate Word, San Antonio, TX.

Lama, A. (2005). *Transitory' reserves for Mashco-Piro Indians.* Tierrámerica. Retrieved from http:// www.tierramerica.org/2005/0416/iacentos.shtml

Lee, V.E., & Lockheed, M.E. (1990). The effects of single-sex school on achievement and attitudes in Nigeria. *Comparative Education Review,* 34(2), 209–231.

Lewis-Williams, D. (2004). *The mind in the cave: Consciousness and the origins of art.* London: Thames & Hudson. (Original work published 2002).

Lillard, A.S., & Peterson, J. (2011, September 12). *The immediate Impact of different types of television on young children's executive function.* Pediatrics. Retrieved from http://pediatrics.aappublications. org/content/early/011/09/08/peds.2010-1919.full.pdf

Liptak A. (2008, April 23). *Inmate count in U.S. dwarfs other nations.* New York Times. Retrieved from http://www.nytimes.com/2008/04/23/us/23prison.html?pagewanted=all

Louv, R. (2008). *Last child in the woods.* Chapel Hill: Algonquin Books.

Ludwig, M. (2010, July 18). *Remedying remedial college classes.* San Antonio Express News, p. 1A.

Malone, A., & McConnell, A. (Writers), & Maybury-Lewis, D. (host). (1992). *The shock of the other/ strange relations,* pt. 1 of Millennium: Tribal wisdom and the modern world [VHS]. Los Angeles, CA: PBS Home Video.

Mann, C. C. (2006). 1491: *New revelations of the Americas before Columbus.* New York: Vintage Books.

Martin, P. (2011, June 21). *Migration's economic tradeoffs: Farm worker wages and food costs.* Population Reference Bureau. Retrieved from http://www.prb.org/Articles/ 2010/usfarmworkersfoodprices.aspx

Matthews, J. (2012, July 30). *Large study says great teachers get little respect.* Washington Post. Retrieved from http://www.washingtonpost.com/blogs/class-struggle/post/large-study-says-great-teachers-get-little-respect/2012/07/30/gJQAy6NqKX_blog.html

McGivern R.F., Mutter K.L., Anderson J., Wideman G., Bodnar M., & Huston P.J. (1998). Gender differences in incidental learning and visual recognition memory: Support for sex difference in unconscious environmental awareness. *Personality and Individual Differences,* 25(2), 231.

McMurtry, L. (2005). *Crazy Horse: A life (Penguin Lives biographies).* New York: Penguin Books.

Means, R. (1980, July). *On what to call indigenous people of North America.* Speech presented at the Black Hills International Survival Gathering, South Dakota.

Misra, N. (2005, January 4). *Stone age cultures survive tsunami waves: Indian islanders apparently heeded ancient lore.* Associated Press. Retrieved from http://www.msnbc.msn.com/id/6786476/ns/ world_news-tsunami_a_year_later/

Momaday, N. S. (1998). *The man made of words: Essays, stories, passages.* New York: St. Martin's Griffin.

Moore, T. (1992). *Care of the soul: A guide for cultivating depth and sacredness in everyday life.* New York: HarperColins.

Morris, F. (2007, February 21). *Cherokee tribe faces decision on freedmen*, National Public Radio.

Mott, M. (2005, January 4). *Did animals sense tsunami was coming? National Geographic News.* Retrieved from http://news.nationalgeographic.com/news/ 2005/01/0104_050104_tsunami_animals.html

Nabokov, P. (Ed.). (1991). *Native American testimony: A chronicle of Indian-White relations from prophecy to present*, 1492–1992. New York: Penguin

National Center for Education Statistics. (2012). *Fast facts: Students with disabilities, inclusion of. Institute of Education Sciences.* Retrieved from http://nces.ed.gov/fastfacts/ display.asp?id=59

National Geographic Expeditions (2012). *National Geographic adventures: Tanzania: Walking safari with the Maasi.* Retrieved from http://www.nationalgeographicexpeditions.com/expeditions/maasai-walking-safari/detail

Nature Conservancy. *Connecting America's youth to nature.* Retrieved from http://www. nature.org/ newsfeatures/kids-in-nature/youth-and-nature-poll-results.pdf

Nerburn, K. (1994). *Neither wolf nor dog: On forgotten roads with an Indian elder.* Novato, CA: New World Library.

Noriega J, (1992). *American Indian education in the United States: Indoctrination for subordination to colonialism.* In M.A. Jaimes (ed.), *The state of Native America: Genocide, colonization, and resistance.* Boston: South End Press.

North American Association for Environmental Education (NAAEE) Guidelines for K-12 Learning. Retrieved from http://eelinked.naaee.net/n/guidelines/topics/Excellence-in-EE-Guidelines-for-Learning-K-12

Nowell, C.J. (1995). Play potlaches. In Hirschfelder, A. (Ed.), Native heritage: Personal accounts by American Indians 1790 to the present (pp. 103–104). New York: Macmillan.

One step toward bridging the racial computer gap. (2000). *The Journal of Blacks in Higher Education*, 26, 62. Retrieved from http://www.highbeam.com/doc/1P3-494183301.html/print

Ollivier, C. (2008, August 20). *France bans broadcasting of TV programs for babies.* San Antonio Express News.

Olson, S. (1964, May 23). *Testimony before the Selke Committee on the fate of the Boundary Waters Canoe Area.* Saint Paul, MN.

Ornstein, A.C., & Levine, D.U. (2008). *Foundations of education*, Boston: Houghton Mifflin Company.

Overholt, T.W., & Callicott, J.B. (1982). *Clothed-in-Fur and Other Tales: An Introduction to an Ojibwa World View.* Washington, DC: University Press of America.

Pack, W. (2010, June 18). *Panel envisions more frugal college athletics.* San Antonio Express News.

Perry, W. (1998). *Forms of intellectual and ethical development in the college years: A scheme.* San Francisco, CA: Jossey-Bass.

Perrault, F. (1930, May 2). [Letter to Frank Edwards, Department of Indian Affairs]. National Archives of Canada (CN 65-4, Vol. 1, File 494/25-1-015), Ottawa, CA.

PestalozziWorld. (2012). *Educating children for a better world.* Retrieved from http://www. pestalozziworld.com/pestalozzi/methods/html

Plato. (1945). *The republic of Plato*, (F.M. Cornford, Trans.) New York: Oxford University Press.

Pomerantz, J. (2005, September 6). *ADHD: More prevalent or better recognized.* MedScape News Today. Retrieved from http://www.medscape.com/viewarticle/511173_print.

Pomeroy, S. B. (1975). *Goddesses, whores, wives, and slaves: Women in classical antiquity.* New York: Schocken Books.

Postman, N. (1983). The disappearing child: Americans are confused about how they should be educating children because American culture is the enemy of childhood. *Educational Leadership, 40*(6), 10–15. Retrieved from http://www.ascd.org/ASCD/pdf/journals/ed_lead/el_198303_postman.pdf

Pratt. R. H. (1964). *Battlefield and Classroom: Four Decades with the American Indian, 1867–1904.* R. M. Utley (Ed.). New Haven, CT: Yale University Press.

Price, A. (1995). *Playing wickiup.* In Hirschfelder, A. (Ed.), Native heritage: Personal accounts by American Indians 1790 to the present (p. 100). New York: Macmillan.

Progress on graduation rate stalls; 1.3 million students fail to earn diplomas. (2010, June). Education Week. Retrieved from http://www.edweek.org/go/dc10

Radio New Zealand International. (2010, July 14). Legendary FSM master navigator dies. Radio New Zealand International. Retrieved from http://www.rnzi.com/pages/news.php?op=read&id=54698

Radin, P. (1927). Primitive man as philosopher. New York: D. Appleton.

Ransom, W., & Moulton, M. M. (2001, December). Why girls' schools? The difference in girl-centered education. Fordham Urban Law Journal 29(2). Retrieved from http:www.thefreelibrary.com/why+girls'+schools%3f+the+ difference+in+girl-centered+education-a083701146

Rasmussen, K. (1975). Magic words. In Field, E. (Trans. & Ed.), Eskimo Songs and Stories (pp. 7–8). Cambridge: Delcorte Press/Seymour Lawrence.

Redfield, J. (1993). The celestine prophecy. New York: Warner Books.

Redfield, J. (1997). The celestine vision: Living the new spiritual awareness. New York: Warner Books.

Redfield, J. (2007). Celestine vision: James Redfield and the celestine prophecy movie. Retrieved from http://www.celestinevision.com

Rennie Center for Education Research and Policy. (2009). Rise the age lower the dropout rate? Retrieved from http://www.renniecenter.org/research_docs/Compulsory%20Age%20Brief-FINAL%20 4.9.09.pdf

Rideout, V.J., Foehr, U.G., & Roberts, D.E. (2010). Generation M2: Media in the lives of 8 to 18-year-olds. Menlo Park, CA: Kaiser Family Foundation. Retrieved from http://www.kff.org/entmedia/upload/8010.pdf.

Risku, M.T. (1996). American Indian learning style: The illusion. In Schacher, S.M., (Ed.), Celebration of Indigenous Thought and Expression (pp. 267–272). Sault Ste. Marie, MI: Lake Superior State University Press.

Rodriguez, R. (1982). Hunger of memory: The education of Richard Rodriguez. New York: Dial Press.

Rodriguez, R., & Villarreal, A. (2000, August). Development through engagement: Valuing the at-promise community. Intercultural Development Research Association. Retrieved from http://www.idra.org/IDRA_Newsletters/August_2000%3A_Educational_Pipeline/Development_Through_Engagement/

Russell, J. (2005, May 22). Teachers figure into the school gap. San Antonio Express News, p.1A.

Sabine, C. (2005, January 6). Senses helped animals survive the tsunami: Few carcasses turning up in affected region, NBC Nightly News. Retrieved from http://www.msnbc.msn.com /id/6795562/#. UDJ1A7_CKes.

Salamon, M. (2011, June 14). Too much TV raises risk of diabetes, heart disease and death. Health. Retrieved from http://news.health.com/2011/06/14/too-much-tv-raises-risk-of-diabetes-heart-disease-and-death/

Sandoz, M. (1997). Crazy Horse. New York: Fine Communications.

Saxon, R. (2009, August 26). L.A. school board OKs school choice plan with private operators. USA Today. Retrieved from http://www.usatoday.com/news/ education/2009-08-26-los-angeles-schools_N.htm

Scharrer, G. (2010, July 20). Students need great teachers. San Antonio Express News. Retrieved from http://www.mysanantonio.com/news/education/article/Students-need-great-teachers-781469.php

Scharrer, G. (2010, July 21). Teacher quality Is called 'critical' to educational gains. San Antonio Express News.

Scharrer, G, & Lloyd, J.R. (2011, July 19). Texas education report on discipline: 60% of kids in trouble, San Antonio Express News.

Scharrer, G. (2010, April 8). White flunks Perry's handling of dropouts. San Antonio Express News.

Selfe, C.L. & Selfe, R.J. Jr. (1994). The politics of the interface: Power and its exercise in electronic contact zones. College Composition and Communication, 45(4), 481–482.

Shannon, K. (2010, April 8). Governor makes a pitch for electronic schoolbooks. San Antonio Express News.

Sheingold, K., Martin, L.M.W., & Endreweit, M.E. (1987, July). Preparing urban teachers for the technological future. Paper presented at the meeting of the World Assembly of the International Council on Education for Teaching, Eindhoven, NL.

Shield, P. (1995). I tried to be like my mother. In Hirschfelder, A. (Ed.), Native heritage: Personal accounts by American Indians 1790 to the present (p. 97). New York: Macmillan.

Sioui, G. E. (1992). *For an Amerindian autohistory, An essay on the foundations of a social ethic.* S. Fischman (trans.). Montreal: McGill-Queen's University Press.

Smith, M. K. (2008). *Howard Gardner, multiple intelligences and education.* In The encyclopedia of informal education. Retrieved from http://www.infed.org/thinkers/gardner.htm

Society for Neuroscience. (2004, October, 24). *Mothers have brains primed for care and certain techniques may reverse problems in offspring related to poor parenting.* Society for Neuroscience News Release. Retrieved from http://www.sfn.org/index.aspx?pagename=news_102404c

Spring, J. (2010). *American education.* Boston, MA: McGraw Hill.

Spak, K. (2011, May 27). *Report: Over a third of students entering college need remedial help.* Chicago Sun-Times. Retrieved from 9336-418/college-can-be-a-rude-remedial-awakening.html

Standing Bear, L. (1978). *Land of the Spotted Eagle.* Lincoln: University of Nebraska Press. (Original work published 1933).

Standing Bear, L. (1988). *My Indian boyhood.* Lincoln: University of Nebraska Press. (Original work published 1931).

Standing Bear, L. (1975). *My People the Sioux.* Lincoln: University of Nebraska Press. (Original work published 1928).

Starr, L. (2000, August 22). Solving the substitute shortage. *Education World.* Retrieved from http://www.educationworld.com/a admin/admin185.shtml

State board wants calculators out of grade schoolers' hands. (2012, April). *Houston Chronicle.* Retrieved from www.chron.com/.../Early-math-lesson-Put-calculators-aside-3496172.php

Strasberber, V. C. (2007, October). First do no harm: Why have parents and pediatricians missed the boat on children and media. *Journal of Pediatrics, 151*(4). pp. 334–336. Retrieved from http://www.jpeds.com/article/S0022-3476(07)00491-X/fulltext

Swaminathan, N. (2010, August 17). Is public education failing black male students? *Good Education.* Retrieved from http://www.good.is/post/is-public-education-failing-black-mal students/

Swartman, G. (1945, December 31) [Letter to Department of Indian Affairs]. National Archives of Canada (CN 65-4, Vol. 1, File 494/25-1-015).

Sweezy, C. (1995). *We counted time by sleeps.* In Hirschfelder, A. (Ed.) Native Heritage: Personal accounts by American Indians 1790 to the present (p. 174). New York: Macmillan.

Tafoya, T. (1995). *The old ways teach us.* In Hirschfelder, A. (Ed.). Native heritage: Personal accounts by American Indians 1790 to the present (p. 113). New York: Macmillan,

Tamaoka, K. (1986, October). *Congruence between learning styles of Cree, Dene and Métis students, and instructional styles of Native and Non-Native teachers.* Paper presented at the Mokakit Conference of the Indian Education Research Association, Winnipeg, MB.

Tanner, L. (2004, April 5). *Watching TV linked to attention deficit problems.* San Antonio Express News.

Tatum, B. (2008). *Can we talk about race? And other conversations in an era of school resegregation.* Simmons College: Beacon Press.

Tedlock, B. (2005). *The woman in the shaman's body.* New York: Bantam.

Tikly, L, (2004). Education and the new imperialism. *Comparative Education, 40*(2), 173.

Tileston, D. W. (2004). *What every teacher should know about: Instructional planning.* Thousand Oaks, CA: Corwin Press.

Times-Dispatch (2009, July 16). *Times-Dispatch Editorial Expresses Regret for Massive Resistance.* Richmond Times-Dispatch. Retrieved from http://www2.timesdispatch.com/news/2009/jul/16/ed-mass16_20090715-183204-ar-37136/

Toor, R. (2007). The care and feeding of the reader. *The Chronicle of Higher Education, 54*(3). Retrieved from http://chronicle.com/article/The-CareFeeding-of-the/46632/

Tucker, N. C., Kojetin, B. A., & Harrison, R. (1996). *A statistical analysis of the CPS supplement on race and ethnic origin.* Proceedings of the Bureau of the Census' 1996 Annual Research Conference. p. 5. Retrieved from http://www.census.gov/prod/2/gen/96arc/arc96.html

Vandal, B. (2010, May). *Rebuilding the remedial education bridge to college success.* Retrieved from http://www.gettingpastgo.org/docs/GPGpaper.pdf

Van der Post, L. (1986). *The lost world of the Kalahari.* San Diego: Harcourt Brace. (Original work published 1958).

Vitousek, P. M., D'Antonio, C.M., Loope, L.L., Rejmanek, M., & Westbrooks, R. (1997). Introduced species: A significant component of human-caused global change. *New Zealand Journal of Ecology*, *21*(1), 2.

Vitousek, P. M., Mooney, H.A., Lubchenco, J., & Melillo, J.M. (1997). Human domination of earth's ecosystems. *Science*, *277*, 495.

Wagamese, R. (1994). *Keeper'n Me*. Toronto, Canada: Doubleday.

Webb, P. K. (1980). Piaget: Implications for teaching. *Theory into Practice*, *19*(2), 93–97.

Wilson, C. (1969). *The philosopher's stone*. New York: Warner Books.

Winchester, S. (2003). *Krakatoa*. New York: HarperCollins.

Wolff, R. (2001). *Original wisdom: Stories of an ancient way of knowing*. Rochester, VT: Inner Traditions.

Yanko, D. (2010, November 4). *Visions on rock*. Virtual Saskatchewan. Retrieved from http://www.virtualsk.com/current_issue/visions_on_rock.html

SUBJECT INDEX

CPSIA information can be obtained at www.ICGtesting.com
Printed in the USA
BVOW031749170313

315695BV00004B/69/P

Education for Tomorrow